SPIN THIS!

SPIN THIS!

ALL THE WAYS WE DON'T TELL THE TRUTH

BILL PRESS

FOREWORD BY BILL MAHER

POCKET BOOKS
New York   London   Toronto   Sydney   Singapore

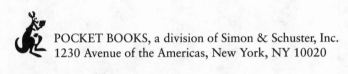

POCKET BOOKS, a division of Simon & Schuster, Inc.
1230 Avenue of the Americas, New York, NY 10020

ISBN: 0-7434-4267-9

First Pocket Books hardcover printing November 2001

10 9 8 7 6 5 4 3 2 1

POCKET and colophon are registered trademarks of
Simon & Schuster, Inc.

For information regarding special discounts for bulk purchases, please
contact Simon & Schuster Special Sales at 1-800-456-6798 or
business@simonandschuster.com

Printed in the U.S.A.

Cartoons on pp. 44, 112, and 131 reprinted with permission of Tribute
Media Services Incorporated, 2001.
Original cartoon on page 54 courtesy of George Booth.

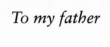

To my father

Consider the lilies of the field, how they grow;
they toil not, neither do they . . . SPIN.

—Matthew 6:28

CONTENTS

FOREWORD

BY BILL MAHER

Bill Press ought to know from spin. After all, he's been spinning for a long time. He's a good guide to help us wiggle our way through the spin of others.

What is spin, really, but a lie communicated through the veneer of vague truth? Whitney Houston suffering from "exhaustion," and New Jersey being labeled the "Garden State."

Glaring political examples come to mind: the Nixon cover-up's "previous statements are inoperative," Gary Condit's "cooperating fully," and, of course, any discussion of Dick Cheney's "health."

But, by far, my favorite instance of unabashed spin occurred during the 1996 presidential campaign. When asked whether or not cigarettes are addictive, Bob Dole replied, "I don't know. I'm not a doctor."

Why, that's just as preposterous as if President Bush were to say global warming "needs more study."

Oh wait. He *did* say that.

SPINNING THIS BOOK

"Then you should say what you mean," the March Hare went on.

"I do," Alice hastily replied; "at least—at least I mean what I say—that's the same thing, you know."

"Not the same thing a bit!" said the Hatter. "Why, you might as well say that 'I see what I eat' is the same thing as "I eat what I see'!"

"You might just as well say," added the March Hare, "that 'I like what I get' is the same thing as 'I get what I like'!"

"You might just as well say," added the Dormouse, which seemed to be talking in its sleep, "that 'I breathe when I sleep' is the same thing as 'I sleep when I breathe'!"

"It *is* the same thing with you," said the Hatter, and here the conversation dropped.

—Lewis Carroll, *Alice's Adventures in
Wonderland,* Chapter VII: A Mad
Tea Party

This book was born in shock: the shock of sitting down as co-host of *Crossfire* for the very first time, in February 1996. I asked a straightforward question, expecting a straightforward answer. What I got instead was spin.

Our guest was conservative Republican Senator Don Nickles of Oklahoma. But it could have been liberal Democratic Senator Teddy Kennedy of Massachusetts. No matter. The result's the same. We ask. They spin.

There is no good definition of spin. It's easier to say what it's not than what it is: It's not the truth. Neither is it a lie. Spin lies somewhere in between: almost telling the truth, but not quite; bending the truth to make things look as good—or as bad—as possible; painting things in the best possible—or worst possible—light.

Spin is nothing new. As we shall see, it has been around since Adam and Eve. But we are more aware of it today. It is used more outrageously today. And we've finally given it a name.

Spin is everywhere. It is part of our daily vocabulary. It colors and shapes every arena of human endeavor. Grownups do it; kids do it. We live in a world of spin.

Of course, politics is one of spin's most fertile breeding grounds. Many political campaigns establish official "spin rooms." Consultants are hired to put the "best spin" on a candidate's résumé. The candidate himself learns to spin, rather than answer a question directly. Party leaders are recruited to parachute into campaigns and serve as "master spinners." Today's variation of an old cynicism reads: *How can you tell when a politician is spinning? When his lips are moving!*

Spin is not limited to political campaigns. It not only helps people to get elected, it helps them to stay in office and build public support for their programs. Whether in the city council, or in the U.S. Congress, spin is a big part of getting bills passed. When Tom Daschle took over as Senate majority leader in June 2001, he created a special "intensive care unit" for members of the media with questions on the pending patients' bill of rights. Reported the *Washington Post:* "No media ICU would be complete without spin doctors, who will offer reporters quick rebuttals to attacks by the health care industry and its allies in Congress."

But the political realm has no monopoly on spin. In fact, politicians may not even be the worst offenders:

- Defense lawyers are paid to put the best possible spin on their client's criminal behavior: "Yes, Your Honor, she did stab her husband 30 times with a butcher knife while he was watching the evening news, but she's a good mother to her 6 children and she volunteers for the Red Cross every Saturday."
- Salesmen spin the supposed magic of their products: "This new vacuum cleaner actually makes housework fun!"
- TV networks spin their nightly newscast: "Ten reasons why all children hate their parents. Tape at 11."
- Over cocktails, men and women spin their sex appeal: "No, actually, there's no one in my life right now." Meaning, of course, no one I want to tell you about.

And that's just for starters. Look around you. Spin is in the air. There is a magazine called *Spin*. A Tom Lowe novel about politics called *Spin*. A TV show called *Spin City*. *The Nation* magazine advertises itself as "Spin Control." There was a rock band called "Spin Doctors." Howard Kurtz, media critic for the *Washington Post,* wrote a book about the White House called *Spin Cycle*. In June 2001, the mighty Smithsonian Institution sponsored a workshop on "Who Spins the News?". And, during the 2000 election, conservative columnist Tucker Carlson and I hosted a popular nightly primetime show on CNN called *The Spin Room*.

Tucker and I compare spin to obscenity, and borrowing a phrase from Supreme Court Justice Potter Stewart, we may not be able to define it, but we know it when we see it. According to Tucker, spin is when you hear a politician say something so patently untrue that you want to throw a beer bottle at the TV set. As a former student of theology, I take a loftier road: spin is when somebody says something so outrageous that you expect God to send a bolt of lightning to strike the spinner dead on the spot.

Unfortunately, spin is not always so obvious. Sometimes, it's much more insidious. When George W. Bush said that politics had nothing to do with his decision on stem-cell research, some people didn't see the spin. Some people actually believed him.

GEORGE ORWELL AND SPIN

Spin has its roots in what was first described as "Newspeak" by George Orwell in his novel *1984*. (Orwell may have gotten the date wrong, but he was right about everything else.) In the totalitarian state he described, the ruling party controlled thought by controlling the language. The key was "doublethink," as expressed in "doublespeak"—by which one says the exact opposite of what one means, yet ends up believing it to be true: "War Is Peace," "Freedom Is Slavery," and "Ignorance Is Strength."

Another disturbing parallel between Washingtonspeak and Newspeak is the shrinking vocabulary. In Orwell's *1984*, certain words are dropped from the language each year until, in the end, Oldspeak disappears entirely and only Newspeak is left. If you can't express a thought in Newspeak, that thought cannot be expressed at all. The leaders of our nation do not operate with the same level of efficiency, but they do play the same game with words: they drop certain words or phrases and replace them with others, in order to control or change what we think about a proposal by giving it a new name.

Thus, "late-term" abortion becomes "partial-birth" abortion and "fast track" authority becomes "trade promotion" authority. Ronald Reagan's original proposal to build a Strategic Defense Initiative has undergone many name changes over the years—from SDI, or Strategic Defense Initiative, to "Brilliant Pebbles" to "National Missile Defense" to simply "missile defense" today, although the best name was and remains "Star Wars."

In Orwell's classic essay, "Politics and the English Language," he compares those who so deftly manipulate language to "a cuttlefish spurting out ink." It's all part of politics, he argues. From those who inhabit the corrupt world of politics, says Orwell, we can expect to encounter equally corrupt speech. After all, he continues: "Political language—and with variations this is true of all political parties, from Conservatives to Anarchists—is designed to make lies sound truthful and murder respectable, and to give an appearance of solidity to pure wind."

"Giving solidity to pure wind": how closely that resembles the contemporary news conference. Over the years, I have listened to politicians of all stripes and ideologies attempting to give "solidity to pure wind."

I confess: I had done a little spinning of my own before joining CNN. For almost fifteen years, with one year out to run for political office, I worked on radio and TV in Los Angeles, the second-biggest market in the country. My specialty was nightly political commentary as part of the evening news—first on KABC-TV, later on KCOP-TV. In only two and a half minutes, I'd not only tell you everything you needed to know about an issue, I'd tell you what you should think about it. On the late news, at 11 P.M., I'd do the same thing in only thirty seconds. The formula was: "Here are the facts. Here is my spin. Thank you for listening."

Soon after starting in TV, I branched out into talk radio, first, as guest host for the vacationing Michael Jackson (the talk show host, not the Gloved One) on KABC Radio. Next, I was presenting political commentary during morning drive. Then, I was debating the issues every afternoon with conservative sidekick Bill Pearl, where we were immediately dubbed "The Dueling Bills." Eager to have my own show, I moved to KFI Radio and launched *Bill Press, True American* on weekend afternoons. When Republican spokesman Tony Blankley first heard of my radio moniker, "True American," he sniffed, "Talk about spin!"

More so than television news, talk radio is spin heaven. The talk show host begins with an opening spin on the topic of the hour. Then listeners call to spin the talk show host. It's great fun, and it's the most democratic forum that exists for the debate and discussion of ideas. Talk radio is the home of equal opportunity spinning.

I've always been comfortable in politics: While working in TV and radio, I also held down the volunteer job of Chairman of the California Democratic Party and took time out in 1990 to run unsuccessfully in the Democratic primary for California State Insurance Commissioner. I started out volunteering for Gene McCarthy in 1968 and ran a campaign in San Francisco for Supervisor Roger Boas. I worked for nine years in Sacramento as Chief of Staff for State Senator Peter Behr; as Executive Director of the Planning and Conservation League, an environmental lobby; and as Director of the California Office of Planning and Research for Governor Jerry Brown. By the time I began broadcasting, I knew almost every elected official in the state, Republican and Democrat, starting with Pat Brown, Jesse Unruh and Ronald Reagan, and I had worked with many of them on various issues.

But my first introduction to spin—real spin, as practiced by a master—was with California Governor Jerry Brown. Whenever the governor gave a news conference, his team of advisers would immediately gather in Press Secretary Bill Stall's office, anxiously awaiting the first story about his remarks to come over the Associated Press wire. If the coverage did not match their expectations, either Stall or Chief of Staff Gray Davis (now governor himself) or top adviser Tom Quinn—or sometimes even the governor—would get the reporter on the phone, harangue him and demand a different lead to the story. Most of the time, the poor reporter, perhaps stunned by the immediate and urgent attention, usually agreed to provide it.

First, the governor spun the news in his statement. Then, if he didn't get the spin he wanted, he was able to spin it again—all before the wire story was picked up by the papers or radio or TV. This was virtual spin control. In state capitols, it still happens every day.

So, before joining *Crossfire,* I'd been around the block—the relatively small block that California is. Nevertheless, I was unprepared for the total verbal disconnect in the nation's capital. In many ways, Washington really did resemble

Alice's Mad Tea Party. With every *Crossfire* guest, I understood the words they spoke well enough, but they didn't exactly say what they meant, or mean what they said.

After one year in Washington, I was afraid I might end up believing things like "People are homeless by choice," "Guns don't kill," "Conservatives are compassionate" and "Arsenic is good for drinking water."

I soon came to realize that the twists and turns of language I was hearing in Washington were not as evil as Orwell's Newspeak (not yet, anyway). What I was hearing was much more banal. Somewhere between lies and the truth, these were not the words of tyrants seeking to control; they were the utterings of politicians seeking to confuse. But they were also the words of politicians who were confused themselves, because they were leading double lives. And not just the politicians, unfortunately; most of the people around them were leading double lives as well. Welcome to Washington.

WASHINGTON AS SPIN

The late Meg Greenfield, editorial page editor of the *Washington Post,* discovered that people inside the Beltway had developed a language of their own, speaking on two levels at once: "The two-track conversation is as close as the capitol comes to having its own language," she notes in her memoir *Washington.* In every conversation, in other words, almost in every statement, there is the literal meaning and the implied meaning. In a world of spin, we hear the literal meaning, but respond to the implied.

Greenfield also discovered that people didn't just talk in two tracks, they also lived in those same two tracks. They pretended to be someone who, in fact, they were not, and they pretended so successfully that they soon forgot which persona was the real one and which was the phony. "It is as if everyone who came to the place were put into the witness protection program," Greenfield explained, "furnished with a complete new public identity, and left with much untended anxiety about the vestiges of the old one. We are, most of us, much of the time, in disguise. We present ourselves as we think we are meant to be."

So Washington veterans, both in and around the Congress and the White House, all have their public persona and their private persona. After a while, they're not sure which is which.

In such an environment, spin is essential to enabling one to mask the truth—both in speech and in life. Spin is the only way to survive, or to advance one's personal or political agenda.

As novices, our first reaction is to flee. Our second is to scream out loud, "Cut the bullshit!" Our third, which most fall into, is simply to accept it and begin cultivating our own double personality. That's the way it is, it's not going to change, and you might as well adapt accordingly.

Like Meg Greenfield and countless others, I learned to survive in Washington by learning to recognize spin, deal with it, laugh at it, see through it—and even do a little spinning myself. Why not? When in Rome, spin as the Romans spin.

But while Washington may be the capital of spin, it's not alone. Wherever we live today, we live in a world of mutual dependency between spinners and spun. Spinners feel they must spin in order to gain any respect or attention. Spinnees, in turn, expect a certain amount of freedom with the truth from others. We are constantly spinning each other in circles. And we are spinning our discourse downward.

Today, spin is no longer a secret. It's openly talked about—and bragged about. If, earlier, politicians or consultants were occasionally derided as mere "spinners," they now proudly label themselves "spin doctors" or "spinmeisters." If gatherings of supporters were once mocked as "spin alley," campaigns now openly organize "spin rooms," where spokespeople come to spin and reporters come to be spun.

Every celebrity today has his or her own spokesperson, or spinperson. And not just celebrities, almost anybody who lands in the news gets one.

- O.J. still has a spin doctor.
- Congressman Gary Condit hired one along with a criminal attorney. So did Chandra Levy's parents.
- When a little boy in Florida lost his arm to a shark, his uncle first yanked his severed arm out of the shark's jaws—and then hired a spin doctor.

Even spin doctors need spin doctors. When New York's celebrity flack Lizzie Grubman got into hot water for backing her SUV into the crowd outside a Hamptons night club, she hired two of them.

Life is tough. By the time you pay for your personal trainer and your personal spin doctor, there's no money left for groceries.

THE SPIN ROOM

By the 2000 election, spin had become such an important component of political campaigns that CNN decided to launch a new show about spin called the *Spin Room.* Conservative columnist Tucker Carlson and I got the lucky assignment. We parsed the spin every night throughout the election, the long recount and into the first months of the new administration, when Tucker moved over to join me and Bob Novak on *Crossfire.*

Tucker's great fun to work with (and I'm not just spinning!). Neither one of us takes ourselves, or our political parties, too seriously. Unlike any other political show on television, *Spin Room* was a casual, meandering conversation: a chance to kick back at the end of the day, chew over the latest news, poke holes into the most outrageous spins of the day, read e-mails and chat room comments from viewers and, most important, enjoy a few laughs.

But what started out as a show about political spin became a show about universal spin. Once Tucker and I started talking about political spin—and the more examples of spin we heard from viewers—we realized that spin was not limited to politics. Spin was everywhere. In every profession and every human experience, we are bombarded with spin: from doctors, lawyers, car salesmen, advertisers, businessmen, professors, journalists, preachers, boyfriends, girlfriends, even husbands and wives. Parents spin their kids, and kids spin their parents. Spin makes the world go round.

Before anybody spins us, before we spin anybody else, it all starts closer to home: we spin ourselves. What is self-esteem but spinning oneself in a positive manner? Who wants to go around all day feeling down in the dumps? Do yourself a favor. Take a cue from Al Franken's Stuart Smalley on *Saturday Night Live:* "I'm good enough, I'm smart enough, and doggone it, some people like me." Start your day by telling yourself how smart, good-looking, clever, witty and sexy you are.

Spin yourself.

GOOD SPIN/BAD SPIN

The obvious question: *Is spin bad?*

That's what most people think. Spin has a bad reputation, which is unfortunate, because not all spin is bad. For the most part, it's benign. And sometimes, it can actually be a good thing. (The best answer, in the end, is what the old man said when asked whether he wore boxers or briefs: "Depends . . .")

Spin can be bad. Spin can be evil. It can be used deliberately to deceive, to cover up, to distort the facts and to justify the most foul acts a person or government can commit. In those cases, spin is more accurately called a "lie." However, as Lanny Davis—former spinner for Bill Clinton and one of the world's best—observes in his book *Truth to Tell,* that kind of spin often backfires, because the truth comes out and the liar is caught with egg on his face. In which case, Davis concludes: "Bad spinning is not only dishonest, it is ineffective."

Unfortunately, lies don't always backfire. Sometimes people get away with lies. Always have, and always will.

But most spin is garden-variety harmless. It is nowhere near a lie. It is simply toying with the truth:

- When a movie critic gushes: "You'll be rolling in the aisles. The worst that could happen is missing this film." That's spin.
- When your son comes home from fishing, stretches out his hands and says: "Mom, you should have seen the one that got away!" That's spin.
- When the golf pro tells you: "All you have to do is buy this new titanium club. It'll take ten strokes off your game." That's spin.
- When we dignify the job of trash collector by calling him "a sanitation engineer." That's spin.
- When Reno, Nevada, promotes itself as "The Biggest Little City in the World." That's spin.
- When the minister tells a grieving widow: "God loved your husband so much, He wanted him right up there alongside Him." That's spin.
- When a national politician gets off the plane from an early foray into Iowa and New Hampshire and swears to reporters: "I haven't even thought about running for president. For the next two years, all I want is to do the best possible job for the people of my home state." Don't believe a word he says. He doesn't expect you to. That's spin.
- When a man tells a woman: "That's the best sex I've ever had in my entire life." He's just happy he got laid. That's spin.

Spin (n): something between truth and a lie.

HELPFUL SPIN

Spin can also be a positive force to help us through some sticky situations.

- After twenty-seven years of marriage and four kids, a famous couple gets divorced and a spokesman insists they're "still friends—they just discovered they weren't compatible anymore." Now, everybody knows he's been cheating on her for years, they haven't lived as man and wife for years, and they were just waiting for their youngest to start college before making it official. But spin makes it easier for them to hold their heads up high. Why not?

- You hate your job. You hate your boss even more, and the feeling is mutual. Along comes a new job, so you quit your old job. But you don't burn your bridges behind you. You spin your way out of it: "I really enjoyed this job. It's been a great learning experience for me. In many ways, I hate to go, but it's time to move on." And, sure enough, the boss even says a few nice things about you, no matter how happy she is to see you finally walk out the door for good. Spin gets you both through what could have been a painful situation.

- In May 2001, after reporting huge losses and being slammed with an SEC investigation, Lucent Technologies canned its hot shot CFO Deborah C. Hopkins—but made her a sweetheart deal. In addition to providing her full $650,000 base salary and a severance payment of at least $1.95 million, Lucent agreed to hire a public relations executive for six months to protect her reputation by spinning the reasons for her departure. The deal later fell through, but the precedent was set. From now on, when fired, every powerful Wall Street executive will be entitled to his or her own spin doctor. Never again will anyone dare say: "So-and-so did a lousy job, so we fired his ass!"

Spin is also used in applying for a job. After all, what's a good job interview but good spin?

- If you're serious about getting the job, you're sure as hell not going to slink in, shoulders drooping, eyes downcast and whisper, "I'm not really sure I can handle all the pressure, but I'd be willing to give it a try, if you'd be so kind as to be patient with me." Instead, you stride in, standing tall, and proudly declare, "I was born to do this job. I'm the best person you could find, no matter how many you interview." You know it's spin. They know it's spin. But that's the way you get the job.

Spin helps in less dramatic ways, too.

- Question: "Hey, how goes it?" Answer: "Great!" or "No complaints" or "Never been better"—not "Life really sucks, big time." Putting it more positively makes us feel more positive about ourselves.

Spin is a self-help technique as old as Dale Carnegie's 1936 classic *How to Win Friends and Influence People.* It builds us up in the eyes of others. In the section of his book on "How to Win People to Your Way of Thinking," Carnegie advises: "Let the other person feel that the idea is his or hers." Now that is nothing but spin, but it works. We all do it.

Sometimes spin is a means toward a greater end. If you really value a friendship, you don't have to destroy it by telling the guy how much your wife can't stand him. Spin the reason he's never invited over, spare him the truth, save the friendship. Spin may also be the way to keep a job, save a marriage or salvage a business relationship. If so, it's worth it. The end doesn't always justify the means, but in this case it does.

During time of war, spin can also serve to unite an entire nation and help us through adversity. After the horrendous attacks against the World Trade Center and the Pentagon, the first time foreign terrorists struck the American mainland, there were many strong statements from President Bush and other leaders. "We are the greatest people on earth." "We will not be scared off." "We have declared war on terrorism." "This is World War III." "We will win this war." "We will find those responsible and wipe them off the face of the planet." "He can run but he can't hide." "We will bring Osama bin Laden back dead or alive."

Some of it was true. Some of it was hyperbole. Some of it was spin. Some of it was more suited to a Super Bowl game than national policy. But all of it was welcome, helping us pull together, survive, steel ourselves for the difficult days ahead, start rebuilding, and return to as close to normalcy as we will ever get. Spin works.

Most important, spin builds us up in our own eyes as well. Spinning ourselves helps us gain self-confidence. In today's competitive world, spin is an essential survival technique.

This book is a look at spin in its many dimensions: good and bad; political, professional and personal; historical and current. After reading it, you will be better equipped to live in the world of spin. You will know how to spot spin better. You will know how to recognize it, decipher it, see through it, respond to it—and, perhaps, even how to better practice it yourself.

You will, in fact, be spin-proof.

ONE

THE BEST
POSSIBLE LIGHT

You can fool all of the people some of the time, and
some of the people all of the time, but you can not fool
all of the people all of the time.

Abraham Lincoln

In May 2001, when former Independent Counsel Ken Starr
appeared on CNN's *Crossfire,* I asked him to comment on a
charge by Senator Charles Schumer that Republicans under
George W. Bush were attempting an ideological takeover of
the federal courts. Starr didn't hesitate one second. "Look,
that is spin," he sniffed. "That is absolute spin."

He didn't define the term. He didn't have to. A few years
ago, nobody would have known what Starr meant. Today,
everyone listening did. We live in the Age of Spin.

Advertising critic Randall Rothenberg, in fact, suggests
there is something called the "Media-Spindustrial Complex,"
which encompasses advertising, public relations, lobbying,
polling, direct mail, investor relations, focus groups, jury
consulting, speechwriting, radio and television stations and
newspapers—all joined together in the business of twisting
the truth. He's not being cynical. In fact, he may be naïve.
Spin may be even more widespread than that.

*   *   *

Today, truth is relative. We are not obliged, or expected, to speak the truth. Instead, we routinely manipulate the truth in order to shine the best possible light on the worst of circumstances. We no longer say what we mean, nor mean what we say. We say what we want people to think, and, if we say it often and well enough, people will.

THE BEGINNINGS OF SPIN

There are two origins of the word "spin" as we commonly use it today. The first relates to the ancient art of spinning. That's what the good, old spinning wheel was for. If fibers can be spun, so can words. So it wasn't long before the word "spin" took on the meaning of telling a story. Homer makes this point dramatically in the *Iliad*: Penelope spins and weaves all day long—then, at the end of the day, she pulls the fabric apart and starts all over again the next morning. As she spins the thread, Homer spins the adventures of her missing husband Odysseus. Thus was spin born.

Later, spin took on the additional meaning of using words in a way that even more closely resembled the spinning of thread: not just telling a story, but drawing it out, twisting the facts, exaggerating to make a point. Think of walking along the waterfront in New Bedford, Massachusetts. There, pulling on his pipe, sits a bearded, long-retired sea captain, telling stories of sailing ships and codfish harvest and whaling adventures. Oh, what a yarn he "spins"!

The second, more modern, origin of the word has its roots in that other American pastime: baseball! When a pitcher throws the ball a certain way, he puts "spin" on it, giving it a deviant, rather than a straight, track. He throws a curve. Well, of course, you can put the same spin on words.

The popular English *Bloomsbury Good Word Guide* defines a spin doctor as "a person employed by a political party, government department, etc., to present or interpret facts or events in a favourable light." As an example of current, correct usage of the term, Bloomsbury cites an article from *The Observer:* "Almost everyone who took part in the travelling circus of the election became so bewitched by the spin doctors, photo opportunities and in-jokes of each campaign that we lost sight of one fundamental reality."

But Bloomsbury does not pretend that England invented the spin doctor. It admits that the term, although increasingly popular in the U.K., is actually "a vogue expression of American origin," which has its origin on the playing field. "The expression derives from the spin given to a ball in certain sports in order to control its direction through the air or the way in which it bounces."

Spin as practiced today is neither so innocent nor so one-dimensional. It comes in many varieties, but it is always used to camouflage the truth, rather than to tell it.

THE TEN ESSENTIAL SPINS

THE HAPPY-FACE SPIN

In its most innocent and innocuous form, spin is simply putting bad news in a better light: If you're dealt a handful of bad cards, bluff and pretend it's a royal flush. Or, as San Francisco's legendary advertising genius Jerry Mander once famously spun: "When you're handed a lemon, make lemonade."

Putting a spin on bad news is something we do naturally. It's how we survive. Any bad news can be turned into a positive. So what if Jake got canned? He still has his health, doesn't he? And isn't good health more important than a good job? Sure, her house burned down, but she saved her family photographs. Yes, he totaled his car, but at least he had insurance. The Mets lost, but they played a great game.

In the media, you quickly learn to put the best spin on everything, even total failure. When Dr. Laura Schlesinger's TV show bombed in the ratings and was canceled after only seven months, she still saw a sliver of sunshine. "I think the good news is, people got to see the mettle of my character," she told an interviewer for *World* magazine. "If there were ever a question of my character, there isn't anymore. I guess in every pile of poop, there is a flower that grows."

Only Dr. Laura would say "pile of poop" instead of "pile of shit." But, then again, she was speaking to a conservative Christian publication. And who but Dr. Laura would compare herself to a flower that feasts on feces?

As former Democratic Chairman of California, I was called upon more than once to put a happy-face spin on losing an election. "The important thing is not that we didn't win the election. The important thing is that we received 57 percent of the women's vote and 49 percent of the minority vote. That is a great victory." Nonsense, I would think to myself. We still lost, Bozo.

Variations on this same lame excuse were heard from Los Angeles in June 2001, when Antonio Villaraigosa lost his chance to become the first Latino mayor of Los Angeles in modern times. It was a huge embarrassment for Hispanics, who make up almost 50 percent of L.A.'s population. Still, supporters insisted they were not disappointed. "Just the fact that he came so close," psychologist Mauricio Murillo, told the *New York Times*. "I think he did the most he could've done."

Being sent to jail, too, could be a good thing. Sentenced for 90 days for protesting the American bombing of Vieques Island, the Rev. Al Sharpton, potential presidential candidate in 2004, beamed, "Nelson Mandela went from prison to president."

A serious heart condition can even be happy-face spun into good news, as long as you have the right cardiologist—and the right spin doctor. When Vice President Dick Cheney was rushed to the hospital for his second heart procedure in three months, Mary Matalin, my former co-host on *Crossfire*, now Cheney's communications director, faced a real challenge: how to paint this as a routine procedure that would not interfere with performance of his official duties.

In order to help meet this challenge, *Brill's Content* magazine sought advice from several expert spin doctors, including Michael Deaver, the man who succeeded in making people believe Ronald Reagan actually understood the issues he was talking about. Here was Deaver's prescription for Cheney:

"I'd keep Vice President Cheney's schedule as public as possible: Get him out there. I'd show him walking on Capitol Hill, talking to senators, going to his Senate office. Show him active when he's in the Senate and walking around the White House complex." Even before the magazine appeared, Mary Matalin, acting on her own instinct for good spin, followed Deaver's advice and had Cheney out walking.

Indeed, with enough imagination, even the most gruesome situation can be positively portrayed. When it came time for the execution of Oklahoma City bomber Timothy McVeigh at the federal penitentiary in Terre Haute, Indiana, Mayor Judy Anderson was asked by the *New Yorker*'s Marc Singer how she felt about her city's being the center of such morbid international attention. "It's not something we chose," admitted the mayor, "but because it's going to happen we're trying to put a positive spin on the activities that will take place here." Her spin: that the people of Terre Haute are really very friendly, unlike your typical executioner, and that the federal prison is really a wonderful institution that employs a lot of local people. The death chamber is just one, unfortunate, part of the prison that, after all, is rarely used.

The gallant mayor also found positive things to say about all the hucksters who suddenly showed up in Terre Haute to make a buck off the execution by hawking buttons, souvenir programs and T-shirts. "We have no control over what they sell," she acknowledged, "We're just asking that it be in very good taste." Sounds good, unless you know, as Singer reports, that the hottest-selling item at the souvenir stands was the front page of a phony newspaper called "The Hangin' Times," with a photograph of McVeigh and the headline: "Die Motherfucker Die." Hard to spin that one as good taste. Indeed, it's hard to imagine any execution souvenir that could be considered good taste.

The risk with spinning bad news as good news is that you sometimes get caught—and exposed. In May 2001, Republican Senator James Jeffords of Vermont—exasperated by an increasingly right-wing and intolerant Republican party, and snubbed one too many times by the Bush White House—sud-

denly left the GOP and became an Independent, thereby handing power over to Senate Democrats and leaving the Bush policy agenda up the proverbial shit creek without a paddle. An
embarrassed George W. Bush unleashed political counselor
Karl Rove to absolve the White House of any blame by slam-
ming Jeffords's motives: The White House did nothing to push
Jeffords out of the party, Rove insisted. His defection was mo-
tivated only by "committee chairs and deals and bargains and
pledges" with Democrats. Exposing this double-dealing was
considered good news for the White House.

Rove's gambit backfired. An outraged Jeffords declared
that his decision was based on principle, not expediency. As a
Republican, he felt he could no longer represent his state or the
nation on the issues he cared about: education, energy, choice,
the environment. As a moderate, he felt unwelcome in a party
and administration led by George W. Bush. That's why he left.
Any other explanation, Jeffords sneered, was mere "spinning."

THE BOY-SCOUT (OR GIRL-SCOUT) SPIN

An equally common form of spin is the pious denial. Why
admit you did something wrong when you can save face—
and, perhaps, fool the world—by casting your crime, or some
embarrassing action or statement, in the best possible light?

When Linda Chavez was nominated by President George
W. Bush to be Labor Secretary, she was roundly condemned
for having hired an illegal alien to work in her home at a sub-
minimum wage. Forced to withdraw her nomination, Chavez
did not deny that she had employed a woman from
Guatemala illegally. But, she insisted, she had not knowingly
broken the law. She was simply being a good Samaritan. Or,
to use George Bush's now-classic spin, she was just living the
role of a "compassionate conservative."

For obvious reasons, getting caught with your pants down
seems to bring out the most colorful spin in people—and not
just in Washington. When Eddie Murphy was caught with a
transvestite prostitute in his car on Hollywood's Santa Monica

Boulevard—actually, he was driving his wife's car!—the free-wheeling, fast-talking Eddie was lost for words, but his publicist issued a classic denial that the comedian had done nothing wrong: Eddie was just offering a downtrodden woman a ride home. "Nothing happened at all," insisted the flack, "but Eddie said he will never do this again." Of course not. Eddie will never again troll Hollywood Boulevard, looking for hookers to give free rides to—especially not in his wife's car.

But for the most imaginative boy-scout spin, it's hard to top controversial Ohio Congressman James Traficant, a favorite *Spin Room* guest. His hair defies gravity, as does his spin. In his first trial for racketeering, back in the early '80s, when he was county sheriff, Traficant successfully defended himself against charges he had pocketed Mafia money in return for looking the other way on mob activities. How? By convincing a jury that he had not accepted bribes from the mob. Rather, in a secret, one-man sting operation, Traficant insisted, he was simply helping take their money "out of circulation"—and thereby performing a valuable public service.

This type of spin is clearly just a fancy word for bullshit. But I'm willing to bet that neither Linda Chavez, Eddie Murphy, nor James Traficant actually believed their crazy stories. Not only that, they didn't expect us to believe them, either. That's just the way it works. It's the standard response when shit happens today. Spin it the best you can because you know nobody believes what you're saying anyway, and it's less painful for everyone involved than telling the truth.

THE TWILIGHT-ZONE SPIN

Sometimes spin is used to express the exact opposite of what one means.

Politicians often spin this way and, remarkably, do so with a straight face. In the early days of the Bush administration—with the Senate tied 50–50 and Republicans holding an edge only because of the tie-breaking vote of Vice President Dick Cheney—Minority Leader Tom Daschle stood in front of reporters and declared, "We look forward to working closely with Republicans in a constructive, bipartisan manner." Reporters dutifully jotted it down, but they didn't believe it. Neither did Daschle. Everybody knew what he really meant was, "We'll go along as best we can for now. But, as soon as Strom Thurmond dies and we get control of the Senate, we'll cut their balls off." Then Jim Jeffords switched parties and that's exactly what Daschle did.

Consider the courtroom: How many times does the defendant who pleads "not guilty" really mean it? More often than not, when he tells the judge "not guilty," what he means is, "I'm guilty as sin, but I don't think you have enough evidence to prove it, so go ahead and take your best shot."

Failure to recognize this brand of spin can prove dangerous to your relationship. When your significant other, for example, insists, "My birthday's no big deal. I don't want to do anything special"—don't you believe it. Order the flowers, make a reservation for dinner, light the candles, or your goose is cooked. Silly you—you missed the twilight-zone spin.

SPIN HALL OF FAME NOMINATION

By Robert D. Novak

NOMINEE: Al Gore

OCCASION: Al Gore at the 1996 Democratic Convention.

SPIN: "Three thousand young people will start smoking tomorrow. One thousand of them will die a death not unlike my sister's. And that's why, until I draw my last breath, I will pour my heart and soul into the cause of protecting our children from the danger of smoking."

TRANSLATION: "Looks like anti-smoking is the way to go right now. So I'll run with it."

While Al Gore's speech may have sounded heartfelt at the time, in fact it stands as a hallmark of spin. Not only had Al received $16,000 in tobacco money during his tenure as a Tennessee congressman, his party had received more than $900,000 in tobacco funds from 1992 to 1995. And Gore is the man who once proudly boasted of tobacco, "I want you to know that with my own hands all of my life, I put it in the plant beds and transferred it. I've hoed it. I've dug in it. I've sprayed it, I've chopped it, I've shredded it, spiked it, put it in the barn and stripped it and sold it." For invoking his deceased sister to mask his earlier political and vocational ventures in tobacco, Al Gore reached a new low in spin.

Robert Novak is the co-host of CNN's Crossfire *and a nationally syndicated columnist for the* Chicago Sun-Times.

This form of spin is not just saying one thing while meaning another. There's another variation: pretending to *be* one thing when, in fact, you're just the opposite. In the 2000 presidential campaign, Al Gore pretended to be a Tennessee farmer, when his entire lifetime was spent at three different addresses along Washington, D.C.'s Massachusetts Avenue, with only summer vacations in Tennessee. But he wasn't the only pretender: George W. Bush also painted himself as the Washington outsider, the Western maverick. Bush was born in Connecticut; educated at Andover, Yale and Harvard; helped manage his daddy's campaign for president; and lived and worked for a while in the White House. Forget the 10-gallon hat. Bush is a Beltway boy with a twilight-zone spin.

What's interesting is that this phenomenon of pretending to be someone you're not is not unique to Bush and Gore. It's expected, or required, of anyone aspiring to the White House or Congress. There's a certain personal transformation necessary for anyone who comes to live and work in the nation's capital. As we saw earlier, they're asked to join what Meg Greenfield called "the witness protection program." That duality of personality may exist elsewhere in the country, but nowhere to the degree it does in Washington.

Here spin is a fancy word for camouflage. And, again, people believe what they want to believe. They believed Bush, even though they knew it wasn't true, because they liked him. They didn't believe Gore, because they didn't trust him. His cowboy boots didn't look like they'd ever stepped in a cowflop.

THE BLAME-IT-ON-MY-YOUTH SPIN

Kids can get away with murder. We all know that, because we all did. And just like, in some ways, we never want to grow up, in other ways, we never want to lose the innocence of childhood—especially the ability to do something wrong, bad, or just plain stupid, and get away with it because "after all, he's just a kid."

Illinois Congressman Henry Hyde. As Chairman of the House Judiciary Committee, Hyde was riding his white horse, leading the Republican charge against that wife-cheating Bill Clinton, when Salon.com reported that Hyde was quite the wife-cheater himself as a state legislator. In fact, as a married man, he had enjoyed a very public fling with a female legislative assistant. Hyde testily denied that his transgression bore any similarity to Clinton's playing around. Cheating on his own wife, Hyde piously insisted, had been but "a youthful indiscretion." That's the classic blame-it-on-my-youth spin. At the time of his affair, Hyde was 41 years old, married, with two kids. Indiscreet, yes. Youthful, no.

Interestingly enough, the Hyde spin proved to be contagious. George W. Bush caught it toward the end of his campaign. Just days before the election, news broke of his long-covered-up drunk driving arrest: an event that happened in 1976 in Kennebunkport, Maine, but had never been reported.

His handlers dismissed the news as too long ago to matter. It was just another "youthful indiscretion." Bush was thirty when arrested. Old enough to know better. And he was fifty and governor of Texas when he instructed his attorney, Al Gonzales, now White House counsel, to get him out of serving on a DWI jury, so he wouldn't have to lie about his own driving record.

As transparent as Bush's don't-blame-me-I-was-only-a-kid spin was, it worked. In fact, it was the entire basis of George W. Bush's campaign for president. He successfully spun the theory that he had led a wild and woolly life up until the age of forty—thereby self-extending his youth by at least twenty years—and refused to talk about anything that happened during all that time. Under this life-begins-at-forty rule, Bush never had to answer questions about alcohol, drugs or playing hooky from the National Guard. He stuck to his guns that the first forty years of his life were one giant "youthful indiscretion"—that the only part of his life that counted was after he found Jesus—and reporters let him get away with it.

THE VAST-CONSPIRACY SPIN

One of the easiest ways of dealing with bad news is to blame somebody else. It's the grown-up version of the kid who couldn't turn in his homework because his dog ate it. No self-respecting teacher would accept that excuse today, even though they may have once tried it themselves. But you'd be surprised how many self-respecting journalists will still accept a politician's version of the my-dog-ate-my-homework story and report it straight-faced.

This version of spin could, of course, be called the Hillary Clinton defense, because she is its most famous practitioner. Thanks to the miracle of videotape, what Hillary said may be remembered longer than what Bill and Monica did. Interviewed by Matt Lauer, on NBC's *Today* show, the morning of January 27, 1998, she sprang to her husband's defense: "The great story here, for anybody willing to find it and write about it and explain it, is this vast right-wing conspiracy that has been conspiring against my husband since the day he announced for president." And, the sad part is, she believed it at the time.

SPIN HALL OF FAME NOMINATION

ఞఞ

By Kate O'Beirne

NOMINEE: Hillary Clinton

SPIN: "Our role-playing helped Chelsea to experience, in the privacy of our home, the feelings of any person who sees someone she loves being personally attacked."

OCCASION: Hillary describing in her 1996 book *It Takes a Village* how she and Bill Clinton would say horrible things about the future president in front of their six-year-old daughter to steel her against political invective.

TRANSLATION: "By telling that story about Chelsea, we put reporters and political opponents on notice that any time they attacked Bill they were hurting a little girl."

Brilliant spin. By arguing "not in front of the children," Hillary deflects all manner of Clinton criticism back on the critics. Of course, Chelsea wouldn't have had to hear so many horrible things about her father if he hadn't done so many horrible things over the course of his career, but never mind that one nagging fact.

Kate O'Beirne is the Washington Editor of National Review *and a member of CNN's* Capital Gang.

But, even though Republicans later slammed Hillary for accusing them of being responsible for her husband's philandering, they quickly sang the same song when they, too, got into trouble. When the House Judicial Committee was preparing to begin hearings on President Clinton's dalliance with Monica Lewinsky and it was reported that Judiciary Chairman Henry Hyde, while still a state legislator in Springfield, Illinois, had enjoyed his own adulterous fling with Cheryl Snodgrass, Hyde borrowed a page from Hillary's book. In addition to his blame-it-on-my-youth spin, Hyde questioned the motives and the timing of those who had released this bombshell. "The only purpose for this being dredged up now is an obvious attempt to intimidate me and it won't work. I intend to fulfill my constitutional duty and deal judiciously with the serious felony allegations presented to Congress in the Starr report." In other words, when forced to defend the low road, take the high road.

Hyde wasn't the only Republican to grab for the Hillary/conspiracy life preserver when his boat started to sink. When Dubya's drunk-driving arrest was made public, the evidence of drunk driving, plus the fact that he had denied ever breaking the law, threatened to derail Bush's candidacy and cost him the election. Bush spinners went to work and had Dubya painted as the victim of a vast, *left*-wing conspiracy. "Why now, four days before the election?" he asked. "I've got my suspicions." His staff blamed the conspiracy on a local Democratic attorney and, of course, the liberal media, even though his arrest was first reported by Maine's Fox News station, hardly a bastion of the liberal press.

THE IT-DEPENDS-ON-THE-DEFINITION SPIN

Every president leaves behind one memorable phrase for the history books. Of all the great things he said, Abe Lincoln will be remembered most for: "With malice toward none, and charity for all." For Franklin Roosevelt it was: "The only thing we have to fear is fear itself." Of Richard Nixon, we will always remember: "I am not a crook." But Bill Clinton takes the cake. In one way, at least, he outshines them all: "I did not have sex with that woman, Miss Lewinsky."

This, we soon learned, was pure spin. Clinton was not lying to the American people, he was just spinning them. He did not have "sex" with that woman, Miss Lewinsky, as long as we all agree on what the definition of sex is. In Clinton's dictionary, we soon learned—and it may be true on most college campuses today–the definition of sex does not include oral sex. Yes, Virginia, you can still give blow jobs and be a virgin. Yes, Bill, you can still get blow jobs from your intern and not cheat on your wife. When sex is spun according to the it-depends-on-the-definition spin, only vaginal sex counts as adultery.

You would think that, once he'd been caught stretching the truth, Clinton would have learned his lesson. But, no, for months, he continued trying to wiggle out of taking responsibility for his irresponsible acts by redefining terms. Asked if his denial of sexual relations with Monica Lewinsky before the judge in the Paula Jones case had been a lie, Clinton said not necessarily: "It depends on what your definition of is is." As if everybody didn't know the meaning of is!

In the end, Clinton was impeached, not for having sex with Monica—that did not meet the definition of an impeachable offense—but for lying about it under oath. That in turn inspired Newt Gingrich to play his own word games. When news broke that Gingrich was having a secret affair with congressional aide Calista Bisek, at the very same time he was leading the Republican charge against Clinton, Newt and fellow Republicans insisted it was not the same thing. Yes, he had cheated on his wife, but he had not *lied* about it when caught, and that made all the difference. In other words, it depends on the meaning of the word "adultery": If you don't lie about it, it's not adultery. Unfortunately for Newt, his aggrieved wife, Marianne, didn't buy his depends-on-the-definition spin.

A couple of *Spin Room* viewers sent in another example of definitional spin. This one from the world of sports: "Just to show you that spin is not confined to politics," e-mailed Joan Seltzer and Don LoCrasto from San Francisco, "Manager Dusty Baker of the San Francisco Giants made the following comment when asked why pitcher Kirk Reuter gave up 8 runs in one inning. 'Kirk was hurt by a number of near strikes,' Baker replied." As Joan and Don pointed out, most people define "near strikes" as "balls"—and, unlike in horseshoes or hand grenades, in baseball near misses don't count.

THE FREE-LUNCH SPIN

Of course, there's no such thing as a free lunch. Everybody knows that. But some things we want to believe, even though we know they're not true, and the free lunch is one of them. Which, of course, as P. T. Barnum knew, makes us born targets for spin, and born suckers for anybody who spins us that we're about to get something for nothing.

The free-lunch spin is everywhere you look in the world of sales and business. How often do we hear the phrase: "no money down"? Or, better yet, as "Paul, the King of Big Screen," used to advertise on KFI Radio in Los Angeles: "no money down, no interest, no payments—until next year's Super Bowl game."

The implication, of course, is that it hurts less, or costs less, if you simply defer the payments, when, in fact, the exact opposite is true. By putting no money down, you end up paying more, not less. Even if you wait a whole, interest-free year before starting to make payments, you'll still be more in the hole than ever, and deeper in debt, because you've probably already spent all the money you could have been using to make regular payments on other irresistible bargains. Plus, you've had the big screen for a year, so it's no longer a novelty, and you're probably wondering why you bought the damned thing in the first place. Or else you're dying for this year's even bigger model. Great free lunch, wasn't it?

Perhaps the most widespread free-lunch spin comes from credit-card companies. If you believe the advertising, you never have to pay for anything anymore. You don't even have to fill out any forms or qualify for credit. As long as you have a mailing address, valid personalized credit cards will start arriving in the mail. Then, all you have to do is hand over a piece of plastic, and the objects of your desire are all yours. Of course, it only follows that the more plastic cards you have, the more toys you can acquire. You can have it all for nothing—until the bill comes. Then you can still have it for next to nothing, as long as you make the bare minimum payment, just enough to keep your line of credit alive.

Why spoil the fun by warning people that credit-card companies charge the highest rate of interest of any financial institution? Why point out they'd be better off applying for and getting a consumer loan from a bank? Why warn eager shoppers they could soon get themselves into so deep a hole they'll never dig their way out? What the hell? Why ruin the spin of a free lunch? Just charge the free lunch to your credit card!

Whether they're shopping with cash or credit card, consumers are hooked by another spin: the bargain price. It's so phony, it's comical, but it still works. And we're all suckers. You've had your heart set on those new $5,000 golf clubs forever, but they were just too damned expensive to justify. Then, one day, you're walking through the pro shop and there they are, at a big discount: "Special! Today only! Save $1,000." You can't resist. You hand over your plastic, you load the clubs into the car, you drive home and walk in the door with the good news: "Honey, I just saved $1,000!" No, idiot, you just spent $4,000 for clubs you don't need and that are not going to improve your hopeless game.

The other spin with pricing is the 99-cent trick. Yes, we all know there's no difference between $11 and $10.99—but somehow, $10.99 sounds a lot more reasonable and affordable. Suckers that we are, we'll fall for it everytime.

In sales and advertising, just remember the rule: If it sounds too good to be true, it undoubtedly is.

THE STATISTICS SPIN

When all else fails, overwhelm them with numbers. This kind of spin works, frankly, because people are usually so impressed with statistics, they don't pause to question the valid-ity of the numbers or what they really mean. As the saying goes, 73.5% of statistics are made up.

General Barry McCaffrey, President Clinton's drug czar, was a real spinmeister. Good thing, too. The war on drugs is such a spectacular failure, only spin can make it appear worth all the billions of dollars we continue to spend trying to plug the holes in our leaky border—when the real problem is one of demand, not supply.

In July 1998, attempting to justify spending even more good money on top of bad, McCaffrey warned that loosening up on drugs would turn the United States into another crime-ridden country like the Netherlands. "The murder rate in Holland is double that in the United States," McCaffrey told reporters. "The overall crime rate in Holland is probably forty percent higher than the United States. That's drugs."

Wow! That's scary enough to make you put down that joint, except that McCaffrey was doing the statistics spin. Some enterprising researcher at The *L.A. Times* checked the figures, and in an editorial a few days later titled "The Drug War Can't Abide Honest Stats," the *Times* rebutted: "In fact, the U.S. murder rate as a percentage of the population is 4.5 times higher than in Holland." General, what were you smoking?

Politicians often use phony stats. In a classic use of the statistics spin to make things seem better than they seem, George W. Bush sold us his massive $1.8 trillion tax cut. When critics pointed out that the bulk of his tax cut went to the wealthiest one percent of Americans, Bush countered that this was only fair because the richest one percent pay most of the taxes and therefore deserve the biggest tax break . . . as if the wealthiest one percent is some disadvantaged group.

Baloney! As a percentage of income, which is the only gauge that matters, Donald Trump pays a much smaller share of taxes than the average, middle-class working stiff, who, unlike Trump, is subject to the regressive payroll tax, which Bush's tax cut doesn't touch. Still, after Bush got finished spinning, it's amazing how many Americans ended up feeling sorry for those poor, deprived one percenters.

Outrageous claims based on faulty numbers, of course,

are what advertising is all about—the more outrageous, the more believable.

Have you heard about the Incredible Expanding Toyota? A recent ad for the new Toyota Camry asks: "How can it be that an automobile that's a mere nine inches longer on the outside gives you over two feet more room on the inside? Maybe it's the new math!" Or, maybe it's the fact that Toyota deliberately mixes cubic feet with linear inches. Either way, it doesn't add up. But enough suckers will believe it.

Just like some suckers will believe this one, too: "You'd have to eat four bowls of Raisin Bran to get the vitamin nutrition in one bowl of Total." How *big* a bowl? Same size bowl? Which vitamins? All vitamins? Please, don't give us too much detail—it would ruin the statistics spin.

But the true home of statistical spin is in public opinion polls, which today dominate and determine both advertising and political campaigns. They are only, as they say, a snapshot in time. Their results are only as valid as the sample surveyed. They can be slanted to prove any side of any issue, depending on how the question is asked. They are, in short, unscientific, undependable, unreliable—meaningless, in fact.

So why does the media breathlessly report every latest poll? Because we all subscribe to the same fallacy. We believe that public opinion is so ephemeral, so fickle and so unquantifiable that if anybody can catch it in their net, nail it down and pin a number on it, it must be true.

Never forget Mark Twain's warning: "There are three kinds of lies: lies, damned lies, and statistics."

THE VICTIM SPIN

The great Samuel Johnson wrote that "the last refuge of a scoundrel is patriotism." He was right, but today he'd have to add, "or sympathy." Today's scoundrels are less likely to hide behind the flag than they are to masquerade as victims, and then expect people to feel sorry for them.

Victimhood is often the first way station on the highway of spin. But the reasoning is so tortured, we're usually moved to laughter, rather than tears. Especially when men spin themselves as victims of women.

When Chandra Levy was first reported missing in May 2001, aides to Congressman Gary Condit denied he had any romantic relationship with the young woman. They were just "good friends," was the official spin—a state of innocence later contradicted by the congressman himself. But the spin went further than that. It was privately suggested that Levy was actively pursuing him, that she wanted more of a relationship than just friendship, that she was, in fact, pressuring him to break up his marriage and marry her—but that he, the virtuous one, was resisting. He, poor guy, was one more victim of a horny, aggressive female.

Yeah, sure. We all remember that the same rumors were spread by the Clinton White House about Monica Lewinsky. What is it about those Washington interns? They just won't stop picking on older, powerful men!

However, Condit's attempts to paint himself as a victim, as outrageous as they are, pale alongside Rudy Giuliani's. Let's face it. There are some people who will never pass the victim test, mainly because, for most of their lives, they've been such successful thugs. Rudy Giuliani a victim? Who's he kidding?

True, in those scary hours and days following the terrorist attacks on New York City of September 11, 2001, Mayor Giuliani proved himself a great leader. He was everywhere. He was in control. He was reassuring. He held the city—and nation—together. He suddenly became, one friend told me, "the Giuliani we'd been looking for for the last eight years." But, up until that time, he more often than not had proved to be a royal pain in the ass.

As U.S. Attorney or mayor of New York, Rudy Giuliani's speciality was making other people victims of his inquisition-like politics: jaywalkers, taxi drivers, streetwalkers, homeless. You name it, he waged war on them all. So for this guy to turn around and spin himself as a victim was kind of a stretch.

But there he was, telling his sad story, spinning himself as a victim of his wife, Donna Hanover, in their God's-gift-to-the-tabloids divorce battles. Some might call him a cad for not only having a public affair with another woman, Judith Nathan, but also for daring to invite her to receptions in his own home, while his wife and children were under the same roof. To all outward appearances, cad indeed. Not so, countered Giuliani. His victim spin: he lived miserable and alone, apart from his wife and kids, in a remote corner of the mayor's mansion; and he was so sick from chemotherapy for his prostate cancer treatments that he spent half the night vomiting his guts out in the bathroom down the hall, because there was no private bath in his forced in-home exile.

Do you feel sorry for him yet? Well, then, try this: It's not true that Ms. Nathan is his lover, we were told. Yes, they are friends. But he's not her lover. In fact, he cannot possibly, *physically*, be her lover—because his radiation treatments have left him impotent. In other words, the mayor who could get it up for everybody else, can't get it up for himself and Judith. Not even Viagra could help.

What a sad case. Usually, we expect a little vigor in our elected officials. Giuliani is the only politician I can remember who tried to make a virtue of being both sick and impotent. Unfortunately for him, the public didn't buy it. He had been such a pest for so long, to so many people, it was simply impossible to accept him as a victim, no matter how hard he tried the victim spin.

THE DON'T-BELIEVE-A-WORD-I-SAY SPIN

We started with the most innocent form of spin. We end with the most evil. So far, the spin we've talked about has been misleading, but fun. But sometimes spin can be more sinister. Sometimes, it's used to mask the truth.

The person whose reputation was hurt most in the Monica Lewinsky affair was neither Monica nor Bill. It was Linda Tripp. Not just because she betrayed and ratted on her co-worker, although that didn't help much either, but because she told such blatant lies about why she did it.

Depending on which day you asked, Tripp had two explanations for why she taped her conversations with the gullible

Lewinsky, turned her over to the FBI, then ran to Independent Counsel Ken Starr and spilled the beans. On Mondays, Wednesdays and Fridays, Tripp said she did so because she had such great respect for the White House that she could not silently bear Clinton's sullying of it. On Tuesdays, Thursdays and Saturdays, she said she was forced to act only because she feared for her life. On Sundays, presumably, she prayed for forgiveness.

Such spin! Such nonsense! As her no-nonsense book agent, Lucianne Goldberg, informed the world, Linda Tripp's motivation was purely personal and financial. She had previously tried to peddle a book about sex in the Bush White House—which, of course, she could never sell because of lack of material. She struck gold in the Clinton White House, but Goldberg pressed her for factual evidence. It was Goldberg, in fact, who suggested that Tripp betray the guileless Lewinsky, an act of treachery the money-grubbing Tripp gleefully agreed to.

Live for greed, spin for patriotism. Does it get any lower?

Of course, that wasn't the only black lie told during the Lewinsky scandal. It was all a sordid collection of lies, by all players involved. One of the worst was the White House's contention, spread to many journalists, that there was nothing to the rumors that President Clinton had a sexual relationship with the White House intern. It was obvious that Miss Lewinsky was a troubled young woman, we were assured, but the president was merely spending time with her to counsel her, just as he had counseled so many other young people.

Yeah, sure. That kind of counseling is called a "blow job."

In defense of White House spinners, however, they probably didn't believe that spin. Loyal soldiers all, they were just repeating the spin they'd been told by you know who.

SPIN AND LIES

Having told you what I think spin is, I want to tell what I think it is not. Spin is not a lie, although many people, chief among them the legendary former *Washington Post* editor Ben Bradlee, consider it synonymous with lying. Comparing the days of Watergate to the days of Monica Lewinsky, Bradlee bemoaned: "People lie now in a way that they never lied before—and the ease with which they lie, the total ease. . . . People expect no consequences. This word spinning is a nice uptown way of saying lying."

I agree with Bradlee about the ease and impunity of lying today, but I disagree in dignifying lying by equating it with spin. I don't even think it should be lumped under the broadest definition of spin. At best, it's what Lanny Davis calls "bad spin"; intended to deceive or betray.

There are clear distinctions between good spin and bad, or between spinning and lying:

- Spin is a variation on the truth; lying has no connection to the truth.
- Spin can go close to the line; lying is over the line.
- Spin is acceptable; lying is not.
- Everybody can get away with spin; nobody should be allowed to get away with lying.
- Spin is positive; lying is negative.
- Spin is good; lying is bad.

How to tell the difference? When somebody says something of a serious nature that is flat out untrue and intended to deceive or hurt another person—or keep the public in the dark about an issue of vital importance—that's a lie. When somebody twists, bends, toys, exaggerates or plays with the truth in order to make it sound better or give oneself a tactical advantage, that's spin.

For practitioners, there's one other difference: If you're caught *spinning* once, no problem. You can spin again and again. If you're caught *lying* once, you're dead.

- Professor Smith gets fired, but tells his colleagues he has decided to leave because he wants to try his luck in the business world. That's OK. That's just face-saving spin. But if Professor Smith tells his friends he could have stayed forever if he wanted to, but told the dean to "take that job and shove it," that's not so cool. That's a lie—and an unnecessary lie, when spin would do the job just as well.

The rule is: spin, yes; lies, no—unless you're under oath, when only the truth, and nothing but the truth, will do.

SPIN ON!

And so the spin continues. On *Crossfire,* we're equipped to deal with it on a nightly basis—even from the Bush White House.

Former presidents are usually reluctant to criticize their successors. But, about six months into the Bush administration, former President Jimmy Carter blew his top. He had earlier criticized Bush and Cheney for pretending there was a serious energy crisis, serious enough to justify drilling for the oil in the Arctic. But this time Carter went much further. He blasted Bush for abandoning the Kyoto treaty, for pushing missile defense, for doing nothing in the Middle East, for ignoring human rights and for refusing to listen to moderates within his own administration. In fact, Carter said, he was disappointed in *everything* Bush had done so far in office.

That was material for a great *Crossfire.* Of course, Bush wouldn't answer Carter directly, but we were fortunate to book as our guest White House Media Affairs Director Tucker Eskew, as smooth a spinner as there ever was. If anybody expected Bush's spokesman to rip Carter a new one, however, they too were disappointed.

"You can't deny it, can you? Everything Jimmy Carter said is true, isn't it?" I challenged Eskew.

"Not at all," crooned Eskew. "Just two months ago, this president, former President Carter, said that he really didn't have much to quarrel with, with the new administration, so you can kind of take these new comments with a grain of salt.

"This president—our current president—ran as a compassionate conservative. He's doing in office what he said he'd do. Maybe that is a surprise to some people, but not to most Americans."

I asked for a direct answer. I wasn't surprised to get spin.

IT DIDN'T START WITH CLINTON

History is more or less bunk.
—Henry Ford

SPIN HALL OF FAME NOMINATION

⮂

By Cal Thomas

NOMINEE: Satan

OCCASION: Satan, in the form of a serpent, spoke these words to Eve, on eating from the tree of knowledge despite God's prohibition against it.

SPIN: "You will not surely die." (Genesis 3:4)

TRANSLATION: "Better pack your bags, darlin', because you and Adam are on your way out of Dodge for good."

In terms of the spin that has had the greatest impact on the world and its inhabitants, this moment is huge. Thanks to the devil's spin in this instance, Adam and

---

Eve were cast out of Paradise and forced to make their way in the rough-and-tumble world as we know it today. Thus entered sin into the world and with it, lies, damned lies and spin.

Cal Thomas is a syndicated columnist and commentator for Fox News.

Typically proud, obnoxious, ignorant Americans, we think we invented everything—including sex and spin. We didn't invent—and we're not experts in—either.

History is full of spin. Like everything else, spin began in the Garden of Eden. And ever since, we've all been cursed with original spin!

Appropriately enough, the serpent started it all: assuring Eve she would not die if she ate the fruit of the forbidden tree. She would instead become like a god, knowing good and evil. And when Eve, realizing for the first time she was naked, then said to Adam, "Come over here and take a bite of my apple," she clearly had something else in mind. She was just spinning.

For his part, Adam launched the spin that has lasted men through the ages. Asked by God for an explanation, Adam blamed it all on Eve, thereby becoming the role model for every boyfriend and husband that followed him.

In addition, for those who take the time to read it carefully, the Old Testament is teeming with examples of spin used to cover up scandalous behavior.

- To save his life, Abraham spun the story that his wife Sarah was actually his sister—and let the Egyptians make her part of Pharaoh's harem.
- God chose Aaron to be the prophet, or spokesperson, for his brother Moses—thereby making Aaron the first official spin doctor.
- After fleeing from Sodom, Lot's daughters got their old man drunk and had sex with him. Not, of course, because they were horny and there were no other men

around, but for the noble cause of serving as vessels in order to carry on the family bloodline. "Come, let us make our father drink wine, and we will lie with him," says the older daughter to the younger, "that we may preserve the seed of our father."

- When David asked Saul for the hand of his daughter Michal, the king said he didn't want a dowry, he'd rather have the foreskins of 100 Philistines. That, of course, was spin for: I don't want you marrying my daughter, I want to see you killed in battle, instead. But David had the last laugh. He killed 200 Philistines, cut off their foreskins and presented them proudly to Saul.

The Gospels are one of the earliest examples of spin in print. The four evangelists did more than just tell the story of the life of Jesus. Each of them juggled, selected or rearranged the events of His short time on earth to present Him in the most positive light and emphasize the message they were trying to deliver. For Mark, He was the secret Messiah who suffered for our sins; for Matthew, the teacher; for Luke, the Savior; for John, the divine Son of God.

Not even Jesus was above spinning. When He assured his disciples: "My yoke is easy and my burden is light," He was just spinning them. He meant just the opposite, as anyone who has tried to practice Christianity knows all too well.

And so it continues. From ancient times to modern, world leaders—kings, queens, philosophers, even popes—have stooped to spin to make a point or to paint their cause or country as morally superior. During the Crusades, the killing of millions of Muslims and Jews was justified as the only way to protect sacred biblical sites—for Christians only. How many medieval wars, celebrated as spreading Western civilization, were nothing more than mere land grabs? Henry VIII insisted he was dumping Catherine of Aragon, not to jump into bed with Anne Boleyn, but to comply with the biblical proscription against marrying his brother's widow. And, still today, the Vatican insists that, even though he knew what was going on, Pope Pius XII did not speak out against the horror of the Holocaust because he was actually trying to help the Jews.

If there were a Father of Spin, perhaps it would have to be Herodotus. Rightly celebrated as the Father of History, he was a mighty spinmeister, too—certainly in the literal sense of spinning tall tales. While reporting on the Greco-Persian wars, he also tells of gold-digging ants the size of foxes; of races of people bald from birth, or with only one eye; and of plants which, when thrown on a fire, emit smoke that makes people drunk, just as wine did the Greeks. Herodotus thus learned early on the number one rule of television news: It's not enough to report the news, you also have to make it entertaining!

Another early spinmeister, Pericles, leading statesman of Athens, declared his city-state to be the model for civilized society. In his famous funeral oration for those killed in the Peloponnesian War, he asserted: "We alone do kindness to others, not because we stop to calculate whether this will be to our advantage, but in the spirit of liberality, which motivates us." Damned good spin, wouldn't you say? We still believe it today.

We all know Nero fiddled while Rome burned, and many a hapless politician has been accused of, figuratively, doing the same thing. But wouldn't you know? It's all spin. For one thing, the fiddle wasn't even invented until centuries later. Nero may have been strumming the lute, or simply reciting poetry, but he certainly wasn't fiddling. Historians tell us that the fire probably started accidentally, one of countless conflagrations in ancient cities that swept through and destroyed crowded, dirty, unsafe and unsanitary dwellings. Then the spinning started. Citizens blamed it on Nero, saying he started it to make room for his massive rebuilding plans. Nero blamed it on Christians, and used it as an excuse to step up persecutions of the early sect. Spin vs. spin.

Eugene McCarthy, who helped drive Lyndon Johnson from the White House in 1968, has a better ear for bullshit than most—and also a keen sense of history. Writing in *The Progressive Populist* in May 1997, McCarthy outlined the duties undertaken by Cassiodorus, an obscure fifth-century Roman official who served in the court of Theodoric. "His continuing and significant work . . . appears to have been that of praising the emperor, of reassuring him, of advising him and of protecting him and his family from harsh public judgment. He was early into damage control, taking on the task of explaining and defending Theodoric's murder of his predecessor. . . . He also wrote the equivalent of bulletins and press releases for the emperor, identifying three classes of readers or listeners to whom addresses should be made in different styles: the superior, those of mediocre taste and understanding, and those of little intelligence."

Give that man a job in the White House.

In advising the princes of Florence how to govern, Machiavelli rejected the optimism of the Athenians. They thought all men were good; he knew all men were inherently evil. "Whoever desires to found a state and give it laws, must start with assuming that all men are bad and ever ready to display their vicious nature, whenever they may find occasion for it."

In such a society, not so unlike ours, Machiavelli understood that spin would be the language of the realm, because the truth would be intolerable. "There is no other way of guarding oneself against flattery than by letting men understand that they will not offend you by speaking the truth; but when everyone can tell you the truth, you lose their respect." Doesn't that remind you of Washington, D.C.?

Among historical masters of spin must also be included Martin Luther. The spin is that he tacked his ninety-five theses to the church door at Wittenberg to protest the selling of indulgences by the pope. Of course, Luther was right. Indulgences were a giant scam: the more money you contributed, the less time you had to spend in purgatory. No longer, as Jesus warned, was it as difficult for a rich man to enter Heaven as for a camel to pass through the eye of a needle. All he had to do was pay for enough indulgences. As Johann Tetzel, the most notorious huckster of indulgences promised,

"As soon as the coin in the coffer rings, the soul from purgatory springs!"

But the truth is that Luther had long supported the selling of indulgences—as long as they were attached to the sacred relics his patron Frederick had assembled in his own castle chapel. In addition to suggesting that salvation was based more on faith than good works, Luther's famous declaration only protested the selling of one particular indulgence: a so-called jubilee indulgence, which Frederick had prohibited in his territory, for rebuilding St. Peter's basilica in Rome. In other words, Luther was only against indulgences that competed with his own self-interest. He was not against indulgences, as long as his boss was making money off them.

Having suffered a life of temptation, Luther was a strong believer in the active presence of the devil: "For where God built a church, there the Devil would also build a chapel." And, no doubt remembering the story of the serpent in the garden, he believed the devil was still at work, spinning away, and influencing others to spin. "If Satan can turn God's Word upside down and pervert the Scriptures, what will he do with my words—or the words of others?"

So there you have Luther's explanation: I didn't mean to spin, the devil made me do it. That serpent again. How handy.

There is, of course, no greater repository of spin than the work of our greatest poet and playwright, William Shakespeare. In effect, his entire opus is about spin, because Shakespeare's central premise is that all of us, not just the actors on stage, have roles to play. Therefore, in life, as well as in theater, you have to interpret what people are saying in order to get at the real meaning. Could he have said it more clearly: "All the world's a stage, and all the men and women merely players: they have their exits and their entrances."

Shakespeare scholar John Andrews suggests that, of all the Bard's plays, *Hamlet* is the most abundant in spin—down to the final scene, where, as he lays dying, Hamlet begs his friend Horatio not to commit suicide, but to stay alive so he can spin Hamlet's tale:

If thou did'st ever hold me in thy Heart,
Absent thee from Felicity a while
And in this harsh World draw thy Breath in Pain
  to tell my Story.

NEW WORLD SPIN

How did spin first make its way across the Atlantic? Easy. Christopher Columbus brought it. Columbus, ironically, was the son of a weaver and an accomplished weaver himself. He had spinning in his genes.

As incentive for discovering the New World, Queen Isabella had offered a lifelong pension of 10,000 maravedis a year to the first man who sighted land. In his monumental work *A People's History of the United States* (putting a different spin on history), Howard Zinn relates what happened. Early on October 12, 1492, a sailor named Rodrigo, serving as lookout while Columbus and the rest of the crew slept, saw the moon reflected off the white sands of a Caribbean island beach and cried out. Rodrigo never got his reward, however. Captain Columbus insisted that he had seen a distant light the evening before. No surprise, Columbus got the pension.

Columbus also spun the native Americans he encountered as "Indians." After all, he and his crew had landed in India, hadn't they? The name stuck, even though his geography was off by half the globe.

Of course, historians are guilty in glorifying Columbus as a great navigator and discoverer—and glossing over the fact that he was also a mass murderer. As Zinn argues: "To state the facts, however, and then to bury them in a mass of information (about other things) is to say to the reader with a certain infectious calm: yes, mass murder took place, but it's not that important."

Once in the New World, spin found fertile ground. Early colonists pledged their continued loyalty to the king, when what they were really saying was: "We'll be loyal subjects, as long as you just leave us alone!" Puritans cited Scripture to justify the use of force to seize land from the natives: "Whosoever therefore resisteth the power, resisteth the ordinance of God; and they that resist shall receive to themselves damnation" (Rom. 13:2). As they baptized men, women and children from Africa being unloaded off slave ships in chains, preachers bragged about "freeing" them—but only from heresy, not from their chains.

When colonial leaders began their drive toward independence, they justified breaking from the motherland on a new spin: that all men are created equal . . . except, of course, for women, blacks, native Americans and men without property. In *Common Sense,* perhaps the most powerful piece of propaganda ever printed, Tom Paine painted the revolution as necessary to get rid of government—"Society in every state is a blessing, but Government even in its best state is but a necessary evil"—when what the revolution really did was replace one government with another, albeit better, more democratic and homegrown. And that new government only won approval thanks to the convincing spin of Alexander Hamilton and James Madison in *The Federalist.*

What happened when colonists ran out of land and forests in the East? They simply pushed westward, seizing more land from the Indians under the banner of "Manifest Destiny": the manifestation of the supreme plan that white men shall rule and red men shall simply disappear, as captured so powerfully by Bob Dylan in song: "The cavalries charged, the Indians died, / Oh, the country was young, with God on its side."

Once independence was won, some way had to be found to build public confidence in the new government and its new leader. The answer: spin. How could you not trust a man who, as a little boy, 'fessed up to his father about cutting down the cherry tree? It worked to make George Washington a legend in his own lifetime, even though historians now tell us there's no chance it ever really happened. The first president's first recorded statement, not published until the year after his death, was the nation's first whopper. But what else could we expect from a man whose family motto was *"Exitus acta probat"*—the ends justifies the means?

Washington set the course that all candidates, presidents and elected officials after him automatically followed: paint the worst as the best—and let the public, or history, sort it out. As novelist E. L. Doctorow said in 1998: "I've been trying to think of an American president in my lifetime who didn't lie to the American people." He couldn't. Neither can we.

- Thomas Jefferson declared all men equal and free, unless he owned them.
- President Lincoln's Emancipation Proclamation didn't free all the slaves, only those in enemy, Southern, territory.
- The Civil War, spun in the history books as a crusade to end slavery, is precisely what it was not. As Lincoln made clear in a famous letter to journalist Horace Greeley, his primary motivation in warring against the Southern states was to keep the nation intact: "My paramount object in this struggle is to save the Union, and is not either to save or to destroy slavery."
- Franklin Roosevelt tried to justify packing the Supreme Court, by arguing that the Justices were overworked and needed relief.
- Senator Joseph McCarthy insisted his anti-communist crusade was a bipartisan effort, yet he accused only Democrats of being secret Communist Party members or sympathizers.
- President Kennedy denied that withdrawal of Soviet missiles from Cuba amounted to a quid pro quo—when, in fact, he had made a deal to pull American missiles out of Turkey.
- During the Vietnam War, we stopped talking about dead soldiers or civilians and started talking about "body bags" or "collateral damage." American planes bombed villages in order to save them, not destroy them.
- Richard Nixon insisted that if a president did it, it could not be illegal.

- Ronald Reagan railed against government spending, while spending the nation into record deficits.

But all of their spin was just a warm-up to Bill Clinton and George W. Bush.

So how do politicians get away with it? Surely, reporters see through the spin. Why don't they expose it? They know the facts. Why don't they print the truth behind the spin? Well, once in a while, they do. Every so often, you read a good article that compares what a politician says with what he does or with the way things really are. But that's rare. Usually, we're just fed the blather they spin, without commentary or correction. In a way, reporters and politicians feed each other. In a more perverse, co-dependent way, reporters can even become the enablers of the politician's spin.

There are two reasons for this. First, reporters believe their job is to be neutral: simply to report what a politician says, without telling the public what he really means. Let people figure it out for themselves.

Second, reporters don't puncture the politician's spin because they're too busy, and so good, at spinning, themselves.

In fact, nobody's better at spinning than they are. Reporters spin for a living.

THREE

ALL THE SPIN THAT'S FIT TO PRINT

People everywhere confuse what they read in the newspapers with news.

—A. J. Liebling

The best spinners are not the politicians reporters cover. The best spinners are the reporters themselves. In order to truly appreciate spin, consider the source.

After every political debate, it's become standard practice for candidates and their supporters, win or lose, to rush into an adjoining press room and try to convince reporters how well they did, what points they scored and why the debate put new life into their campaign.

There's a good reason this gathering place is called the Spin Room—but not because the candidates are such good spinners. The reporters themselves are masters of the art. Up against reporters, politicians don't stand a chance. In the end, it's the reporters who spin, for all the world to read, what supposedly happened in the debate. They can, and do, spin winners into losers, and losers into winners.

Journalists are people who spin for a living. It goes to the very heart of what they do. Media critic Malcolm Gladwell made the connection in the July 6, 1998, edition of the *Brown University Alumni Magazine:* "Spinning is the art of telling a story, even when there is no story to tell," he observed, "and this is irresistible, particularly to journalists, who make a living by telling stories even when there is no story to tell."

The idea that reporters don't spin, that they always shoot straight, is simply naïve. A conservative and a liberal can look at the same facts, and effortlessly spin them in totally different directions. In fact, Tucker and I pride ourselves on it.

And it's getting worse, not better. Consider the impact of new technology. The quicker news reaches us, the more immediate the spin. The faster the news cycle, the faster the spin cycle. The more news/talk cable channels, the more opportunities for spin.

Yes, there are a few solid reporters left. Those who merely gather and report the news. No bias, just the facts, ma'am. God bless 'em. But they are few and far between. Many reporters are willing to let their bias show. Not only that, more and more reporters make themselves available on radio and television as part-time commentators or pundits, where they are put in the unique position of analyzing a politician's spin by offering spin of their own. Spinners spinning the spinners' spin!

The news business itself is steeped in spin. When a veteran reporter starts out "My sources tell me . . . ," he really means: "I called a lot of people until I finally found somebody who agrees with me." Or, when a talk show host brags about "an exclusive interview with O.J. Simpson," he doesn't really mean "exclusive." He simply means exclusive between the hours of 6 and 7 P.M., that particular day.

Such has always been the case with the American press, ever since 1735, when Alexander Hamilton successfully defended Peter Zenger, publisher of the *New York Weekly Journal,* who had been accused of libel against the colonial British government. Hamilton convinced the jury that it was impossible to libel the Crown because intelligent readers were capable of deciding themselves what was fact and what was not. Thus was born freedom of the press—and freedom to spin.

The first challenge that newspaper publishers faced was how to handle spin. Did they allow their publication to spin to the right? Or spin to the left? Benjamin Franklin, the first successful American newspaper publisher, resolved the dilemma by accepting and publishing whatever spin crossed his desk, no matter whom it offended. "If all printers were determined not to print anything till they were sure it would offend nobody, there would be very little printed," Franklin noted. In truth, he was spinning. For him, his newspaper was primarily a business. He printed all sides of every issue, not to practice freedom of the press, but to sell the maximum number of newspapers.

The notorious publisher James Callendar lived by a different standard: he printed whatever spin he was paid to spin. As long as he was being subsidized by Vice President Thomas Jefferson, he blasted President John Adams and Treasury Secretary Alexander Hamilton as traitors. But later, when President Jefferson refused to nominate his former co-conspirator as postmaster of Richmond, Callendar turned his wrath on the Sage of Monticello: "It is well known that the man, whom it delighteth the people to honor, keeps and for many years, has kept as his concubine, one of his own slaves. Her name is Sally."

A royally pissed-off Jefferson got even with Callendar by denouncing newspaper publishers for eternity: "The man who reads nothing at all is better educated than the man who reads nothing but newspapers."

In Quincy, Massachusetts, the woman who had suffered the most from Jefferson's double-dealing against her husband could not resist telling him: I told you so. "The serpent you cherished and warmed, bit the hand that nourished him," Abigail Adams wrote Jefferson about Callendar. "When such vipers are let loose . . . all distinctions between virtue and vice are leveled."

There's that serpent again!

Internet gossip columnist Matt Drudge, Callendar's direct descendant, has rattled today's establishment media by admitting he doesn't always get his facts right. But he has a quick defense handy. In being loose with the truth in order to scoop the competition, Drudge argues, he represents the future of American journalism. What Drudge doesn't realize is that he doesn't represent the future. He's actually a link to the past.

After Callendar, many American journalists never contented themselves with telling the truth when invention could make for such a better story—and sell so many more newspapers. Pure spin even gave way to pure hoax. In 1835, the *New York Sun,* led by publisher Benjamin Day, electrified the nation with reports of life on the moon, as discovered by British astronomer Sir John Herschel. In four installments, the *Sun* ran detailed descriptions of lunar trees and vegetation, oceans and beaches, bison and goats, cranes and pelicans, before dropping the bomb: the existence on the moon of furry, winged men resembling bats!

Even when unmasked as "the Great Moon Hoax," the Herschel reports didn't damage the reputation of the *Sun.* It remained the largest-circulation newspaper in the world.

There's a straight line from the Great Moon Hoax to the Great Election Hoax of November 2000, when all the networks first called the election for Al Gore before all the polls had closed on the East Coast—and then called Florida for Bush, before all the votes were counted. Despite their collective gaffe, they still retain the undeserved reputation for objective, or at least competent, reporting.

And why not? Even the venerable Mark Twain got in on the act. As a young reporter, Twain first gained fame with a story about a "petrified man" discovered in a sitting position, still winking and thumbing his nose. He thereafter made no bones of his willingness to stretch the truth: "I am not one of those who in expressing opinion confine themselves to facts," he said in a 1907 speech to London's Savage Club. Earlier, he had confessed to W. D. Howells: "Journalism is the one solitary respectable profession which honors theft (when committed in the pecuniary interest of a journal) and admires the thief."

William Randolph Hearst followed in the footsteps of Callendar and Twain, but outdid them in his audacity. Like Joseph Pulitzer before him, Hearst became an expert at making news out of nothing. In his masterful biography of Hearst, David Nasaw explains the famous publisher's guiding principle: "News is not a phenomenon that exists in the real world, waiting to be discovered. . . . An event becomes news only when journalists and editors decide to record it. More often than not, what determines whether an occurrence is newsworthy or not is the ease with which it can be plotted and narrated so that readers will want to read about it." Thus spin feeds the beast of corporate-driven journalism.

Hearst discovered there was no limit to his ability to spin something from nothing. Determined to stir trouble between the United States and Spain, he sent an artist to Cuba to provide drawings of the growing hemispheric conflict between the two major powers. Finding no evidence of discord in Cuba, the artist wired that he was returning to New York. Whereupon Hearst sent back the famous retort: "You furnish the pictures, and I'll furnish the war." Fortunately for Hearst, the USS *Maine* exploded in Havana harbor. With zero evidence, he blamed the sinking of the ship on Spanish terrorists. Americans were outraged—and the Spanish-American War was born.

Walter Lippmann was arguably the most famous journalist of the last century. His column strongly shaped the public opinion of his day. Presidents often called him to the White House and asked his advice before making policy decisions. Lippmann knew his words were powerful, but he also knew—and was proud of the fact—that they were also spin: the kind of spin, Lippmann believed, that was necessary to persuade readers.

Lippmann was a firm believer in democracy. However, he worried that society was growing too complex for people to appreciate the basic principles of democracy. The only answer, he believed, was what he called "the manufacture of consent"—as good a definition of spin as I've ever heard.

According to Lippmann, public opinion is shaped by three factors: (1) the world of our direct experience; (2) the pictures we have of the world outside our direct experience; and (3) the thoughts, feelings and actions that we take in response to the pictures in our heads. Who puts those pictures in our heads? Journalists! What pictures do they paint? It's up to them! Will we believe them? It depends on how convincing they are!

Nobody ever laid it out any clearer. What journalists or politicians are doing when spinning is attempting to paint a certain picture in order to manufacture the consent of the governed.

Lippmann at least pretended to be dispassionate. Not so, Hunter S. Thompson or Thomas Wolfe. Believing that objectivity in news reporting is more myth than fact, they threw all illusions of objectivity out the window, sought out characters or events they wanted to write about, chose up sides and spun wild tales, usually about subjects—peace demonstrations, drugs, what goes on among reporters in a political campaign—ignored by the mainstream press. A friend of Thompson's branded it "gonzo journalism," which HST defined as "a style of reporting based on William Faulkner's idea that the best fiction is far more true than any kind of journalism."

Sadly, perhaps, not every reporter is equipped, physically or emotionally, to follow. A good gonzo journalist, Hunter said, "needs the talent of a master journalist, the eye of an artist/photographer and the heavy balls of an actor."

TODAY'S TOP SPINNERS

Among today's media spinners, no one—day in, day out—can match conservative radio talk-show host Rush Limbaugh. Three hours a day, he relishes in praising conservatives and sucking up to whatever Republican happens to be in power, while blaming liberals for everything from flu epidemics to snowstorms. Most of the time. The rest of the time is simply spent puffing himself up. He may even have inspired the title of Howard Kurtz's excellent book on pundits, *Hot Air.*

As a classic example of his own spin, Rush describes himself in the first chapter of his book *See, I Told You So* as just a humble country boy: "I'm a nice guy—a harmless little fuzzball with a strong live-and-let-live credo. The furthest thing from my mind is to carry out some devious master plan to take over the airwaves and impose my views on anyone." The furthest thing from his mind? That's not the impression you get from reading his introduction to the same book: "Let's see now: I've conquered radio, television, the newsletter business and the book world. Now [this book] will eclipse all publishing records known in the English-speaking world."

For a few years, every Saturday, I followed the Rush Limbaugh show on KFI Radio in Los Angeles, with my own talk show, which I called, just to piss Rush's listeners off, *Bill Press, True American.* To further piss them off, I would spend a few minutes each show refuting some outrageous statement, or spin, Rush had made during the previous week. At first, I would spend hours each day listening to Rush, making notes, searching for some easy-to-pop balloon. I soon realized that was a waste of time. I didn't have to spend hours listening for spin. I could just tune in for any two minutes of any show and find exactly what I needed. Rush didn't sprinkle spin throughout his show. The whole damned show was spin—was then, and still is. Which is not to condemn his show, but simply to say: Don't tune in expecting to hear the truth.

One thing for sure, spin pays. Very well. Limbaugh's latest contract guarantees him $250 million for the next eight years, on top of a hefty $35 million signing bonus—making him, by far, the highest paid performer on radio or television. And that won't be his last contract, either. An exultant Limbaugh declared he will only retire when everyone in America agrees with him. And he's not kidding.

Editorial pages are, by nature, full of spin. Sometimes, humorously. Implying some left-wing conspiracy, the *Wall Street Journal* moaned editorially during the 2000 presidential election's long Florida recount: "Poor Florida. It is being put under a national microscope to determine the credibility of its voting system." Why feel sorry for Florida? No one had to force Florida under a microscope. The defects in its voting machines, voting procedures and recount rules—plus the partisanship of its elected officals—were so glaring the whole world could see them with the naked eye.

Same with the op-ed page. That's where you expect to find spin because that's what commentators do. It could be called "The Spin Page." Nevertheless, sometimes the spin is more obvious than others. In the aftermath of the Marc Rich pardon, the ever-so-pompous Bill O'Reilly blasted President Bush for suggesting there were more important issues facing the country than continuing to talk about Bill Clinton. "Apparently, Mr. Bush is more interested in the short-term success of his administration than the long-term strength of the country," O'Reilly trumpeted in the conservatives' house organ, the *Washington Times*.

What Mr. O'Reilly was really saying, of course, is: "Don't try to stop me from talking about Bill Clinton, because that's all I know how to talk about." And, besides, for conservatives, bashing Clinton is more fun than trying to defend Bush's tax cut for the rich.

Actually, O'Reilly deserves a special spin award for opening his ever-so-predictable nightly TV show with the warning "Caution: you're about to enter a no-spin zone." He's just published a book with the same title: *The No-Spin Zone*. It should be called: "The Nothing-but-Spin Zone," because his show consists of nothing but his conservative spin on the issues of the day—spiced up by his self-righteous spin about how wonderful and powerful he is. As in his book's subtitle: *Confrontations with the Powerful and Famous in America*. Oh, please.

There's only one reason O'Reilly poses as the Anti-Spin: because he think it's in his best interest as an entertainer. And ratings prove him right. His conservative viewers, God bless 'em, actually believe that he's free of spin and that everybody else is full of spin.

Speaking of confrontations with the powerful and famous, Tucker Carlson and I tried very hard to arrange one on the *Spin Room*. After Tucker got into a public spat with O'Reilly on the Don Imus show one morning, over negative comments Tucker made about O'Reilly's first book in *Time* magazine, Tucker invited the pompous pontificator to appear on the *Spin Room*. To Imus's vast audience, O'Reilly immediately accepted. Tucker announced on the air that evening that O'Reilly would soon be our guest. But then, despite many invitations, he turned us down flat. Refused to appear, and never gave any reason why. Does he lack the courage of his convictions? Was he afraid his own spin might have been punctured on the *Spin Room?* We'll never know.

There's nothing wrong with being a conservative commentator. It's just dishonest to deny that's what you are, like O'Reilly does every night. Check out his nightly "Talking Points." On Friday, May 25, 2001, for example, he blasted the thirty-eight Senate Democrats who failed to vote for the compromise tax cut: "How can the American economy start growing if Americans themselves have less money in their pockets?" A quick check of the facts would show, of course, that the American economy was actually quite strong and, since retail, new home and new car sales were up, Americans seemed to have lots of money in their pockets. Not only that, the people who most needed the money to spend would be the last to get it under the Bush tax plan.

But, what the hell. O'Reilly is entitled to his point of view. What's misleading is for him to add: "Ideology has nothing to do with this." That's pure spin. Ideology, O'Reilly's conservative ideology, has everything to do with it. His talking points that day were the same talking points used by every other conservative commentator on Fox or CNN. Wonder if they all come from the same source?

Or, try this out for balance. From *The O'Reilly Factor* on March 23, 2001: "Coming next, drug-addicted pregnant women no longer have anything to fear from the authorities, thanks to the Supreme Court. Both sides on this in a moment." Both sides follow, after he's already told you there is only one side.

Here's one more example. On May 3, 2001, O'Reilly opened his show with this preamble:

"Tonight, violent demonstrations on the rise all over the world, as capitalism comes under assault and America's college campuses are being besieged with socialistic messages. We'll have a report.

"The first hundred days of Hillary Clinton in the Senate. Did she actually do anything? We'll find out.

"And was Al Gore antagonistic toward some of his students at Columbia? That's the word.

"Caution: You're about to enter a no-spin zone."

Wait a minute. Socialism on the rise, Hillary goofs off, Al Gore antagonizes students—this is a "no-spin zone"? Anybody who doesn't laugh out loud at that preposterous claim must be brain dead.

There's also nothing wrong with being a man of the people, as O'Reilly claims to be in every interview, except that, in his case, it's just not true. He talks often of growing up in Levittown, Long Island, son of an accountant who never made more than $35,000 a year (which translates into something closer to $92,000 today). "You don't come from any lower than I came from on an economic scale," he asserts. The hell you don't. How about *my* father, a gas station owner in Delaware City, Delaware, who never made much more than $10,000? Or how about kids in the inner city who don't even *know* who their father is? Come on, Bill, don't make it any worse than it was. And with a chance to go to high school, college and graduate school, you seem to have made out OK.

Even today, O'Reilly says he's just an average, working stiff. "I drive in here in my 1994 automobile and I come up and I do this show," he told the *New York Observer*. Before you feel sorry for him, you should know his 1994 automobile was a Lexus—and he now makes $4 million a year. He can no longer complain about being ignored by the media elite—he *is* one of them. And he acts like one of them.

You know a journalist has lost all sense of reality when he starts believing his own spin. A sure sign O'Reilly's lost it forever is what he told Gore campaign manager Donna Brazile, June 5, 2001, when she foolishly agreed to appear as his guest: "Do you know, Ms. Brazile, that if Al Gore had appeared on "The Factor," he'd be President of the United States. I believe that firmly. If he had acquitted himself well on this program with our enormous audience in Florida—we have an enormous audience there—if he had acquitted himself well and answered the tough questions, he would have won."

Don't look for the tongue in that cheek. There is none. This guy is serious. That's the problem.

Of course, O'Reilly is just an arm of the Fox News Channel, which is itself a marvel of spin. To his credit, Roger Ailes has built a very successful TV network around strong conservative personalities like O'Reilly, Brit Hume, and Tony Snow. But the guy's also a marketing genius: He still spins his net-

work as a place to find objective news coverage, under the slogan: "We report. You decide."

Talk about spin. Ben Bagdikian, esteemed former journalism dean at UC Berkeley, charges that the Fox slogan translates into: "We decide what news you hear, and you make up your mind based on what we tell you." The media watchdog group FAIR calls Fox "the most biased name in news."

Yes, it's pure spin, masquerading as counter-spin, but it's still very effective. The number of Fox viewers have soared, while MSNBC and CNN's numbers have declined. Some nights, the upstart Fox kicks CNN's butt in the ratings.

No matter how hard Ailes tries to camouflage Fox's bias, sometimes its slip will show, as it did on election night 2000. Working inside the Fox newsroom, with the all-important job of deciding when the network would call which states for Bush or Gore, was John Ellis—who also happens to be George W. Bush's first cousin. Rejecting any pretense of objectivity, Ellis admitted he was on the phone with Bush, and brother "Jebby," several times on election day, and that he consulted Bush before first calling Florida for Gore and phoned him again, early the next morning, before calling the state for Bush. As Ellis described that early-morning call to the *New Yorker's* Jane Mayer: "It was just the three of us guys handing the phone back and forth—me with the numbers, one of them a governor, the other the president-elect. Now that was cool."

Cool to him, no doubt, but not so cool to the viewers who stayed up expecting information reported by news gatherers, not a Bush-family cheerleader. At the time, Tom Rosentiel, director of the Project for Excellence in Journalism, said that Fox's slogan "We report. You decide" was "obliterated by the fact that one candidate's first cousin is actually deciding, and then they report."

But conservatives have no monopoly on spin. Seeking to tarnish President Bush's reputation by tagging him with Ronald Reagan, the president most despised by liberals, columnist Helen Thomas wrote: "Like Reagan, Bush's day is scripted from the start, from the time he arrives at the Oval Office until he leaves."

Nice spin, but not fair. Helen Thomas knows better than anybody that *every* president's day in the Oval Office is scripted from the start. Bush is no exception.

The real problem with spin in newspapers, of course, is not its presence on editorial or op-ed pages. That's where we expect it, and that's where it belongs. The problem is when spin ends up in news articles on page one. The *Washington Times,* for example, on page one, reported on Democratic reaction to President George W. Bush's first address to Congress: "Many, apparently speaking from talking points, said the president's plan 'doesn't add up.' " That's pure Republican spin.

It's not surprising to discover spin from the propagandist *Washington Times,* even in so-called news articles. After all, The *Times* reads like it was written by the Republican National Committee, and it probably was. But how about this, from the national newspaper of record: the great, gray *New York Times.* On February 10, 2001, the *Times* ran Frank Bruni's profile of the new occupant of the White House on page one under the giddy headline: "Presidency Takes Shape with No Fuss, No Sweat." Inside, the *Times* headline was even more rhapsodic: "Bush's Leadership Style is Simply Presidential." And Bruni's reporting was equally enthusiastic: "Every new chief executive inhabits the role in a distinctive way, and George W. Bush is establishing a no-fuss, no-sweat, "look-Ma-no-hands" presidency, his exertions never measured, his outlook always mirthful." If that's not spin, what is? Why didn't Bruni point out that the real reason Bush seemed to have nothing to do was because he'd delegated all the heavy lifting to Dick Cheney?

In this case, the usually objective Bruni was either caught up in the thrill of the moment—watching the new president cavort worry-free in his new playpen—or, worse yet, he simply swallowed the White House spin: that Bush is such a good CEO he can run the country without lifting a finger— and regurgitated it on his readers. Either way, he became an unwitting White House enabler. It proves why reporters should stick to hard facts. Once they start reporting their personal impressions, they lose credibility.

One reason reporters get caught up in spin is because they tend to behave like sheep. This is especially true in Washington, D.C. Ever notice this? One pundit makes some outrageous assertion, usually with little or no evidence to back him up, and before you know it, everybody's repeating the same nonsense as fact. Or, what appears on the front page of the *New York Times* becomes the lead on the evening news and the subject of debate on most talk shows. Some call it "pack journalism," which is a pretty fancy term for people who are just too lazy to do their own research or thinking.

I don't know who it was, for example, in Spring 2000, who first suggested that voters were suffering from "Clinton fatigue," but before you could say "semen-stained dress," Clinton Fatigue was the topic du jour on all the talk shows. Few bothered to point out that Clinton's approval rating was about 65 percent, higher than Ronald Reagan's at the same time. So, if voters were suffering from Clinton fatigue, they didn't seem to be aware of it themselves.

Still, by repeating the same old nonsense, reporters were helping to spread the Republicans' spin that Clinton was political dead meat, and so, by extension, was anyone connected with him. Unfortunately for Al Gore, he bought into it, too, and failed to talk about Clinton's record or invite Clinton to campaign for him. Big mistake.

In my experience, the worst example of pack journalism was the rush to report on how Clinton aides had trashed the White House and Old Executive Office Building before leaving town. It started as an amusing leak to Lloyd Grove's column in the *Washington Post* about some prankster removing all the "w's" on White House typewriters. Followed by reports someone had switched the signs on the men's rooms and women's rooms—adolescent practical jokes, right?

Two days later, according to press accounts, damage was so extensive we were lucky the White House was still standing. Fed by the new White House spin machine, print and electronic media pulsed with reports of widespread damage:

expletive-laced graffiti on sacred walls, presidential seals steamed off doors, obscene messages left in copy machines and stolen art works. On the front page of the *Washington Post,* White House reporter Mike Allen cited "numerous acts of apparent vandalism." On the NBC *Nightly News,* veteran reporter Andrea Mitchell bemoaned "Phone lines cut, drawers filled with glue, door locks jimmied so that arriving Bush staff got locked inside their new offices."

And, of course, editorial writers piled on. "Such trashy behavior and disrespect for the White House comes as little surprise," harrumphed the *Houston Chronicle.* "These vandals deserve to be exposed," demanded the *Indianapolis Star.*

For Clinton haters, it seemed too bad to be true—and it was! It was all a hoax. Four months later, after an investigation requested by perennial Clinton-hating Congressman Bob Barr of Georgia, the Government Accounting Office concluded there were "no records of damage." The condition of the offices was just what you would expect, reported the GAO, when one business moves out and another moves in.

I kept waiting for an apology from the Bush White House. It never came.

I kept waiting for the *Washington Post* to admit it was wrong on page one. Instead, they buried word of the GAO report inside the paper.

Most other major papers carried no correction at all. Having helped to spread the White House spin, they were not about to admit how they'd been taken, how they'd let themselves become enablers, once again.

Only Tony Snow of *Fox News Sunday* had the guts to stand up and say he was wrong.

So, how do you keep track of what's real and what's not in the way the news is reported?

Fortunately, for those who have the time, there's an excellent guide to journalistic spin. You can find it on the Internet. It's called the *Daily Howler* (dailyhowler.com). Every day, editor Bob Somerby mercilessly punctures the spin of reporters, both print and broadcast. Nobody escapes. It's an invaluable tool. If we could all read the *Daily Howler* every day, after we read the morning paper or watch the evening news, we'd be a hell of a lot better informed—and a hell of a lot less confused.

THE LIBERAL MEDIA

Surely, the greatest media spin of all is the conservatives' favorite whipping boy, the liberal media. What a total crock. Every time someone asks me a question about the liberal media, I say: "You want to see the liberal media? Here I am!" OK, to be fair, add Paul Begala and Geraldo Rivera. We're the only three I know in the entire country who dare stand up on national television and proudly call ourselves liberals.

Two things about the so-called liberal media: First, it is absolutely, demonstrably false. Check it out yourself.

- Look at the op-ed pages. Compare the number of conservative columnists with liberal columnists.
- Listen to talk radio. Count the number of nationally-syndicated liberal talk-show hosts. I know of none. Jim Hightower was the last.
- Watch the cable-TV talk shows. Count the number of liberal pundits. The balance is overwhelmingly tilted toward conservative voices. They own, they dominate the airwaves and op-ed pages.

Don't stop there. Check out the platforms:

- Name one TV channel as openly liberal as Fox is blatantly conservative. There is none. Certainly not CNN. CNN bends over so hard to be balanced, I never appear without a conservative by my side.
- Check out the newspapers. Name one major paper that is 100 percent liberal, the way the *Washington Times* is nothing but a Republican propaganda sheet. There is none. Don't say the *New York Times* or *Washington*

Post, either. No papers in the country, not even the *Washington Times,* were more critical of Bill Clinton.
- Check the national magazines. *The Nation, Mother Jones* and *American Prospect* magazines are the only three liberal publications. Compared to the right-wing's *National Review, Weekly Standard, American Spectator, Commentary* and several others.

There is no liberal media. It is a myth. It is a total invention of the far-right—pure spin—but very effective. Even conservative high-priest William Kristol, editor of the *Weekly Standard,* admitted to the *New Yorker:* "The liberal media were never that powerful, and the whole thing was often used as an excuse by conservatives for conservative failures."

The myth of the liberal media is kept alive, and conservatives keep complaining about it, for two reasons: One, it helps to raise money from paranoid followers. Two, it unnerves the media and puts producers on notice that their coverage had better be more friendly to conservatives, or else. As former RNC Chairman Rich Bond admitted, it's all a mind game. In a 1992 interview with the *Washington Post,* he compared complaining about bias among reporters to complaining about calls by sports officials. "If you watch any great coach," Bond explained, "what they try to do is work the refs. Maybe the ref will cut you a little slack next time."

And, boy, does it work. I discovered that myself. Once when CNN's Washington staff met with a new CNN executive, a colleague noted that House Majority Whip Tom DeLay was not pleased with CNN's news coverage and, consequently, would not appear on some CNN shows. This was followed by a long discussion about what could be done to mollify DeLay: Should CNN brass call him, go meet with him, get other conservative friends to intervene? All options were on the table except the obvious: *Do nothing.* Who cares if Tom DeLay is unhappy? CNN could never please him unless we read his press releases on the air verbatim.

It was a surreal experience. Throughout it all, I kept

wondering what Roger Ailes would do if one of his staff reported that Dick Gephardt had complained about Fox's coverage. Roger would settle it in two words: The first one starts with *f*.

STRAIGHT SHOOTERS

Not all reporters are mindless, malleable mutton. Over the years, even among journalists, there have been exceptions. Most notably, the legendary sage of Baltimore, H. L. Mencken. Whatever his ugly side—he didn't like Jews, blacks, Asians, women, WASPs, Brits or the Appalachian poor—Mencken was a straight shooter. He never minced words. He never twisted the truth. He never tried to be politically correct. As reporter and commentator for the *Baltimore Sun,* he followed this creed: "I believe it is better to tell the truth than to lie. I believe it is better to be free than to be a slave. And I believe that it is better to know than to be ignorant."

He made no secret of his contempt for religion, marriage and politics. He scorned both Democrats and Republicans, and was a Libertarian before the term was invented. He was even painfully cynical about his own profession of journalism: "No one in this world, so far as I know, has ever lost money by underestimating the intelligence of the great masses of the plain people."

But, whether writing about schoolteachers, lawyers or members of Congress, Mencken was quick to spot, and even understand, the spin of others. "It is hard to believe that a man is telling the truth," he wrote, "when you know that you would lie if you were in his place."

CBS giants Edward R. Murrow and Walter Cronkite also deserve mention in the near-spin-free pantheon. Murrow saw through the evil spin of Joseph McCarthy and destroyed him, on television. Cronkite saw through the claims of American success in Vietnam and did as much as anyone to destroy public support for the war. He prided himself in simply telling the truth. "And that's the way it is," he ended every broadcast.

But even Cronkite was forced to admit later: "We can't cover the news in a half hour every evening. That's ridiculous."

Unfortunately, Cronkite successor Dan Rather has fallen short of the mark. Often unfairly accused of bringing a liberal bias to the nightly news, Rather nonetheless gave his critics plenty of ammunition in March 2001 when he was guest of honor at a fundraiser for the Democratic Committee of Travis County, Texas. Even if his daughter was one of the sponsors, Rather should have known better than to agree to a political fundraiser. And he certainly should have come up with a better excuse than spinning that he hadn't realized beforehand that the event was a political fundraiser. Didn't he learn anything from Al Gore and the Buddhist Temple?

Another straight shooter was the great Mike Royko, who chronicled the streets and people of Chicago so insightfully that millions of people around the country found meaning, as well as humor, in his columns. With such a national reputation, Royko was beset with invitations to join the professional spinners by appearing on radio and television. He declined them all. And he scorned those who accepted, ridiculing members of the McLaughlin Group as "the McGoofy Group." As *Washington Post* book critic Jonathan Yardley wrote in praising a new edition of Royko's columns: "Royko was as gritty and real as too much of Washington journalism is self-regarding and phony."

Once warned by the *Washington Post*'s Ben Bradlee that he would have to move to Washington if he ever wanted to cast a "long shadow," Royko told Bradlee: "I never thought about my shadow, how far I can cast it. I know how far I can cast a lure, if I'm fishing. But my shadow? I've never worried about casting a long shadow."

Too bad there aren't more like him left.

FOUR

POLITICS: SLIPPERY NOT ONLY WHEN WET

All issues are political issues, and politics itself is a mass
of lies, evasions, folly, hatred, and schizophrenia.

—George Orwell

Politics is not the only place spin thrives, but it thrives there
better than anyplace else. All those connected to politics—
candidates, office-holders, consultants, press secretaries, finance chairs and lobbyists—seem born to spin. After all,
what is politics but one man or woman, spinning him or her
self as better than another? Before convincing others, he must
first convince himself that he, more than anyone else, deserves to be mayor, governor or president. Then he proceeds
to spin his ideas as better than the next guy's. It's left up to us
poor voters to sort through the spin and make decisions.

POLITICAL SPINS

Politicians find many inventive ways to spin. Here are a few
of my favorites.

"The boys down at the barber shop want me to run for governor."

THE ALL-IN-THE-FAMILY SPIN

How many times do we hear a politician say he's going to retire, or he's decided not to run for some higher office, because he wants to "spend more time with his family"? That's one of the oldest chestnuts in the book. Most of these guys haven't seen their families in years. They'd rather be three thousand miles away. They only drag the family out when they need them, politically.

Indiana Senator Evan Bayh used this excuse when he announced he was pulling out of the 2004 presidential sweepstakes. "To run for president means I would abandon my kids for the next three and a half years," Bayh told the *Indianapolis Star*. He insisted his decision had nothing to with politics, that he just wanted to spend as much time as possible with his twin five-year-old sons.

That was spin, and everybody knew it. What really drove Evan Bayh out of the race was the early certainty he couldn't win the nomination—not up against stiff competition from fellow Senators John Kerry, John Edwards and Joe Lieberman. (And, besides, if Al Gore might even come back from his political grave.) In the same breath, Bayh as much as acknowledged that family wasn't his only consideration—he welcomed the possibility of being nominated for vice president. Which, of course, post-convention, would require the same amount of campaigning, and time away from the twins, as running for president.

SPIN HALL OF FAME NOMINATION

⤬⤬

By Margaret Carlson

NOMINEE:	Max Kennedy
OCCASION:	Kennedy's reason for abruptly dropping out of the congressional race to succeed the much-beloved Joe Moakley of Massachusetts.
SPIN:	"Looking into my children's eyes, I thought, I don't want to make the decision to be away from them, not just for the period of the four months of the

campaign, but for what it would take to be an effective congressman over the period of the next 10 or 20 or 30 years."

TRANSLATION: "Looking into the polls, I realized, I don't want to be the first Kennedy to lose a race in Massachusetts."

Looking into the *Boston Herald,* Kennedy could have found the story that he'd been arrested as a teenager (along with his cousin, alleged murderer Michael Skakel), for assaulting a Harvard University police officer. And Kennedy had been widely ridiculed for a speech gaffe earlier in the month, in which he lost his place and started laughing. But, of course his decision "had nothing to do with the setbacks" he had suffered in recent weeks.

Margaret Carlson is a columnist for Newsweek *and a member of CNN's* Capital Gang.

THE LOOK-FOR-THE-SILVER-LINING SPIN

The one unwritten rule of politics is *"Never admit things went bad."* But wouldn't it be refreshing to hear some candidate stand up, the morning after an election, and say: "I lost because I ran a lousy campaign. I deserved to lose"? Instead, we get all the bullshit about how well they did . . . given the circumstances.

Terry McAuliffe, spinner-in-chief of the Democratic National Committee, is a good example. Long after Al Gore lost, having run one of the least inspiring presidential campaigns in memory, McAuliffe was still insisting that Gore had actually won the popular vote; he would have won Florida if all the votes had been counted and the Supreme Court had not intervened.

Which may be true, but . . . hello? Who's in the White House now? And who lost the state of Tennessee?

Democrats fell back on the same lame excuse in June 2001 when they lost a special congressional election in southern Virginia to replace veteran Democrat Norm Sisisky, who died in March. Even though Republican Randy Forbes beat Democrat Louise Lucas 52–48—giving Republicans one more seat in Congress and an early leg up for the 2002 elections—Congresswoman Nita Lowey insisted it was no big loss: "When you consider that at one time we were nineteen points behind in the polls and we only lost by four points," she spun, "this was a big victory for us."

Republicans searched for the silver lining when Vermont's Senator James Jeffords suddenly abandoned the GOP and became an Independent. It was a severe body blow to President Bush and the Republican party, giving Democrats control of both the Senate and the legislative agenda. But party strategists insisted it was no defeat. In fact, they argued, Jeffords's defection might actually turn out to be a blessing for Bush and a curse for Democrats. Their spin was that, as long as the GOP controlled both chambers, Bush was under pressure from conservatives to deliver on his campaign promises. But, with Democrats in control, the onus was now on them to deliver. Bush could just sit back and take credit for whatever they passed and he signed into law. This was a brave attempt to turn their lemon into lemonade.

THE NOT-ME-I'M-DIFFERENT SPIN

One of the funniest ways politicians spin is to insist that what they're doing is different—when they're up to the exact same tricks they were excoriating others for, not so long ago. It's so transparent, yet both Democrats and Republicans do it, all the time.

Thanks to the *New Republic* magazine (July 2, 2001) for pointing this one out. During his presidential campaign, Al Gore was pilloried by Republicans for promising to move the U.S. Embassy in Israel from Tel Aviv to Jerusalem, and then having second thoughts. "In a blatant display of pandering,

Al Gore changed his position on moving the U.S. Embassy in Israel to Jerusalem," thundered Bush spokesman Dan Bartlett on October 30, 2000. "Al Gore is once again showing that he can't be counted on to take a principled stand."

Oops! On June 12, 2001, the Associated Press reported: "President Bush has backed off a campaign pledge to move the U.S. Embassy in Israel to Jerusalem and will keep it in Tel Aviv, at least for now." As this book goes to print, Dan Bartlett has not yet conceded that President Bush can't be counted on to take a principled stand, either.

And what about all those White House parties?

During the Clinton administration, both Clinton and Gore held many receptions for big donors in the White House and vice president's residence. When I was chair of the California Democratic Party, I went to a few of them myself. Plus, there were those infamous White House coffees and all those Lincoln Bedroom sleepovers (to which I was never invited). Technically, they were not fundraisers. They were simply "meet and greet" or "thank you" events, but since only high rollers were invited, they sure looked and smelled like political fundraisers—on government property, no less. Republicans howled with outrage. Dan Burton held hearings. Janet Reno was asked to name still another Independent Counsel. You might think Washington had never seen anything so scandalous.

Well, what do you know? The more things change, the more they stay the same.

Early in the Bush administration, both the president and vice president held the very same kind of big parties for Republican fat cats—and Republicans defended them as different as night and day. White House press secretary Ari Fleischer called Cheney's gala reception—get this!—"nothing more than a thank you to longtime Republicans." GOP strategist Ed Gillespie went even further, defending the White House event. "What we have here is the president, in this instance, also acting as the head of the party, raising money for the party, which is nothing out of the ordinary. And that is the difference here. There is no quid pro quo. . . . No one who went there last night gave any money, expecting that that would happen."

Gillespie could have said the same thing about Clinton.

Republicans probably didn't even fool themselves, trying to defend the Bush and Cheney receptions. They certainly didn't fool the *New York Times,* which reported: "Cheney held his own gala reception at his home on Monday night, with his office asserting that it was proper because it was not a fundraising event per se, just an event attended by donors. The distinction was correctly laughed at by Republicans when President Clinton and Vice President Al Gore tried to make it for the events they attended in years past." They didn't fool Common Cause president Scott Harshbarger either, who said, "This is the same thing that the Republicans were criticizing—correctly—Bill Clinton and Al Gore for doing."

There is a risk in becoming such a skilled spinmeister: You start getting a certain reputation, even among members of your own family. In July 2001, Ed Gillespie's wife, Cathy, organized a party to celebrate Ed's fortieth birthday party and invited lots of friends, including me. I saved the invitation. For a spinner, it was a classic.

The invitation read: "He can't spin his way out of this one."

THE BLAME-IT-ON-THE-MEDIA SPIN

This is one of the favorite fallbacks of politicians. Instead of confirming or denying an allegation, you portray yourself as a victim of the media. It's pretty transparent, but, since most people hate reporters as much as—or more than—they hate politicians, it usually works.

For example, when George W. Bush was getting trounced by John McCain in the early primaries, nobody in the Bush camp could believe it was because of any weakness of Dubya's—nor that it was because of any strength of Mc-Cain's. The culprit had to be the media! "That great sucking sound you hear is the sound of the media's lips coming off John McCain's ass," Marvin Bush complained to reporters on his brother's campaign plane.

Four years earlier, Bob Dole lashed out at the media on more than one occasion. Most notably, over tobacco. Campaigning among Kentucky's tobacco farmers, he got carried away and expressed doubts about the dangers of cigarette smoking. But, instead of admitting his mistake, he dug himself in even deeper by blaming the media. Asked by NBC's Katie Couric on the *Today* show to explain why the former Republican Surgeon General C. Everett Koop had declared tobacco addictive, Dole said that Koop had "watched the liberal media and probably got carried away." The good doctor, Dole added, was "a little bit" brainwashed.

Blaming the media is not a Republican specialty; it's a bipartisan affair. Imagine the look of horror on the face of Al Gore when, just before the November 2000 election, he saw the cover of the December issue of *Esquire* magazine. There sat Bill Clinton, the man whose sex scandals Gore had spent an entire year running away from, big as life, his legs spread-eagle, a colorful tie pointed provocatively at his crotch, with a smirk on his face that seemed to say, "Come and get it." It was the last thing the Gore campaign, or Clinton, needed. But, clearly, Clinton had posed for the photograph and given the interview. He couldn't blame that on the media, could he?

Oh, yes, he could. And did. Sure, he'd posed for the photo, but *Esquire* had promised him it wouldn't come out until after the election. "I was promised faithfully by the editor that it'd be done, released after the election, and I believed him," Clinton told reporters. He failed to explain why he thought it was a good idea to strike such a pose in the first place.

But politicians don't have any monopoly on blaming the media, either. Everyone does it, including star athletes. Late in the 2001 season, Red Sox super slugger Carl Everett got mad at plate umpire Ronald Kulpa and confronted him, making contact twice. At first, Everett denied he'd touched him, but television replays saw the umpire stagger away from a bump to the head.

There was only one other person Everett could blame: "The whole thing is that the majority of the media tried to make a monster out of a guy," Everett whined to locker-room reporters. "Everyone is quick to judge. I fault the media. . . . I would say I didn't do the things people said I did."

Maybe Everett should quit baseball and run for public office.

TALKING POINTS

Whatever direction the spin takes, its source is almost always the same: talking points.

For those who are still unfamiliar with the term, here's all you need to know about talking points:

- Talking points are a list of points a politician should make when asked questions about a given topic.
- The list should never be longer than one page.
- No matter what the question, the politician should make those points and only those points.

It is a rare politician, indeed, who would appear on television or hold a news conference without talking points.

Some talking points are written by a politician's own staff. On one *Crossfire* show, I looked over at a member of Congress, our guest on the right, who had unashamedly spread out on the desk in front of him a sheet of paper with the heading: "Talking Points for Crossfire." It was his cheat sheet for the big exam.

Those were retail talking points. But there are also wholesale talking points prepared by the Republican and Democratic National Committees and faxed out every day to party operatives around the country—and to friendly voices in the media. In the Congress, Democratic or Republican committee staff prepare talking points on key legislation and circulate them to all of their members. That's the way they get their message out. And that's the way they get their message spread. By making sure everybody is, literally, reading from the same page.

Just to show you how easy it is for politicians to stick to the script, here is a copy of talking points distributed to Democratic members of Congress on July 27, 2001 by the House Democratic Policy Committee.

A word of background: Two weeks earlier, the House had rejected a rule by House Speaker Dennis Hastert that also had the effect of blocking a vote on the campaign finance reform bill authored by Democrat Marty Meehan of Massachusetts and Republican Christopher Shays of Connecticut. Conservative, or Blue Dog, Democrats then launched an unusual parliamentary maneuver, or discharge petition, to force the bill on the floor for a yes-or-no vote. Now you're ready to step before the cameras.

TALKING POINTS ON CAMPAIGN FINANCE REFORM DISCHARGE EFFORT

- After rigging the rule and losing, the Republican Leadership refuses to bring Campaign Finance Reform back to the floor for a vote. The Discharge Petition is now the only way Members will be able to get a fair and honest debate on Campaign Finance Reform and force the Republican Leadership's hand.

- The Discharge Petition will bring up a fair rule to consider the Shays-Meehan bill and an equal number of Democratic and Republican amendments. Unlike the original rule, the new rule will give Members an up-or-down vote on the Shays-Meehan bill.

- Every time the Blue Dog Democrats have led this type of effort to get campaign reform on the floor, it has been successful—both successful in getting the legislation considered, as well as successful in getting the legislation passed.

- Each time, more than 90% of Democrats have signed the Discharge Petition—just as more than 90% of Democrats have voted for the Shays-Meehan bill.

- The success of the current Discharge Petition will depend on the moderate Republicans and their willingness once again to stand up to their leadership.

Now you know why you hear the same comments coming from so many different voices. Now you know why all politicians sound the same on the Sunday morning talk shows. Talking points: don't leave home without them.

SPINNING THEIR WAY TO THE WHITE HOUSE

We're so inundated with spin these days, we'd like to blame somebody. In fact, we'd like to blame it all on Bill Clinton, because he's such a master of spin. But, as masterful as he is, he didn't start political spin. He's just the latest and greatest in a long line. And, over the years, he's had some pretty stiff competition.

In fact, nowhere is greater political spin to be found than on the way to, or already in, the White House—which makes sense for a couple of reasons. One: the greater the office, the more outrageous the spin. Two: what is the presidency all about anyhow but the giant spin that 42 people so far in our history are better than all the rest of us? (George W. Bush is number 43, but Grover Cleveland is counted twice, having won once, been defeated for reelection, then elected again four years later.) Most Americans buy into the spin that these 42 men were so brilliant and so talented they deserved the most powerful office in the world.

What a joke! The truth is, among the 42, you could count on the fingers of one hand those who really deserved, or excelled in, the position of president. It reminds me of Adlai Stevenson's famous line: "In America, anybody can be President. That's one of the risks you take." He was right. In fact, most of those who did become president simply stumbled into the job and never lived up to it.

So, how did they get there? By political spin, in all its various forms. Long before television, one of the only things people knew about candidates was their nickname. The right nickname would spin one man as better than all the rest. Thus Andrew Jackson was just a man of the people, "Old Hickory"—even though he'd been a member of Congress, a state supreme court judge, a distinguished military officer and a rich businessman. Martin Van Buren was hailed as "The Little Magician"—when the only tricks he ever pulled were stealing elections as New York party boss.

The list goes on. Zachary Taylor was sold as "Old Rough and Ready." James Buchanan, as "Old Buck." Grover Cleveland, as "Grover the Good." Calvin Coolidge, as "Silent Cal." And they were all mediocre presidents. See what spin can do?

Today, nicknames are more often used to tear down a candidate than to build one up. "Slick Willie" was never intended as a term of endearment for Bill Clinton. Neither was "Tricky Dick" for Richard Nixon, or "Shrub," for George W. Bush.

Presidents also use slogans to put the right spin on their agenda. For FDR, it was the "New Deal"; for JFK, the "New Frontier"; for LBJ, the "Great Society."

One clever form of spin deserves special mention. In the presidential campaign of 1840, Martin Van Buren, running for reelection, faced war hero William Henry Harrison, who had defeated the Shawnee Indians in battle near Tippecanoe Creek. His vice-presidential running mate was John Tyler. As political theater, Harrison's supporters assembled a huge ball of scraps of paper and rolled it, literally, from Kentucky to Baltimore, chanting: "It is the ball a-rolling on, for Tippecanoe and Tyler, too." As the ball spins . . .

Political invective is the most potent form of spin, and it started in the United States with the presidential campaign of 1796, which, after two terms of Washington, was the nation's first real political contest. John Adams and Thomas Jefferson did no actual politicking. From beginning to end, they professed their mutual admiration and friendship. But, in newspaper articles, supporters invented the politics of personal destruction, painting their opponent in the most unfavorable light. Adams was denounced as an "avowed friend of the monarchy," a charge repeated four years later. Jefferson didn't get off much easier: atheist, anarchist, demagogue, coward, mountebank, trickster and Franco-maniac. Good thing they never got mean. Adams won. Jefferson, who came in second, became his vice president.

Adams and Jefferson had their rematch in 1800. Both political parties were now well-established, so the spin was even more intense. It's hard to know which candidate was more brutally pummeled.

James Callendar, still at that point on Jefferson's payroll, portrayed John Adams as a "repulsive pedant," a "gross hypocrite" and a "hideous hermaphroditical character which has neither the force and firmness of a man, nor the gentleness and sensibility of a woman." Not to mention "insane." Thomas Jefferson personally reviewed and approved Callendar's spin, assuring his hatchet man, "Such papers cannot fail to produce the best results."

Indeed, throughout his four years as vice president, Jefferson's behavior toward President John Adams would today be grounds for impeachment. Even before the 1800 campaign, Jefferson did everything he could to undermine the policies of his boss—including encouraging, and paying, Callendar to attack Adams in print. Later, when Callendar was arrested under the Alien and Sedition Acts and Jefferson's treachery was exposed, the Sage of Monticello pleaded innocent, insisting to First Lady Abigail Adams that his payments to Callendar were nothing more than pure "charity" toward a needy writer, rather than payments for political propaganda. "Nobody sooner disapproved of his writing than I did," Jefferson piously lied.

He's lucky lightning didn't strike him dead on the spot. Although the fact is, Jefferson may have honestly believed he was as honest as he told Abigail. In his great analysis of the mysterious Virginian, *The American Sphinx,* historian Joseph Ellis argues that the key to understanding Jefferson's character is his talent for self-deception—or spinning himself. It's a theme Ellis returns to in his Pulitzer Prize–winning study of seven Revolutionary leaders, *The Founding Brothers:* "Jefferson was the kind of man who could have passed a lie detector test confirming his integrity, believing as he did that the supreme significance of the larger cause rendered conventional distinctions between truth and falsehood superfluous." That may be the unwritten creed of every politician alive today.

(Ironically, shortly after publishing *The Founding Brothers,* Ellis was discovered to have his own talent for self-deception: wowing his students at Mount Holyoke College about his near-death experiences as a paratrooper in Vietnam, his exciting days in the anti-war and civil rights movements and a big role in a high school football game. Jefferson would have been proud of him. None of it was true.)

Back to the campaign: Adams was also again reviled as a monarchist, the worst insult you could level at an eighteenth-century American. He was accused of planning to marry one of his sons to a daughter of King George III in order to start an American monarchy. Not only that. David McCullough reveals in his masterful biography *John Adams* that, in apparent contradiction to his alleged hermaphrodism, Adams was said to have sent South Carolina Congressman Charles Cotesworth Pinckney to London to bring back four pretty mistresses to divide between them. The 65-year-old Adams could not help but be amused: "I do declare upon my honor, if this is true General Pinckney has kept them all for himself and cheated me out of my two."

And, remember: this was 200 years before Dick Morris! Today's political attacks seem mild by comparison.

For his part, candidate Jefferson was smeared—or spun—as a hopeless visionary, a weakling, a swindler, and one who loved France more than the United States. He was also denounced as an atheist, simply because he had once expressed doubts about the divinity of Christ. In New England, he was considered so dangerous, families were urged to hide their Bibles. There were also rumors that, like all slave owners, Jefferson had slept with his female slaves. Although there is no record of his having said, "I did not have sex with that woman, Miss Hemings."

History treated Thomas Jefferson much kinder than it treated John Adams. There is a Jefferson Memorial in Washington; none is dedicated to Adams. Jefferson's nose protrudes from Mt. Rushmore; Adams's belly does not. Over the years, Jefferson has obviously had better spinners.

Even in his own lifetime, Adams saw this coming—and resented it. It was Adams, after all, who dominated the debate over independence in Congress, almost shaming reluctant delegates into voting to break with England, while Jefferson sat on his hands. Later, it was Adams who asked Jefferson to draft the Declaration of Independence, summing up what Congress had voted and why. And it was Adams who chaired the committee that edited Jefferson's prose into poetry. Yet, as celebrated author of the Declaration—which Adams considered nothing but "a theatrical side show"—Jefferson got all the credit.

In a letter to his friend, Pennsylvania delegate Benjamin Rush, Adams lamented that the signing of the document, not the winning of the debate, had become the defining moment in America's revolutionary history. "Jefferson ran away with the stage effect and all the glory of it." He should have known: you just can't top a good spinner.

It is an interesting comment, not only for its insights into Adams's feelings about Jefferson, but for how Adams sees politics as theater: with its sideshow, stage effects and glory. It was a theme repeated 196 years later by Bill Clinton in June 2001, explaining to graduates of New York's Professional Performing Arts School why he gave up his theatrical ambitions in favor of politics: "If I went into politics, I could stay in acting and never have to change roles." And that was Adams's problem. Unlike Jefferson, Franklin Roosevelt, Ronald Reagan or Bill Clinton, Adams was no actor. He couldn't fake it.

Once in the White House, it was the presidents, and no longer their supporters, who did the spinning. By my reckoning, throughout history, there are three things that cause a president to abandon the truth and spin like mad: war; health; and sex.

SPINNING WAR

President Polk never wanted war with Mexico. He wasn't interested in taking any land from Mexico, either. At least, that's what he told the country. All he sought was justice: punishing Mexico for attacking American troops on American soil. One freshman member of Congress, young Abraham Lincoln, didn't believe Polk's spin. He poked around and discovered that the attack, against an expedition led by Zachary Taylor, had occurred deep inside Mexico—and that Polk was just looking for an excuse to declare war against our southern neighbor in order to seize California for the United States.

Later, Woodrow Wilson didn't want war with Germany, either. He was neutral in the conflict between Western Europe and the Kaiser. So he told the nation, campaigning for reelection in 1916, under the banner "He Kept Us Out of War." Wilson was just spinning. He knew it. The British knew it. The Germans knew it. Only the American people didn't know it. Wilson was already sending aid to England, and promising more. Three months after he was sworn in for a second term, the United States declared war on Germany. President Franklin Roosevelt played the same game in World War II.

Sadly, three recent presidents spun wildly about Vietnam. To justify sending American military advisers in the first place, John F. Kennedy spun South Vietnam as the "cornerstone of the Free World." Lyndon Johnson rationalized stepped-up bombing raids by creating the Gulf of Tonkin incident, even as he declared, "We seek no wider war." And Richard Nixon, explaining his decision to expand the war into Cambodia, maintained, "I have rejected all political considerations in making this decision."

Note how easily, when a president is talking about war, spin goes over the line and becomes a lie. Good spin turns to bad.

SPINNING HEALTH

In dealing with their personal health, presidents are often equally dishonest. President Chester Arthur came down with the debilitating Bright's disease but didn't want anybody to know it. His office said he had a touch of malaria. When he was nominated for president in 1912, Woodrow Wilson told delegates he was in perfect health. He failed to mention he'd already suffered two strokes, one of which left him blind in his left eye. Like Wilson, President Kennedy projected total vigor, but never came clean about his serious affliction with Addison's disease.

Grover Cleveland was one of the most inventive in keeping people in the dark. Diagnosed with cancer of the mouth, he arranged to be secretly operated on aboard a friend's yacht, while Americans believed he was only out for a weekend cruise. Five days later, when the president still hadn't reappeared, the White House spun he was suffering from a bout of rheumatism and having trouble with his teeth. Cancer of the mouth? Trouble with his teeth, indeed!

This kind of spin about health is also called cover-up.

Perhaps the most famous case of presidential cover-up of illness: President Franklin Roosevelt. In a sense, FDR's entire administration was built on spin: the spin that Roosevelt was a robust, healthy man, leading the fight to rebuild the economy and save the world from Nazi Germany. Roosevelt was a great leader, but, as we now know, he was not a healthy man. Seriously disabled, he could not walk on his own. He led the country from a wheelchair. Yet, with the cooperation of White House reporters and photographers, Roosevelt was able to hide his disability from the American people throughout his presidency. It was what he called his "splendid deception"—a wonderful, Rooseveltian synonym for spin.

Ironically, designers of the new Roosevelt Memorial in Washington tried to perpetuate the spin. In its early days, you could walk through the entire four outdoor rooms of the new

Roosevelt Memorial without knowing of his physical disabilities—unless you were curious enough to poke around behind the grand sculpture of FDR—wearing a flowing cape, sitting in an arm chair with his famous dog Fala perched nearby—and notice the little wheels on the back two legs of the chair. That spin has now been corrected with the recent addition of a sculpture of Roosevelt sitting proudly in a wheelchair, prominently placed at the entrance to the memorial.

Of course, in those days, presidents could spin about their medical problems because it was an unwritten rule that this was one area reporters simply did not pry into or write about. How times have changed! Today, in fact, it's just the opposite. We hear more details about every presidential hemorrhoidectomy than we really need, or care, to know. It's impossible for a president to cover up, or spin his way, out of a health crisis. Nevertheless, in February 2001, George W. Bush tried to brush off Dick Cheney's heart surgery—his second in three months, on top of four past heart attacks—as a "routine procedure."

SPINNING SEX

It is sex—what else?—that brings out the true creativity in presidential spin. Starting with Thomas Jefferson. When confronted with allegations of a long relationship with, and children born to, slave Sally Hemings, Jefferson refused to deny the charges, believing that doing so would only bring attention to them. Instead, he chose to change the subject—and plead guilty to a lesser offense. In a letter to Attorney General Lincoln Levi, he admitted to having tried, as a bachelor, to seduce a certain Mrs. Walker (whose husband had challenged him to a duel). That was the only sexual misconduct he would fess up to. "You will perceive that I plead guilty to one of their charges, that when young and single I offered love to a handsome lady," Jefferson wrote to a friend to whom he had sent a copy of his letter to the attorney general. "I acknolege [sic] its incorrectness. It is the only one founded in truth among all their allegations against me."

In other words, like many *Crossfire* guests, Jefferson simply refused to answer the question. But the Sally Hemings issue raised an even larger issue for Jefferson: How could he justify owning slaves in the first place?

Throughout his life, Jefferson was kept busy spinning how the author of the Declaration of Independence—"We hold these truths to be self-evident: that all men are created equal"—could also own slaves, let alone force one of them to sleep with him and bear his children. Yes, in theory, Jefferson argued, all men are created equal. But, in reality, God made some better than others.

Indeed, the spin that Jefferson resorted to in order to justify his position as slave owner is shocking. Blacks were inferior, he wrote, not just because they lacked the superior physical beauty of whites—color, figure and hair–but, he said, because they smelled. "They secrete less by the kidneys, and more by the glands of the skin, which gives them a very strong and disagreeable odour." He also wrote that they were inferior intellectually. "In memory they are equal to the white; in reason much inferior, as I think one could scarcely be found capable of tracing and comprehending the investigations of Euclid; and that in imagination they are dull, tasteless, and anomalous."

Reading those words, one wonders why there are not daily pickets at the Jefferson Memorial in Washington demanding that his statue be unceremoniously tossed into the Tidal Basin.

Among presidents, only Grover Cleveland was forthcoming about sex. When campaigning for president, he was accused by his hometown Buffalo newspaper of illegitimately fathering a child. His consultants told him to deny it. Cleveland, instead, told the truth, admitting both the affair and child-support payments—and won. In vain, opponents had chanted: "Ma, ma, where's my pa? Gone to the White House, ha, ha, ha."

Warren G. Harding also pooh-poohed charges of sexual misbehavior. Despite having already had one affair with a married woman and another with the single Nan Britton, with whom he fathered a child, Harding told power brokers at the 1920 Republican convention: "There is no reason in the sight of God that I cannot be president of the United States." Well, perhaps not in 1920.

It was only after Harding had left the White House that Nan Britton spilled the beans about the closet in the Oval Office where she and Harding continued to meet throughout his presidency—out of the sight of White House staff, but still, one presumes, in the sight of God. "This was a small closet . . . where . . . we repaired . . . many times in the course of my visits to the White House, and in the darkness of a space no more than five feet square the President of the United States and his adoring sweetheart made love."

How touching. How romantic. How sick.

This may be what inspired Bill Clinton to have sex, such as it was, with Monica Lewinsky, in the hidden anteroom and corridor off the Oval Office—and also deny having done so until caught.

Or perhaps, like Jimmy Carter, it was just lust in his heart.

SIX PRESIDENTIAL SPINNERS

Among all of our presidents, on all topics, across the board, six of them stand out as master spinners: Thomas Jefferson, Abraham Lincoln, Teddy Roosevelt, Franklin Roosevelt, Richard Nixon and Ronald Reagan. These, of course, are in addition to the ubermeister spinner: Bill Clinton.

THOMAS JEFFERSON

Sex and slavery weren't the only subjects of Jefferson's spin. He also masked the truth when it came to the use of presidential power. Before assuming the office, he vowed never to take any action not strictly spelled out in the Constitution and never to put the federal government in debt. But when the French offered the entire Louisiana Territory for sale, Jefferson promptly broke both promises. He bought the land, even though the Constitution gave a president no such authority, and paid $15 million, even though doing so increased the national debt by 20 percent. Jefferson's spin: it was too good an offer to refuse, and future generations of Americans would understand.

Actually, he was right. Today we understand both the necessity of the purchase and the value of the spin. Still, such tortured reasoning on so many subjects must have been enough to make even Jefferson's head spin. No wonder the same man invented the swivel chair!

ABRAHAM LINCOLN

"Honest Abe" probably deserved the nickname. He was the greatest, and most honest, of all our presidents. But that doesn't mean he was above spinning. In fact, he was a damned good spin doctor, even before he was elected.

As a result of his own clever self-promotion and the combined spin of scores of historians, Lincoln is revered as close a man to Jesus Christ as ever walked the face of the earth: a selfless, honest, truthful martyr. The truth is, he was a lot more complicated and a hell of a lot more human. He didn't always tell the truth. Campaigning for Congress, he pretended to be for the Mexican War; once elected, he emerged as its chief critic. Nor was he, as we've been led to believe, always a champion of blacks. *Au contraire*. He once boasted: "I am not nor ever have been in favor of making voters or jurors of negroes, not of qualifying them to hold office, nor to intermarry with white people." Before the outbreak of the Civil War, when the North needed black soldiers, Lincoln believed in freeing slaves only on condition that they be immediately exported to Liberia.

Before he was elected president, Lincoln opposed any change to the Constitution, arguing we should consider it "unalterable." As president, he sponsored three amendments to the Constitution, including the Thirteenth, abolishing slavery.

No wonder one critic accused Lincoln of being two-faced, to which he responded, "If I had another face, do you think I'd wear this one?"

TEDDY ROOSEVELT

Nobody spun the public like Teddy Roosevelt. He understood, perhaps more than any president before or since, that he was defined by his media personality and that personality—broadcast from the "bully pulpit"—mattered more than political party. Consequently, even before he got to the White House, Teddy brilliantly used the media to spin the image of himself as an active, vigorous, take-charge kind of leader.

Volunteering for action in the Spanish-American War, he took cameramen to Cuba so they could capture on film his charge up San Juan Hill. In the White House, he gave total access to reporters—even allowing them to film his family in their private quarters—as long as they obeyed his edict never to reprint a word he said outside of public speeches. Reporters who strayed were banished from the White House. How dare they interfere with the president's personal spin machine?

When the government of Colombia resisted his plans to build a canal linking the Pacific and Atlantic oceans, TR gave Panamanian rebels $10 million to start a revolution, then immediately recognized the new government of Panama and started construction of the canal—justifying his imperial actions as necessary because it would have taken Congress too long to debate what to do. When he needed funds for his re-election, he convinced big business he was their best friend, pocketed their money, then double-crossed them by cracking down on corporate "malefactors of great wealth."

Roosevelt's exercise of power was breathtaking, even though it was never enough to satisfy him. "Sometimes I wish I could be president and Congress too," he openly pined. Still, today, nobody else could get away with what he did. He pulled it off only because he was a master self-promoter, a master manipulator of the media, a master spinner.

Did Teddy exceed his legitimate authority? That's not how he spun it. "I did not usurp power, but I did greatly broaden the use of executive power," he explained. You have to admire his style and chutzpah.

FRANKLIN DELANO ROOSEVELT

Must be something about the name. Cousin Franklin comes closer to Teddy than anyone else. We've already noted his spins on attempting to pack the Supreme Court and cover up his disability. But that wasn't all. FDR left behind a whole Bartlett's of famous quotations, of which the most well-known is his declaration upon taking office in the middle of the Great Depression: "The only thing we have to fear is fear itself." Nonsense. There was a lot more to fear at the time, starting with the possibility of total anarchy. What was Roosevelt's declaration other than spin for "Everything is going to be okay"?

One reason Roosevelt was so good at spinning was that he had a powerful new weapon at his disposal: radio. He wasn't the first president to speak on the radio—Wilson was—but Roosevelt was the first to master it. He started out with a perfect speaking voice. Then he became a good actor. Knowing how important it was to sound conversational, he rehearsed every "fireside chat" until he had the cadences just right. It worked. As many as 50 million people—the proportional equivalent of 140 million today—stopped whatever they were doing to listen and remember. No one could match that outreach. No one could outspin that spin.

Seeking reelection in 1940, Roosevelt, like Wilson before him, spun himself as a pillar of neutrality—"I have told you once and I will tell you again: your boys will not be sent into any foreign wars"—when, in fact, he had already made preparations for America's entry into World War II.

Roosevelt also deserves special merit for inventing a new form of spin. It was his own clever twist on the "blame my enemies" approach: blame my enemies by hiding behind my dog. Accused by Republicans of spending millions of taxpayer dollars to send a destroyer to Alaska to retrieve his dog Fala, Roosevelt refused to answer the charges directly. Instead, he thundered: Stop picking on my dog! "I am accustomed to hearing malicious falsehoods about myself. . . . But I think I have a right to resent, to object to libelous statements about my dog."

RICHARD NIXON

The worst president? Richard Nixon. The worst spinner? Richard Nixon. No coincidence.

What do you do when you're president of the United States and your agents are caught breaking into the headquarters of the opposition party? If you're Richard Nixon, you do it all wrong:

- First you dismiss it as a "second-rate burglary."
- Then you seek to hide any White House connection: "I don't give a shit what happens," he says on the tapes, "I want you all to stonewall it."
- When White House involvement is proven, you distance yourself from whatever pranks some low-level aides might have committed: "I am not a crook."
- When your chief of staff is nailed, you force your top aides to resign, go underground and start drinking.
- When the tapes start spinning, revealing you organized a cover-up of the whole damned thing, you resign—but you still don't admit you did anything wrong: "While technically I did not commit a crime, an impeachable offense . . . these are legalisms, as far as the handling of this matter is concerned."
- And when you're out of office, you deny even the possibility of wrongdoing: "When the president does it, that means it is not illegal."

Nixon proves that spin, no matter how outrageous, can't always get you out of trouble. But it does help to soften the pain.

And, of course, Nixon, scoundrel that he was, couldn't resist stooping to the old dog trick, too. In 1952, while he was campaigning for vice president on the Republican ticket, the *New York Post* reported that a wealthy California businessman had set up an $18,000 slush fund for Nixon's personal use. Needless to say, the head of the ticket, boy scout Dwight D. Eisenhower, was not pleased. Nixon went on national television to defend himself. But, like FDR before him, he never answered the charges directly. He hid behind his dog Checkers.

With 55 million Americans watching—the largest television audience until that time—Nixon insisted that the special fund was for political, not personal, use. Then he admitted that he had received another gift (which nobody knew or gave a damn about): a black-and-white spotted cocker spaniel which daughter Tricia had named Checkers. "And you know," oozed Nixon, "the kids love that dog and I just want to say this right now: that regardless of what they say about it, we are going to keep it."

His maudlin handling of the shaggy dog story probably saved Nixon's place on the ticket with Ike. Forty-nine years later, the Nixon family repaid Checkers by exhuming him from his burial plot on Long Island and repotting him at the Nixon Library in Yorba Linda, California, alongside the graves of Dick and Pat. How touching.

SPIN HALL OF FAME NOMINATION

∽◌⟆◌∾

by Hendrik Hertzberg

NOMINEE: Jimmy Carter

OCCASION: Jimmy Carter's speech to North Carolina tobacco farmers in August of 1978.

SPIN:	"The tobacco industry, the federal government, all citizens want to have an accurate and enlightened education program and research program to make the smoking of tobacco even more safe than it is today."
TRANSLATION:	"I'm a peanut farmer from Georgia. These tobacco guys are my only real constituency. Do you really think I'm going to alienate them?"

This is from the same man who as an ex-president wrote in 1995, "If the tobacco companies win, our children lose." Just goes to show, it's a heck of a lot easier to be a statesman when you're no longer a politician.

Hendrik Hertzberg is a longtime writer for the New Yorker.

After Nixon and the honest but hapless Gerry Ford, it's no wonder Jimmy Carter got elected by simply promising: "I'll never tell a lie." Actually, he might have been a better president if he'd learned to lie a little. But he sure did spin a good tale during the campaign. Taking full advantage of public disgust over Washington in general, and Watergate in particular, Carter sold himself as just the opposite: honest, hardworking, smart, trustworthy and, best of all, from outside the Beltway. "I'm not a lawyer, I am not a member of Congress, and I've never served in Washington." Great spin. Trouble is, as someone from outside the Beltway, he proved himself unable to cope, once he moved inside it. Not even spin could save Carter's presidency. Especially not from so skilled a spinner as Ronald Reagan.

RONALD REAGAN

Spin came naturally to Reagan, who started out as a sportscaster—which Garry Wills identifies as "the corner of jour-

nalism where accuracy is least expected and often excluded."
He excelled in the skill of the day: ripping and reading the
wires to see what was happening at a distant baseball game,
while providing a running commentary on the air, as if he
were actually in the stands, watching the play-by-play. But
Reagan was so good at it that, one day, when the wire broke
down, he just carried on and made the whole game up. Nobody noticed the difference. What a spinner!

As an actor, Reagan was always pretending to be what he
was not. And later, in politics, he honed his acting skills to
perfection, first as governor, then as president. Once in the
White House, with the guidance of public relations genius
Michael Deaver, Reagan took spin to new heights by blend-
ing words and pictures. It was a powerful combination. Reagan spoke the words Deaver wrote for him; Deaver staged
the photo-op that magnified the spin of his words. Ronald
Reagan on the shores of the Chesapeake, looking like an environmentalist. Ronald Reagan on the beaches of Normandy,
looking like a combat veteran. Photo opportunities have become the standard spin of every presidency since Reagan:
George H.W. Bush at the flag factory, Bill Clinton at the
Grand Canyon, George W. Bush in the Everglades.

With Reagan, the spin sometimes overpowered the reality. He spoke so much about the horrors of the Holocaust,
for example, that he actually ended up believing he was there
in person, unlocking the gates of the death camps, when, in
fact, he only knew what happened by watching film clips of
the action in the safety of his Hollywood studio.

And that's not the only time he borrowed ideas from the
big screen. In 1940, in the movie *Murder in the Air,* Reagan
played an American secret agent charged with protecting a
secret superweapon capable of destroying all enemy planes in
the air. In 1966, Alfred Hitchcock released a film called *Torn
Curtain,* in which Paul Newman is responsible for develop-
ing an anti-missile missile. Listen to scientist Newman: "We
will produce a defensive weapon that will make all nuclear
weapons obsolete, and thereby abolish the terror of nuclear
warfare." Who does that sound like? Right! Reagan used al-

most the exact same words to first sell his Star Wars plan to the nation in March 1983.

There was no scientific background to Reagan's proposal. The Pentagon knew nothing about it ahead of time. It was pure fiction, right out of the movies, spun as serious public policy by the president. But Reagan sure did a good job of it. He spun it so well, it's still alive—still uncertain, still unproven, still unworkable, but still alive—after all this time. George W. Bush is still selling it.

But Reagan's worst spin was reserved for Iran-Contra. It was his Watergate, and he handled it just like Nixon. Over and over, he assured the American people he would never make a deal with terrorists. "We will never pay off terrorists, because that only encourages more of it." That was the spin: pure mind, pure heart and pure deed. And, of course, he was so good at spinning that people believed it. The reality, however, was a lot more evil. With his authorization, National Security Adviser Bud McFarlane, accompanied by young zealot Ollie North, was making deals to sell arms to Iran, a terrorist nation, in order to secure the release of U.S. hostages in Lebanon—with profits from arms sales going to the contras in Nicaragua.

When the bubble burst and word leaked that the U.S. was in fact making deals with one group of terrorists and providing arms to another, breaking two laws in the process, Reagan retreated to the ultimate spin: He couldn't remember ever approving such a deal. And, of course, he knew nothing about it.

Reagan was so out of it, most of the time, people believed that, too.

Even now, Reagan's former handlers continue to spin his accomplishments as president. Not satisfied with Washington's Ronald Reagan National Airport, the new Ronald Reagan Federal Office Building and the newly-christened destroyer U.S.S. *Ronald Reagan,* conservative Grover Norquist has organized the Ronald Reagan Legacy Project with the goal of having some public structure named for Reagan in every one of the nation's 3,066 counties. And that's not all. They're also sponsoring legislation to have Reagan's face on the $10 bill, replacing Alexander Hamilton. But why stop there? "Do I think in 20 years Reagan could be on Rushmore?" Norquist told the *Washington Post*. "Maybe. Or we could have our own mountain."

Whatever the lasting impact of his policies, Ronald Reagan set new heights in public relations. He was the Great Communicator. Until Bill Clinton came along and broke the mold.

SPINMEISTERS

One important point: all the attention to presidents as spinners obscures the fact that, at least from the time of William McKinley on, presidents or candidates did not act on their own. They put themselves in the hands of master strategists who knew the game of political spin and taught them to spin.

Political consultants used to be seen, but not heard. Today, they are as well known as the candidates they brought into office. Think of George W. Bush, say thank you to Karl Rove. See John McCain's success, look for John Weaver and Mike Murphy standing nearby. Bill Clinton? James Carville, George Stephanopoulos and Paul Begala. For Father Bush, gunslinger James Baker. And so it goes: Ronald Reagan's Michael Deaver, Jimmy Carter's Jody Powell and Hamilton Jordan, Nixon's Murray Chotiner and FDR's Louis Howe, among others.

But the granddaddy of them all, the man who invented the game, was Mark Hanna, who will forever be remembered for summing up what politics was all about, then and now: "There are two important things in politics. The first is the money, and I can't remember the second."

Marcus Alonzo Hanna, a hugely successful businessman from Cleveland, was convinced that having a Republican in the White House was essential to the success of big business. In 1896, he helped McKinley win the Republican nomination for president, then came up with a novel strategy for winning the general election. He planted the candidate down on his front porch, from which he did not budge for the entire campaign, while Hanna himself went off to Wall Street and shook down corporate donors for a record $3.5 million in cold cash, which he used to promote McKinley as a "new Republican."

Political reformers were appalled. "Hanna has advertised McKinley as if he were a patent medicine," complained Teddy Roosevelt, then Police Commissioner of New York City. Ironically, four years later, when he was McKinley's vice-presidential running mate, TR would benefit from Hanna's same tactics—without complaint.

For McKinley, Hanna produced a landslide of campaign coins, pamphlets and posters, buttons and banners. He also organized the first national Flag Day, calling on Republicans nationwide to fly the flag on October 31—after, of course, wrapping William McKinley in it. Roosevelt was right. Yes, it was like selling patent medicine. For Hanna, the candidate was more important than the issues and the spin was more important than the candidate—and it's been that way ever since. The Hanna/McKinley race was a model for Rove/Bush.

POLITICS TODAY

Everywhere you turn today, politics is but a whirlwind of spin where, for one thing, nobody says what they really mean.

Example: When Vermont's James Jeffords bolted from the Republican party in May 2001, upsetting the Republican apple cart and putting Democrats in charge, deposed GOP leader Trent Lott insisted he wasn't upset.

LOTT'S SPIN: "There's something liberating about being in the minority."

TRANSLATION: "I hate no longer being able to wear my leader's uniform, but I'll never publicly give Jeffords the pleasure of knowing how badly he fucked us. What an asshole!"

Example: When Vice-President Dick Cheney started craft-ing the Bush administration's new energy policy in early 2001, he surprised environmentalists by trying to breathe new life into a technology most people thought was dead: nuclear power plants. And, on the spot, top Republicans stood up to salute. Starting with Treasury Secretary Paul O'Neill.

> **O'NEILL'S SPIN:** "If you set aside Three Mile Island and Chernobyl, the safety record of nuclear power is really very good."
>
> **TRANSLATION:** "If you set aside the mountains, Switzerland is really just like New Jersey." Sure, Paul. And what are you going to do with the nu-clear waste?

Example: When Senator Jesse Helms of North Carolina announced his retirement, even most Republicans were glad to see him go, because he was such an embarrassment—not only to the Republican party, but to the whole human race. But, in true Washington style, nobody said: "good-bye, good riddance to this painful reminder of Southern racism." In-stead, even Democrats like Joe Biden searched for something good to say about him.

> **BIDEN'S SPIN:** "Having served with Jese Helms for twenty-eight years, I can tell you on a personal level, he is one of the most thoughtful, considerate and gracious Senators I have ever served with."
>
> **TRANSLATION:** "So what if he's anti-black, anti-gay, anti–women's rights, anti–Martin Luther King's birthday holiday, anti–funding of the United Nations, anti–restrictions on tobacco ads, anti-environment and anti–funding of the arts? He's a real Southern gentleman."

You really don't have to search hard to find evidence of po-litical spin. Just read any newspaper, watch any newscast, listen to any speech or news conference. But there is one special source I recommend: a Web site called Spinsanity.com. Its editors wade through the sea of possibilities and select a few outstanding examples of spin by both Democrats and Republicans to highlight and dissect every day or so. You can even sign up for an e-mail alerting you to the latest outrages. Check it out.

TOMBSTONES

Another manifestation of political spin: the name that Senators or members of Congress stick on their bills. Realizing that most people won't know anything more about the bill than its title, authors look for what used to be called a "tombstone," but in today's media-driven world is more accurately called a "sound bite title." And sometimes, the competition gets tough.

During debate over the patients' bill of rights, there were two competing proposals. The White House-sponsored bill, authored by Republican Bill Frist and Democrat John Breaux, was called: "The Bipartisan Patients' Bill of Rights Act of 2001." Not wanting to be outdone, Democrats Ted Kennedy and John Edwards and Republican John McCain dubbed their measure: "The Bipartisan Patients' Protection Act of 2001." Choose your poison.

This is not a new game. The bipartisan patients' bills follow such monuments as "The Tax Simplification Act of 1993," which was actually hundreds of pages long, and "The Death Tax Elimination Act," which implied that even dead people were forced to pay taxes. Which, of course, the IRS would do, if they could figure out a way. Finding the right name for a bill, says Professor Joseph Cooper of Johns Hopkins University, is "part of the whole game of getting the right kind of spin out to the media."

LE MOT JUSTE

It's not just the right phrase or title that counts in spin, it's also the right word. Finding *le mot juste* is critical to spinning the right message. And nobody knows, or practices, that better than Newt Gingrich.

In 1990, four years before Americans ever heard of the Contract with America, Gingrich published an astounding document called "Language: A Key Mechanism of Control"—and mailed it to Republican leaders across the country. Its object, as Gingrich said later, was to teach fellow Republicans how to "paint a vivid, brilliant word picture." Or, actually, two word pictures: a positive one of themselves and a negative one of Democrats. How? By the very words they use.

Leaving nothing to chance, in his booklet Gingrich included two lists of words. First, the "positive, governing words" Republicans were advised to use when speaking about their own party. And then, the negative words they should use to describe their opponents. Here's the entire list of Republican spin words, courtesy of Newt Gingrich.

Positive Words (for Republicans)

Active	Empower(ment)	Premise
Activist	Fair	Preserve
Building	Family	Principle(d)
Candid(ly)	Freedom	Pristine
Care(ing)	Hard work	Pro-flag,
Challenge	Help	children,
Change	Humane	environment
Children	Inventive	Prosperity
Choice/choose	Initiative	Protect
Citizen	Lead	Proud/pride
Commitment	Learn	Provide
Common sense	Legacy	Reform
Compete	Liberty	Sights
Confident	Light	Share
Conflict	Listen	Strength
Control	Mobilize	Success
Courage	Moral	Tough
Crusade	Movement	Truth
Debate	Opportunity	Unique
Dream	Passionate	Vision
Duty	Peace	We/us/our
Eliminate good	Pioneer	Workfare
time in prison	Precious	

Negative Words (for Democats)

Anti-flag, family, child, jobs	Failure	Self-serving
Betray	Greed	Sensationalists
Coercion	Hypocrisy	Shallow
Collapse	Ideological	Sick
Consequences	Impose	They/them
Corruption	Incompetent	Threaten
Crisis	Insecure	Traitors
Decay	Liberal	Unionized
Deeper	Lie	bureaucracy
Destroy	Limit(s)	Urgent
Destructive	Pathetic	Waste
Devour	Permissive	
Endanger	attitude	
	Radical	

Now that you have the list, my advice is to keep it near your TV set and check off the words you hear, next time you're watching *Crossfire* or the Sunday morning talk shows. Now you know what Republicans do in their limousines, on the way to CNN, Fox, NBC, ABC or CBS. They memorize the list, hoping to blurt as many of Newt's magic words as possible.

IT DOESN'T GET ANY WORSE THAN CONDIT

Throughout this book, you will notice nominations by fellow journalists and pundits for the Spin Hall of Fame. There's only one nominee for the Spin Hall of Shame: Congressman Gary Condit.

The issue is not his relationship with intern Chandra Levy. He's not the first Congressman to have an affair with an intern, and he won't be the last. The issue is: once she was reported missing, and once the nature of his relationship became apparent, he could not have handled it more poorly. His response consisted of one public relations disaster after another.

First, Condit went into denial. Even though he had previously and publicly advised President Clinton to tell the truth about Monica, or else it would leak out "drip by drip," Condit at first refused to tell the truth about Chandra. The two of them, he and his staff insisted, were nothing but "good friends." There was no romantic relationship between them. Not true.

It was all downhill from there. For some strange reason, Condit had difficulty finding time to meet a second time with police, undermining his contention that he had nothing to hide. His publicist Marina Ein declared it a "home run" for Condit when police said he was not a suspect in the case—which did not endear him to Levy's parents. Neither did rumors spread by those close to Condit that Levy had a history of one-night stands and was pressuring the Congressman into busting up his marriage and running off with her. And, throughout it all, Condit played hide-and-seek with the media: appearing in public, pretending to be doing his job, but refusing to make any comment. In the beginning, which only made him look guilty as hell.

And then, when he did finally talk to Connie Chung, he looked even more guilty by refusing to acknowledge a relationship with Chandra Levy or say he was sorry. In fact, he said so little, he would have been better off not doing the interview at all.

In the beginning, there were legitimate reasons for Condit's not talking to the press. Levy's fate was still unknown. And he understandably didn't want to be quizzed on national television about his apparently hyperactive sex life. Still, there was a middle path, as suggested by master Clinton spinner Lanny Davis. He told the *Washington Post* the best solution was for Ein to bring Condit before reporters, beginning with this announcement: "Gary Condit was embarrassed to admit publicly that he had an affair with an intern. He is especially embarrassed that he did not learn the lessons of the recent past. He's sorry he didn't react better and sooner. But he was frightened and was hoping that Chandra Levy would show up and this nightmare would go away. Now he wants to apologize and will answer any question except those that invade his personal life."

For a politician, the moral of the story is: no matter what trouble you get into, you'll never get out of it without the right spin. At the same time, as public relations consultant Eric Dezenhall suggested to MSNBC's Chris Matthews, this was one time where too much spin may have been inappropriate. "You can only spin a public that wants to be spun. You keep hearing all these articles analyzing spin control. This is not a public, in this case, that wants to be spun. This is a public that wants to find a girl who they think was murdered."

Good point: *Where there is a crime, or possible crime involved, spin is not acceptable. Only the truth will do.*

EXPORTING SPIN

Spin is no longer unique to U.S. politics. American political consultants, now international guns-for-hire, have exported spin to Israel, Japan, Mexico, Argentina and many other countries. Anywhere some politician is willing to pay the freight.

Nowhere outside the U.S. has spin found a more welcome climate than the UK. As recounted by Joe Klein in the *New Yorker,* British Prime Minister Tony Blair, who hired Clinton pollster Stan Greenberg and Gore strategist Bob Shrum to help direct his campaign, broke with tradition in 2001: announcing the election to form a new government, not in front of 10 Downing Street, as tradition demanded, but in front of a group of students at a church school in the south of London which, presumably, had benefited from Labor Party funding. The British press was horrified by the American-style photo-op. "The whole event stank of spin doctors' sweat," harrumphed the *Guardian*'s Simon Hoggart.

Toward the end of the campaign, a new play appeared in London, mocking Tony Blair's obsession with controlling his image. But even playwright Alastair Beaten, author of *Feel Good,* was skeptical that exposing Labor's full-time spin machine would do much good. "If the perception at the end of this election campaign . . . is that there was too much spin, that we're going to have to change," Beaten told NPR London reporter Julie McCarthy, "they will figure out a way of putting a spin on that so that there will be a campaign of spin to persuade us that there isn't any spin anymore. I think it's deep in their blood. I don't think they can change. I think it's beyond them."

How true. Once a spinner, always a spinner. It's impossible to stop Tony Blair from spinning.

After all, he learned the art from his pal, the master himself: William Jefferson Clinton.

FIVE

CLINTON: THE MAN WHO BROKE THE SPINNING WHEEL

> He lies by being technically accurate. I wish he would stop it. He's not 14 anymore, trying to outsmart the principal.
>
> —Congressman Barney Frank

By all normal standards, Bill Clinton should never have become president. He had everything going against him. He was from a backwater state, a broken home and an alcoholic stepfather. He had never served in the military, not even the National Guard. He was a blatant womanizer. And he decided to run when incumbent President Bush was enjoying a 90 percent approval rating and was widely considered to be unbeatable.

The fact that he ran and won—and then won reelection—is a tribute to his incomparable campaign skills and his political instincts for adopting policies the vast majority of Americans would support.

It is also a monument to spin, of which Clinton is a master. Spin didn't start with him, but he sure turned it into an art.

In 1992, out of nowhere, it seemed, Bill Clinton burst onto the national scene: a larger-than-life figure with incredible communications skills, insufferable political blather and insatiable appetites. If remembered for anything before that, it was his interminable speech to the 1988 Democratic convention, during which delegates erupted in applause only once: when he finally got around to saying: "In closing . . ."

But Clinton didn't just spring up overnight. For a long time, from his perch in Arkansas—throughout one term as attorney general, six terms as governor and one term as president of the Democratic Leadership Council—he'd been watching politicians on the national stage: learning from their successes, analyzing their mistakes, and waiting for his own opportunity to pounce into the big time. It was never a matter of if, only a question of when.

On that point, too, Clinton did more than a little spinning. When he ran for reelection as governor in 1990, he was pestered with questions about plans to run for national office. Would he absolutely guarantee the people of Arkansas that, if reelected, he would serve out his full term? Clinton's standard, enthusiastic response: "You bet. That's the job I want. That's the job I'll do for the next four years." One year later, he announced his candidacy for president.

For Clinton, of course, it all began much earlier: July 1963, in the White House Rose Garden. The brash, teenage Bill Clinton practically knocked over his fellow Boys Nation members, pushing himself to the front of the line and becoming the first in their group to shake hands with President John F. Kennedy while the White House photographer was clicking away. For Kennedy, it was nothing more than one more meaningless handshake out of millions: nothing felt, soon forgotten. For the Clinton pantheon, it was the sacred anointing, the passing of the baton: that mythological moment when the great JFK reached out to little Billy Clinton of Hope, Arkansas, saw the tremendous potential in his eyes and declared: "You da man!"

In *First in His Class,* Clinton biographer David Maraniss relates how the young Clinton immediately exaggerated the significance of this encounter. Four months after Kennedy's assassination, Clinton was in hot demand as a speaker at civic clubs, relating his memories as one of the last people in Hot Springs to see JFK alive.

When Clinton finally did break out of Arkansas, he was already an accomplished spinner. In fact, his entire rationale for being taken seriously as a presidential candidate was a masterpiece of spin. He was a proven leader, he claimed, even though he'd only presided over the small, dirt-poor state of Arkansas. (George W. Bush would apply the same sleight-of-mouth to his governorship of Texas, eight years later.) He had vastly upgraded the quality of education in his state, he bragged—even though Arkansas had only marginally improved, from 49th to 47th in test scores among the 50 states (another trick Bush would copy).

Spin he was born to do, and spin he did, all the way to and through the White House. And not only Clinton, his entire team as well: Paul Begala, Dee Dee Myers, Joe Lockhart, Rahm Emanuel, Mark Fabiani and Lanny Davis. And none better than the masters: James Carville and George Stephanopoulos.

In his own account of the Clinton campaign, Stephanopoulos admits his first thought whenever sandbagged by another jolt of bad news from Clinton's past was: "How do I spin this?" And he explains the method he perfected for dealing with the press: "A good spinner is like a good lawyer. You highlight the facts that help your client's case and downplay the ones that don't. When the facts are unfavorable, you argue relevance." Even though reporters covering the campaign knew they were being spun and were thus skeptical—once spun, twice shy—Stephanopoulos and company were able to successively beat down every Clinton campaign scandal.

The examples are legion and, now, legend.

Clinton was once against the death penalty. But as candidate, he was not only for it, he even interrupted his 1992 campaign to return to Arkansas and preside over the execution of the feeble-minded Ricky Rector. A contradiction? A self-serving political conversion, now that Clinton was running for president? No way, said Clinton. He had been convinced by his minister that the original wording of the Ten Commandments actually read "Thou shalt not murder," and not "Thou shalt not kill." Exegesis saved the day. The Bible saved the candidate.

Early in the campaign, Clinton aides ran into another problem with their candidate. The damned guy knew too much, and talked too much. At informal coffees in New Hampshire, he would go on and on, in mind-numbing detail, in response to questions on what to do about health care, defense spending, public schools, etc. Reporters, who were starting to fall asleep at campaign events, started whispering that perhaps this guy was too brainy to be taken seriously.

In his White House memoir, *All Too Human*, Stephanopoulos tells how he dealt with this challenge. He came up with the perfect spin. "Specificity is a character issue this year," he told *New York* magazine's Joe Klein. This, the spin doctor admits, was a deliberate stretch. "Like all good spin, it was a hope dressed up as an observation. We wanted Clinton to be seen as the thoughtful candidate—the man with a plan who knew what to do." And it worked . . . until the next, and ultimately most damaging, character issue came along.

There had been rumors before of Clinton's extramarital affairs. So many, he chose not to run for president in 1988. But those that bubbled up in 1992 had been easy to shoot down, until a certain torch singer named Gennifer Flowers.

Clinton denied having sex with Flowers until she produced the audiotapes of their steamy conversations (not the last time Clinton would be tripped up by tapes of phone conversations). Even then, did he admit committing adultery? Of course not. He and his team of advisers came up with the perfect spin. Interviewed by Steve Kroft on *60 Minutes*, while Hillary sat by his side cool as a cucumber, Clinton admitted only to "causing pain" in his marriage. That's all he needed to say. Most Americans would "get it," he insisted. They did.

From sex to drugs. When the host of a local New York Sunday morning interview show surprised Clinton (and his staff) by asking whether he had ever smoked marijuana, the candidate gave his now-infamous answer: "When I was in England [studying at Oxford], I experimented with marijuana a time or two, and I didn't like it. I didn't inhale." This was typical Clinton, trying to have it both ways: identifying with the younger crowd by admitting he'd tried grass; sticking with the older, moralistic crowd by insisting he made sure it never reached his lungs.

"I didn't inhale" joined the lexicon of American political spin.

But Clinton was being more clever than people thought. Too clever. He knew he had a problem that the national media were not yet aware of. Eighteen years earlier, running for Congress, he had been asked the same question and responded: "I never broke the laws of my country [only the laws of England]." That was his dilemma. He couldn't deny trying grass without contradicting himself. But he couldn't fess up to being an occasional user of marijuana without, he felt, destroying his candidacy. So Clinton, on the spot, came up with the ludicrous defense of smoking, but not inhaling.

"Bill Clinton hadn't lied," insists campaign manager James Carville. "He had given an adept political answer at the time." True. He didn't lie. But he sure did spin.

If Clinton wouldn't admit to cheating on his wife or smoking grass, he would never admit to dodging the draft, either. And he never had to. Despite mounting evidence that the draft-ripe young man had left the country while very cleverly stringing out his draft board and the head of his college ROTC until he could get a high lottery number and avoid military service, Clinton stuck to the story that, for him, escaping the draft in 1969, was "just a fluke." "I was just lucky, I guess," he shrugged. Great spin. He got away with it.

And it wasn't just luck. Clinton's entire campaign was a

giant spin machine, run out of the frenzied operations center in Little Rock called the "War Room" and led by Carville, Stephanopoulos, Paul Begala and Mandy Grunwald. Carville describes the process in *All's Fair,* the post-campaign book written with his wife and fellow spinmeister, Bush White House adviser Mary Matalin. Supporters around the country would fax in articles from major newspapers the minute they hit the stands; aides on the road with the candidate would call in comments or questions from reporters—as well as any off-the-wall gaffes Clinton might have made; spies would report on President Bush's latest comments on the trail; and office staff would constantly monitor radio and television to hear the latest coverage. The War Room staff chewed it over and spit out the spin.

They pioneered and perfected what came to be called "instant response." No sooner was a charge made or a story aired than the campaign was out with a statement, clarification, rebuttal or denial. Sometimes they were there even before the story hit. Every night they'd watch the network news to see how well they'd done. Then, says Carville, they'd bring the road crew up to date. "We'd fill them in and they would go back and try and spin the reporters for the next day."

In other words, it was one spin cycle after the next. A better name would have been "Spin Room," which is what they should have called the White House War Room, too. The spin didn't stop once Clinton reached the Oval Office. The eight years of his presidency are a textbook in spin.

It began with his very first initiative: "Don't Ask, Don't Tell." The new Pentagon policy was spun as fulfillment of Clinton's campaign promise to allow gays and lesbians to serve openly in the military. In reality, it forces gay and lesbian soldiers and sailors to live a lie—or else be hounded down and forced out of the military.

Two years of trying to do too much too soon in too haphazard a fashion gave Republicans just the target they needed. Democrats lost control of the House in November 1994. Clinton's arch-enemy Newt Gingrich became Speaker. And Clinton was suddenly no longer the most talked-about politician in the country. Stung by Republican criticism of his 1993 Economic Recovery Act, he told a Houston audience he thought he'd raised taxes too much. Clearly disoriented, if not depressed, he resorted to assuring a White House news conference in April 1995: "The president is still relevant."

But Clinton got his payback when the cocky Gingrich, confusing media puffery with political strength, overplayed his hand and shut down the government—not once, but twice. Gingrich was sure he could persuade the public to blame Clinton. He should have known better than to try and outspin the master spinner. Clinton regretted the inconvenience to those dependent on receiving their government pension checks, but accused Republicans of digging in their heels and creating such havoc in order to kill Social Security.

The Republican case was further weakened when Gingrich complained that one of the reasons he'd stiffed Clinton was because the president had stiffed him while flying home on Air Force One from the funeral of Israeli Prime Minister Yitzhak Rabin, making him sit all alone in the back of the plane—only to have the White House release, the next day, a photo of Clinton, in his airborne presidential office, conferring with Gingrich on board the same flight. For his part, Clinton took the high ground: "I can tell you this," he told reporters. "If it would get the government open, I'd be glad to tell him I'm sorry." Gingrich came off looking like a spoiled brat.

As Stephanopoulos concludes, the battle over the government shutdowns ended in a triumph for the Clinton spin room. "Our strategy was very simple. We couldn't buckle, and we had to say that Republicans were blackmailing the country to get their way. In order to get their tax cut, they were willing to shut down the government, throw the country into default for the first time in its history and cut Medicare, Social Security, education and the environment, just so they could get their way. And we were trying to say that they were basically terrorists. And it worked."

The Clinton spin was not limited to major public policy issues. It extended even to his personal life. Even to his diet. In 1993, the man who never passed a McDonald's without stopping his presidential motorcade long enough to run in for a large order of fries told an interviewer: "I don't eat much junk food." Oops! Realizing there was too much videotape of his fast food frolics to support that statement, Clinton quickly explained: "I don't necessarily consider Mc-Donald's junk food. I eat at McDonald's and Burger King and those other fast-food places. A lot of them have very nutritious food . . . chicken sandwiches . . . salads." I guess it depends on what the definition of "fast" is—or "nutritious."

Clinton staffers, by the way, were never concerned about all the attention to his McDonald's addiction. As media consultant Mandy Grunwald acknowledged, they saw it as a welcome diversion: "We liked hearing jokes about Clinton's weight, because it meant they weren't making jokes about his infidelity."

Clinton also used spin to empathize with each and every one of us. Feeling lonely? Disappointed? Depressed? Suicidal, even? Don't worry, Clinton assured us. We're not alone. "I feel your pain." He became the perfect president for the self-confessional age of Oprah.

Not only that. Clinton didn't just agree with African-Americans on most issues, he *was* an African-American. "That's why I went to Harlem," he told the NAACP in March 2001, "because I think I am the first black president." And he didn't just see eye-to-eye with Native Americans. He was a Native American, too. "My grandmother was one-quarter Cherokee," he told a group of visiting Indians. Finally, he didn't just come from a rural state. "I am the only president who knew something about agriculture when I got there." So much for first farmers, and first framers, George Washington, John Adams and Thomas Jefferson. And what about peanut farmer Jimmy Carter?

No wonder Chicago commentator Paul Green exclaimed in admiration: "If Bill Clinton were the *Titanic,* the iceberg would have sunk."

But even Bill Clinton, as good as he was, couldn't spin fast enough or well enough to stay ahead of the game. So he did what no president before him had ever done. He hired an official spin doctor, separate and apart from the White House press office, whose sole job was to spin the media on the scandal du jour—thus freeing Press Secretary Mike McCurry to talk about the important policy stuff and never get his hands dirty with sex, real estate or campaign cash. First up was Mark Fabiani, responsible for Whitewater. He hired Chris Lehane, who later became Al Gore's campaign press secretary, as his deputy.

Fabiani and Lehane were real pros. Whitewater had been brewing for some time, but it came to a boil just about the time I came to Washington as co-host of *Crossfire* in early 1996. I never had to call the White House to request background information. Every day that we scheduled a debate on Whitewater or some other Clinton scandal, which he would learn by watching promos for the show on CNN, Fabiani would call me at home to make sure I had all the ammunition I needed. And almost every afternoon, before I headed to CNN, a black town car would pull up in front of our house, just long enough for an intern (no, not that intern!) to jump out and deliver to my door a big brown envelope marked "White House: Confidential," stuffed with all the latest material. It was exciting. I felt like I was living a John Le Carré spy novel. *The Spy Who Came in from the Cold*—that was me.

As his next spinner-in-chief, Clinton picked the only man alive who could outspin Mark Fabiani: my friend, Lanny Davis. Lanny already had considerable political experience. He was a prominent attorney, partner of the Capitol's most powerful lobbyist, Tommy Boggs. He had also run for Congress in adjacent Maryland and was a regular commentator on local radio. But he came to fame and to the attention of the White House as a regular guest on *Crossfire,* defending the Clinton administration on Whitewater. When Fabiani resigned and moved back to California, Davis was the logical and perfect choice. He became so adept at spinning that he soon acquired the nickname among reporters of "Doctor Spin."

SPIN HALL OF FAME NOMINATION

‹‹⊙›

by Tony Blankley

NOMINEE: Lanny Davis

OCCASION: The title of spin doctor Lanny Davis's memoirs of his years with the Clinton administration.

SPIN: *Truth to Tell: Tell It Early, Tell It All, Tell It Yourself: Notes from My White House Education*

TRANSLATION: "Lies to Pass Along: Lie Early, Lie About It All, and Get Others to Lie for You"

Given that the book describes in prideful detail how Davis misled, forestalled and bamboozled journalistic investigation of his presidential client, to entitle such a book "Truth to Tell" is staggeringly misleading. It thereby wins my nomination.

Tony Blankley is a nationally syndicated columnist and a regular panelist on The McLaughlin Group.

Poor Lanny had his hands full. Lucky for him, he escaped in January 1998, just as the Monica Lewinsky scandal started to unfold, but he still had to deal with the Lincoln Bedroom sleepovers, the White House Coffees, Roger Tamraz and all the other fundraising scandals. He weathered them all like the master spinner he is. As he explains in his own account of his White House days, *Truth to Tell,* Lanny's M.O. was a version of the old football strategy: The best defense is a good offense. Instead of waiting for bad news to appear in print, and then have to respond to it, Lanny advised Clinton and company, it was better to drop the bad news yourself first—and force the media to dig through it, understand it and respond to it themselves: the classic pre-emptive strike.

It worked like a charm, as *Washington Post* media critic Howard Kurtz describes in his book about the Clinton press operation, *Spin Cycle: Inside the Clinton Propaganda Machine*. In the spring of 1997, Davis released thousands of pages of detailed documents on the White House fundraising operation:

> **SPIN:** The White House had nothing to hide.
> **TRANSLATION:** The White House was burying the truth in a mountain of trivia.

Reporters were so busy trying to sort through the piles of papers and determine what was there and what it meant, they missed the big picture: that the White House was, at least indirectly, for sale. They couldn't see the forest for the trees.

Davis doesn't call this a preemptive strike. He calls it a "predicate story," and explains why it is so effective. "The advantages of the predicate story as a critical tool of damage control cannot be overstated. For damaging stories that have complicated facts, particularly ones mixing facts and legal issues . . . the predicate story is simply mandatory. If it is complete and accurate, it will likely kill or at least diminish follow-up stories, since there won't be much more to report."

Of course, thanks in part to the foundation laid by Fabiani and Davis, Clintonian spin reached its apogee in the Monica Lewinsky affair. As Clinton defined the terms, he was never alone with her, did not have sex with her and did not have a sexual affair with her. In fact, by his definition, he probably never even met the woman.

Listen to his interview, and hear the master at work. Granted, it *was* nobody's business, but nevertheless the question was asked: Were you ever alone with her? Answer: "It depends on how you define alone. Yes, we were alone from time to time, even during 1997, even when there was absolutely no improper contact occurring. Yes, that is accurate. But, there were also a lot of times when, even though no one could see us, the doors were open to the halls, on both ends of the halls, people could hear. . . . So there were a lot of times when we were alone, but I never really thought we were."

That was one clever definition. Here's the next. On the day the Monica story broke in the *Washington Post*, Clinton just happened to have an interview scheduled with Jim Lehrer of PBS. Lehrer went for the kill. "You had no sexual relationship with this young woman?" Clinton went for the spin. "There is not a sexual relationship, that is accurate." Later, Clinton famously defended his obviously misleading answer: "It depends upon what the meaning of the word "is" means. If "is" means is, and never has been, that's one thing. If it means "there is none," that is a completely true statement." Take a deep breath, folks. Spin doesn't get any better than that. Because we all know what the meaning of *is* is. *Is* is *is!*

Once he started hiding behind definitions, Clinton just couldn't stop. Final example: When Paula Jones's lawyers blindsided Clinton into answering questions which, the judge later ruled, had no relevance to her case, he was able to find escape in their own clumsy, and limited, terminology. Just to remind us all how outrageous the Paula Jones deposition was, here is the definition of sexual relations her attorneys finally, after hours of debate, agreed upon with the judge and Clinton's lawyer Bob Bennett as Deposition Exhibit I:

> For the purposes of this deposition, a person knowingly engages in "sexual relations" when the person knowingly engages in or causes—
>
> (1) contact with the genitalia, anus, groin, breast, inner thigh, or buttocks of any person with an intent to arouse or gratify the sexual desire of any person; or
>
> (2) contact between any part of the person's body or an object and the genitals or anus of another person; or
>
> (3) contact between the genitals or anus of the person and any part of another person's body. "Contact" means intentional touching, either directly or through clothing.

Clinton's no dummy. He saw immediately that the special brand of sex he enjoyed with Monica Lewinsky—her performing oral sex on him—was not included. By their own definition, she had had sex with him. But, *mirabile dictu,* he had never had sex with her!

It was like another Immaculate Conception!

Clinton saw the opening and went for it. "I have never had sexual relations with Monica Lewinsky. I've never had an affair with her." Five days later, on January 26, he pointed his finger at the cameras and, red in the face, ended a White House news conference on education with equal finality: "I want you to listen to me. I'm going to say this again. I did not have sexual relations with that woman, Miss Lewinsky." Save that one for the history books.

The funny part is, Clinton didn't have to check the dictionary. He could have asked almost any high school or college student. Among most young people today, only vaginal intercourse is considered sex. Blow jobs don't count.

Bill Clinton was just ahead of his time. . . .

It's only fair to point out that Clinton was not the only one to try to spin his way out of the Lewinsky mess. After illegally taping phone conversations and ratting on her friend Monica, Linda Tripp stood on the steps of the federal courthouse and insisted, "I'm just an average American who found herself in a situation not of her own making." What unbelievable spin! Same for her claim that she only ran to Ken Starr with her juicy story about Monica because she was afraid for her life. Was she afraid that Clinton was going to send Dick Morris to strangle her in her suburban Maryland bed? As we learned later, when he wasn't at the White House, Dick Morris never left the Jefferson Hotel, enjoying his own sexual pleasures.

At least, Tripp's book agent Lucianne Goldberg was honest. She admitted she told Tripp to tape her conversations with Monica, and Tripp eagerly did so, because she was trying, for the second time, to sell a book about sex in the White House. She failed to catch George Bush with his pants down. She just had better luck with Clinton.

At the same time, Hillary was also spinning. When her husband cheated on her (again!), she believed his denials (again!) and told the whole world the entire Lewinsky scandal was the product of a "vast right-wing conspiracy." Poor Hillary. She didn't know how badly she was spinning. But Bill certainly knew, and never tried to stop her.

Naturally, what began in spin and thrived on spin would end in spin. As his final act before leaving the Oval Office, Clinton justified his ignoble pardon of fugitive financier Marc Rich as a case of "compassionate liberalism." Everyone else but Clinton and Rich recognized it as the result of a combination of bad judgment, bad advice, lack of sleep and political payoff.

And, yes, even out of office, Clinton continues to be a serial spinner. On signing the lease for his new headquarters, Clinton crowed that he was opening an office in Harlem as part of his post-presidential crusade to bring new economic development into depressed minority areas. Translation: "I got booted out of the Carnegie Towers because the rent was too high for government offices, so I had no choice but to move to Harlem."

One final word about Bill Clinton that may explain it all. Yes, he spins a lot. But, on the other hand—he's a golfer! And we all know golf is the sport of spinners. It's not your final score that counts; it's your score minus your handicap. Which means a poor player like me could actually beat a much better player—on paper. But it's all spin.

Not to mention the mulligans. I'm not good enough to have played golf with Clinton, but a friend who did so told me that, to put everyone at ease, the president's rules were: three mulligans—one on the tee, one on the fairway, one on the green—for each nine holes. That's not as many as I take in any round of golf. But, hey, who's counting?

In the East, there are also the so-called "leaf rules": if your ball gets lost under too many fallen leaves on the fairway, you get a free drop. And the "winter rules": conditions are so bad, you give yourself a good lie on every shot. And the tree root rule: you can always move your ball when it's too close to a tree or tree root, because you wouldn't want to damage your club. And, winter or summer, who's going to complain about a little nudge with the toe to put the ball in better position?

And then there's the mystique about new equipment. We weekend duffers see an ad in the *Wall Street Journal* for a new titanium driver guaranteed to cut six to eight strokes off our game. With this miraculous club, the ad informs us, a golfer in California shot his first subpar round in twenty years. Another tore the cover off two balls. It's all spin. But we fall for it every time and go out and buy the latest new iron or driver, forgetting the essential fact: it's not the club, it's the swing of the person holding the club, that determines how well and how far the ball goes.

You see what I mean? As a golfer, I think Clinton must be forgiven. It's not his fault. Golf forces you to spin. And he who spins on the golf course will spin anywhere.

Now, it's hard to believe anyone will ever top Bill Clinton in the spin department. But, in his own, low-key way, George W. Bush is already showing great promise. And Al Gore didn't do such a bad job at spin, either. Both spun madly in the 2000 campaign—which turned out to be only a warm-up for the not-so great recount.

SIX

CAMPAIGN 2000: THE SPIN DERBY

> They mis-underestimated me.
> —George W. Bush

It was clear at the beginning of the 2000 presidential campaign that, in spinning their message, both Al Gore and George Bush had decided to imitate Bill Clinton. Surprisingly, it was clear at the end of the campaign that Bush had done a better job.

Neither was a charismatic candidate, nor a born spinner: Gore was too insincere; Bush, too incoherent. It ended up, as *New York Times* columnist Maureen Dowd famously put it, a choice between "the insufficient and the insufferable."

But, despite his limitations, it was soon obvious that Bush had learned more about Clinton from afar than Gore had up close. In the end, Bush emerged more Clintonesque.

If he keeps going, he might end up a better spinner than Clinton ever was.

THE BUSH CAMPAIGN

The entire basis of Bush's candidacy was based on three propositions: that he was an outsider, a successful businessman and, as governor of Texas, a proven leader. All three were pure spin.

Bush was no outsider to the Eastern establishment. He was born in Connecticut, went to Andover Prep School, then to Yale and Harvard. How establishment can you get? He helped run his father's presidential campaign and, for a while, worked in the White House. Sure, before high school and after college, he lived and worked in Texas, but as a transplant from the East Coast.

And Bush didn't exactly set the business world on fire, either in oil or baseball. For a complete account of both ventures, check out the details, never refuted by the Bush campaign, in *Shrub*, by Molly Ivins and Lou Dubose. His one skill was convincing friends of his father to invest in his start-up businesses—and then losing their money. "The governor's oil-field career can be summed up in a single paragraph," write the two Texas journalists. "George W. arrived in Midland in 1977, set up a shell company, lost a congressional election in 1978, restarted building the company he'd put on hold, lost more than $2 million of other people's money, and left Midland with $840,000 in his pocket. Not bad for a guy who showed up with an Olds and $18K."

From oil to baseball. But this time, it was taxpayers, not his daddy's friends, who bankrolled him. When he decided to run for governor, Bush was able to sell his interest in the Texas Rangers for $15.4 million. Not because he'd done such a great job as president—remember, this is the guy who traded Sammy Sosa to the Chicago Cubs—but because the citizens of Arlington, Texas, had voted to raise taxes to build a new stadium, which increased the book value of the team. That public subsidy made Bush a rich man. And poor Hillary got slammed for making only $100,000 in commodity-trading.

Bush was no proven leader, either. How could he be? The governor of Texas is a part-time job. Think about it. The legislature's only in session 165 days—every two years! Cabinet members are elected, not appointed. The real executive power rests with the lieutenant-governor. In fact, Nicolas Lemann of the *New Yorker* calculated that only 137 people report directly to the governor. Only 137? Steve Forbes has more than 137 servants!

So what does a Texas governor do with his time? He works out, has lunch, plays video games. When former White House aide Paul Begala took time off from teaching at the University of Texas to help prep Clinton for his 1996 debates with Bob Dole, Governor Bush actually volunteered—volunteered!—to fill in one night for Begala as a substitute professor. The governor of Texas doesn't have enough responsibility to be a real leader.

Nevertheless, in his early days on the campaign trail, Dubya sounded like a broken record, repeating over and over and louder and louder: "I'm a leader, I'm a leader." It was only after John McCain whipped his ass in New Hampshire that Bush's handlers taught him the much more challenging refrain (one added syllable): "I'm a reformer, I'm a reformer." That was spin, too, just different.

Whatever reforms Bush took credit for are a joke. "I do support a patients' bill of rights," Bush told Al Gore in their third presidential debate. "As a matter of fact, I brought Republicans and Democrats together to do just that in the state of Texas, to get a patients' bill of rights through." Bush wasn't just spinning, he was lying. Yes, Texas has a patients' bill of rights. But that's *despite* him, not because of him. In 1995, Bush vetoed the legislation. When the bill came back in 1997, he first opposed it, then let it become law without his signature. That was leadership? He had nothing to do with it.

Yes, he improved Texas schools: moving them from dead last to next to last among the 50 states (again, similar to Clinton's record, in Arkansas). Yes, he also cut taxes, though not as much as he claimed, but still leaving Texas broke and bleeding. Soon after he left for Washington, Texas officials reported a $700 million budget shortfall and Chris Harris, conservative president of the State Senate, was forced to introduce a constitutional amendment to roll back Bush's 1997 property tax relief.

Only in one area did Governor Bush bring about remarkable change in Texas. While he was governor, Houston replaced Los Angeles as the city with the dirtiest air in the country. And Texas ranked number one in air pollution. But, of course, he didn't brag about that!

All in all, it was a pretty ho-hum five years for Governor Bush. In February 1999, fellow Republican Governor Tommy Thompson from Wisconsin, whom Bush later named Secretary of Health and Human Services, gave this candid assessment: "He hasn't really done much as a governor in regards of doing anything new or innovative." As Cabinet Secretary, Thompson has been much less critical. Fawning, even.

When you examine it closely, you see that Bush's entire career has been, in Paul Begala's marvelous phrase, "a case study in the art of failing upward." But, give him credit. His spin worked. Not only on voters, but on reporters who, for fear of being branded part of the liberal media, never did any serious investigation to discover whether his claims as governor were real or not. When he said he was a leader, they believed it and reported it. When his staff said he had racked up a serious record of reforms, they saluted and replayed it verbatim. Seldom has spin fallen on more fertile ground.

Similarly, Dubya was able to spin his way out of several embarrassing, and potentially fatal, moments in the campaign. Starting with drugs.

Bush admits he was a heavy drinker until the age of forty. He even admits he smoked marijuana. But did he ever do heavy drugs? What about cocaine? We don't know. (Of course, the fact he didn't just say "no" would seem to indicate he had at least tried cocaine.) But we don't know for sure, because Bush so successfully danced his way through the political land mines. First, he spun himself as a different kind of politician. Again, the outsider. He was running a campaign based on "ideas and philosophy," he insisted. (There's a stretch. Bush? Talking philosophy?) He refused to play the "gotcha" game of Beltway insiders. "It's the game where they float a rumor and make the candidate prove a negative and I'm not playing the game," he told a New Hampshire reporter.

Then he decided to play the game, after all, but only so long as he stayed on safe ground. "I could have passed the FBI background check on the standards applied on the most stringent conditions when my dad was president of the United States—a fifteen-year period," he boasted to reporters. Reporters assumed Bush was talking about the beginning of Father Bush's presidency, January 1989—which would take him back to 1974. (That 1974 date would become important later, as we'll see below, when dealing with the National Guard.) He refused to say whether he could have passed the fifteen-year test during his father's years as vice president. Or whether he could clear the much more strict Clinton standard asking information on any drug use after the age of eighteen.

Again, the point is not that Bush may have tried cocaine. Who cares? The point is he was able to spin his way out of answering the question, and get away with it, thanks to a cautious—or fearful—press corps.

And what about that visit to controversial Bob Jones University, his very first stop in the South Carolina primary? To hear Bush spin it, he didn't know anything about their history of segregation. Had no idea they still didn't allow biracial couples. And, he said, nobody ever told him the President of Bob Jones had called the pope a "traitor" and his father, President Bush, "an evil man." Hell, to him, it was just one more campaign event. "I don't have to accept their tenets," he told NBC's *Today* show. "I was trying to convince their college students to accept my tenets. And I reject anyone labeling me because I happened to go to the university."

In other words, they weren't preaching to him, he was preaching to them. They weren't teaching him exclusion, he was teaching them inclusion. He's not a bigot for going there; you're a bigot for labeling him.

On military service: Unlike that draft dodger Bill Clinton, so went the spin, George W. Bush never tried to avoid going to Vietnam. In fact, he risked his life flying dangerous missions for the Texas National Guard. According to his official campaign biography, *A Charge to Keep,* Bush flew fighter planes with his unit for "several years." Nice spin, but not true.

Bush only flew with the Guard for one year and ten months, until he was suspended for failing to take his medical exam and drug test—and never flew again. And, while Bush may not have personally lobbied to avoid the draft, he did enlist a couple of his father's cronies to do so—and bragged about it, later. Thanks to their intervention, he was assigned to the same celebrity Guard unit as Democratic Senator Lloyd Bentsen's son, Republican Senator John Tower's son and seven members of the Dallas Cowboys. Bush was such a famous Guardsman, by the way, that President Nixon sent a jet to pick up the promising young flight student for a date with his daughter Tricia. Good thing they didn't click. Imagine what infernal offspring might have issued from a Nixon/Bush family marriage!

Not only that, no sooner did Bush learn to fly—and get his picture taken in uniform for future political campaigns—than he took a leave of absence in 1968 to work on Edward Gurney's Senate race in Florida. Later, he took another leave, to work on his father's campaign in 1970; and still later, still another leave, to work on an Alabama Senate race in 1972 and 1973. During this period, according to General William Turnipseed, the commander of the Alabama Guard at the time, Bush was never seen or heard from. The Bush campaign never provided a full accounting of Bush's Guard Service. For Dubya, the National Guard seemed to be a place to hang out between political campaigns—much like Pat Buchanan would later hang out at CNN between his own presidential campaigns.

SPIN HALL OF FAME NOMINATION

⌘⌘⌘

By Paul Begala

NOMINEE: George W. Bush

OCCASION: The Dubya campaign's only "proof" that George W. Bush didn't bail out of his commitment to the Alabama Air National Guard in 1972 and go AWOL for a year. No other documentation of his service exists.

SPIN: "You can ask my ex-girlfriend."

TRANSLATION: "I lied to her about it too."

Please. If girlfriends count as proof of military service, let's give the Congressional Medal of Honor to Bill Clinton. Of course this spin was so utterly lame that it worked–the press was either too lazy, too incredulous, or too afraid of showing "liberal bias" to call him on it.

Paul Begala is Research Professor of Public Policy and Government at Georgetown University and the author of Is Our Children Learning?: The Case Against George Bush.

Here's a funny coincidence:

- In April 1972 the Guard announced it would include drug tests as part of its annual physical exams—including urinalysis and close examination of nasal cavities (for cocaine).
- In May 1972 Bush stopped attending Guard duty.
- In August 1972 Bush was suspended from Guard duty for failing to take his physical.

Any connection between Bush's going AWOL and his fear of taking a drug test? We'll never know. No reporter dared ask the question. Karen Hughes might have spanked him.

Bush did have one serious shortcoming the media started to call him on—foreign policy. How could someone pretend he's ready to be president when he has zero foreign policy experience? When, in fact, except for a student trip to Scotland, he'd never even been to Europe? Easy. Spin! Bush just emphasized all the times he'd been to Mexico on official state business. Isn't it amazing how spin works? Once again, the media bought it. Nobody reported that each trip to Mexico lasted no more than a couple of hours, across the border and back, just enough time for a burrito and a Diet Coke. Bush suddenly possessed a foreign policy credential.

The debates were another triumph of spin. In any real test, Bush should have had his clock cleaned. Of course, Al Gore helped a lot by choking and blowing two of three debates: one by underperforming, one by overperforming. But the Bush team also spun the debates brilliantly. Going into the debates, they privately kept reminding reporters that their man was such a novice, they were afraid he'd make a fool of himself. Later, when he'd failed to drool all over his face or collapse off the stage, they declared him the winner. Simply because he was still standing. And the media fell for one of the oldest political tricks in the business: the game of lowered expectations.

And then there was the booze. For a long time, Bush never talked about his drinking days, except to acknowledge it was part of his "wild youth," which ended when he found Jesus. You know, boys will be boys. The only problem is, Bush's wild youth lasted till he was forty years old, married, with two kids. Outrageous spin, to be sure. But it worked for him, until . . . until he got caught.

Bush was riding high—and dry!—until, barely three weeks before election day, a Maine TV station stunned the nation: George W. had been arrested for drunk driving in 1976, they reported, when he was thirty.

He'd lied about it or covered it up ever since.

In Austin, Bush had told reporters he'd never been arrested. Also as governor, he'd hired attorney Alberto Gonzalez, now White House counsel, to get him out of jury duty on the pretext of a possible conflict of interest, so he wouldn't have to answer the standard but loaded question: Have you ever before been arrested for any crime?

But if you think something as serious as lying about a drunk-driving arrest for over twenty years would trip up Dubya, you don't know the power of spin.

First, Bush borrowed a page of spin from Hillary Clinton and fell back on a standard, blame-it-on-your-political-enemies, vast left-wing-conspiracy spin. "Why was this story reported now, four days before the election?" he demanded. "I've got my suspicions." Then Bush outdid Bill and Hillary both. He switched to the traditional, hide-behind-your-family spin, asserting that the reason he'd kept his drunk-driving arrest hidden was only because he was trying "to be a good role model for his daughters." (Clearly, *that* didn't take.)

But did reporters laugh out loud at that one? No, they dutifully wrote it down and reported it. Having given him a free ride on his record, on foreign policy and on drug use, they gave him a free ride here, too. Nobody dared ask the obvious: *How does lying to your daughters make you a good role model?* And, of course, as we learned later, daughters Barbara and Jenna might actually have benefited from some straight talk about alcohol: when to drink, and where, and under whose name.

But no, I haven't forgotten the cornerstone of the Bush campaign—at once its most successful and egregious spin: Dubya's self-anointing as a "compassionate conservative." The phrase was absolutely meaningless. On *Crossfire,* I kept asking, "So what do you call other Texas conservatives like Phil Gramm, Dick Armey and Tom DeLay? 'Cold-hearted conservatives'? 'Cruel conservatives'? 'Asshole conservatives'?"

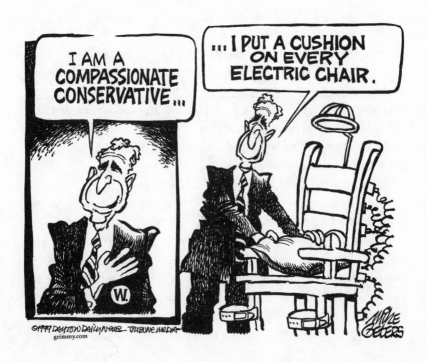

Besides, I could easily see why Bush was considered a conservative. But what did he do to merit the label "compassionate"?

- Preside over the execution of 152 people in 5 years, a new record?
- Veto a patients' bill of rights?
- Veto legislation banning the execution of the mentally-retarded?
- Refuse to sign hate-crimes legislation?

Where exactly had he been hiding his compassion?

But, once again, you have to admire the audacity and the success of the spin. It worked to distinguish Bush from those other conservatives everybody hated in Washington, at least for the duration of the campaign. Once in the White House, we discovered he was just as conservative as all the rest, minus the compassion. But by then it was too late.

The entire Bush campaign was so Clintonesque—and so successful. With the help of the Supreme Court, George W. Bush is now the forty-third president of the United States—and Al Gore is teaching journalism at Middle Tennessee University.

May the best man spin. . . .

THE GORE CAMPAIGN: SPINNING OVER THE TOP

> *Just moments ago, I spoke with George W. Bush and congratulated him on becoming the forty-third president of the United States, and I promised him that I wouldn't call him back this time.*
>
> *—Al Gore*

George W. Bush proved himself a real spinmeister. But Al Gore was no slouch, either. Indeed, if Bush was the King of Spin in 2000, Albert was the Crown Prince. He, too, proved he'd learned a lot at the feet of Bill Clinton. Just not enough.

Gore's campaign was also launched in a mighty swirl of

spin about who he was, where he was coming from and what he had accomplished in life. But, unlike Bill Clinton and George Bush, Al Gore will be remembered not because he spun so well, but because he spun so much . . . over the top, even.

SPIN HALL OF FAME NOMINATION

⌒⌒⌒

By Oliver North

NOMINEE: Al Gore

OCCASION: Al trying to explain away his soliciting DNC funds on federal property in March of 1997.

SPIN: "My counsel advised me that there is no controlling legal authority or case that says that there was any violation of law whatsoever in the manner in which I asked people to contribute to our re-election campaign."

TRANSLATION: "My counsel advised me that I can weasel out of this one if I use a Clintonian hair-splitting definition of 'no controlling legal authority' in front of you today."

This shameful attempt at spin foreshadowed much of the exaggerations and misrepresentations we would hear from Gore the candidate throughout the next election cycle. This includes his renowned "Iced Tea" defense, whereby Gore declared he had left campaign finance meetings at crucial times to use the bathroom. Only Gore's master, Bill Clinton, could've pulled that one off.

Oliver North is the former co-host of MSNBC's Equal Time.

Long before the 2000 campaign, Gore had a problem with exaggeration. He couldn't settle for simply stating the facts. He always felt the need to embellish, despite warnings from his staff. As far back as 1987, when Gore was gearing up to run for president the first time, his deputy press secretary Mike Kopp sounded the alarm: "The point of all this is to caution you about your press image, and how it may continue to suffer if you continue to go out on a limb with remarks that may be impossible to back up."

Gearing up for 2000, Gore proved he still hadn't learned his lesson. Which was crazy because, in his case—even though Gore had to struggle to explain earlier votes against choice and gun control—telling the truth about his early legislative successes would have been powerful enough. There was no need to gild the lily. But every time he stretched the facts, just a little bit, he got himself into trouble. Which was part of the reason he had such a tough time in the primaries against Bill Bradley, who should have been no threat at all. As Gore struggled to explain himself out of misstatement after misstatement, Bradley looked like the real thing.

For example:

True: Gore was one of the first members of Congress to learn about Love Canal and hold hearings on it.
Not true: That he discovered it.

True: Gore was the Senate leader on adapting early computer technology, developed by the Pentagon, into personal and commercial use.
Not true: That he invented the Internet.

True: Gore volunteered to go to Vietnam—unlike George W. Bush or Bill Clinton, who pulled strings to get out of going.
Not true: That he went as a gun-toting soldier, as pictured in earlier campaign brochures. He went as an Army reporter.

By overspinning, Gore turned three positives into negatives.

Like Bush, Gore also tried to paint himself as an outsider—why is it that everyone who wants to rule Washington feels they must first denounce it?—and independent of Bill Clinton.

First, he all but claimed to be a Tennessee farmer. Notice the calluses on both hands? They were proof of a lifetime spent tilling the soil, harvesting the crops and rounding up the cows. He stressed his agricultural experience every time he met with a group of farmers, but not always convincingly. In one such meeting in Iowa, Gore bragged about owning and operating his own farm for twenty-six years. The next day, John Carlson wrote in the *Des Moines Register:* "I think if we'd been in Houston, he would have told us he was an astronaut."

Posing as a farmer in city clothes was quite a stretch for a kid who grew up, son of a United States Senator, in a residential hotel at one end of Massachusetts Avenue, and graduated from St. Alban's School at the other end. But, to hammer his point home even more dramatically, Gore used not words, but geography.

He suddenly upped and moved his entire campaign headquarters—desk, phones, files and staff—from Washington to Nashville. To reporters, campaign aides spun this as a displaced, homesick Al Gore, simply wanting to get back to his roots. They didn't fool anybody. It was obvious this was simply Gore's clumsy attempt to cut any physical ties with the Beltway and put as many miles as he could between himself and the man he now considered that dope-smoking, money-grubbing, skirt-chasing adolescent in the White House.

That move signaled what would turn into a continuing, inexplicable effort by Gore to distance himself from Clinton—staying away from the White House, not calling on Clinton for advice and, in the last weeks of the campaign, not even unleashing Clinton to campaign for him in key states. Which was hard to understand. After all, Gore would not have been where he was without Clinton. And, despite all his problems, Clinton's approval rating soared around 65 percent at the time. He certainly could have helped Gore in places like, let's say Florida—or West Virginia. And there was no way any-body was going to blame Boy Scout Al for Rascal Bill.

Still, it was important for Gore to assert his own identity any way he could, and leap on any contrast with his boss. "Bill Clinton sees a car going down the street and he says, 'What are the political implications of that car?,' " Gore told the *New Yorker*'s Joe Klein and Jane Mayer. "I see the car going down the street and I think, 'How can we replace the internal-combustion engine on that car?' " Which one would you rather vote for?

Later, at the convention, Gore came up with the most cre-ative act of spin in the campaign. How to prove he was not Bill Clinton? The *kiss!* Ninety seconds of "spontaneous" lip-lock with Tipper—which made millions of married women in America green with envy ("They've been married for thirty years and he *still* kisses her like that?") and which nobody could ever imagine Bill doing with Hillary. The spin was ob-vious: *"I'm so in love with my wife you'll never catch me with my pants down around my ankles in the Oval Office."* And, of course, Gore barely mentioned Clinton's name in his Los Angeles acceptance speech.

Gore tried to distance himself from the Clinton fundrais-ing scandals, too. When caught making fundraising calls from his White House office, he came up with an unusual bi-ological spin: during a meeting with Democratic National Committee staff, he surmised, he drank so much iced tea that he must have been out of the room taking a leak when the purpose of the calls was discussed. And, of course, even if he did make calls to potential donors, there was "no controlling legal authority" against it. Translation: what I did was flat-ass wrong and stupid, but at least I didn't break the law.

With that inauspicious beginning, the Gore campaign be-came a story of Big Al tripping over his own Big Spin. He just couldn't help himself. When brush fires ravaged millions of acres in Texas, it was Vice President Gore, not Governor Bush, who rode to the rescue. Why, just the year before, he remembered accompanying Federal Emergency Management Director James Lee Witt to Texas to deliver federal aid.

Oops! It turned out Gore went a lot of places with Witt, but Texas wasn't one of them. *Sigh . . .*

Same with campaign reform: It could have been—*should* have been—a good issue for Al Gore. After all, Bush was against it, Gore was for it. McCain had won big with that issue in the primaries. So, all candidate Al Gore had to do was announce his support for the McCain-Feingold legislation. Instead, Gore spun that, as Senator, he was one of the first co-authors of the McCain-Feingold legislation, which sounded pretty good, until reporters discovered he had already left the Senate by the time McCain-Feingold was introduced. *Sigh, sigh . . .*

Gore also enjoyed strong support from organized labor. But, again, he had to take it one step too far. Addressing a union convention in Las Vegas in September 2000, Gore reminisced: "You know I still remember the lullabies that I heard as a child." At which point he broke into song: "Look for the union label." Unfortunately for him, that lullaby wasn't written until Gore was 27 years old. *Sigh, sigh, sigh . . .*

Give Gore credit for one more innovation. He was the first to use clothing, not just words, as spin. On the advice of consultant Naomi Wolf, he switched from his standard white dress shirt, red tie, dark-blue suit to earth-tone sports shirt and slacks. It was his way of spinning: I'm my own man. I'm a different man. I'm the new, loose-as-a-goose, get-down-and-dirty, just-your-average-guy-next-door funster. But, once again, the old adage rang true. Clothes don't make the man. The debates proved he was still the same old, stiff, preachy, insufferable Al Gore.

His excessive spin cost Al Gore greatly. By election day, he'd lost all credibility with the media. Reporters parsed his every word, searching for overspin. As a result, even when it was all over, he didn't get any credit for accepting reality. He knew he'd won the popular vote. He knew, if all the votes were ever counted, he'd probably win Florida and the electoral vote, too. But nevertheless, in the end—when the five Supremes ruled "Enough democracy, let's shut this baby down while our guy is still ahead"—Gore stood up in front of the cameras and declared: "The U.S. Supreme Court has spoken. Let there be no doubt: While I strongly disagree with the Court's decision, I accept it. I accept the finality of this outcome."

It was an act of courage, a true class act. But nobody believed him. For once, he wasn't spinning; he was telling the truth.

Too bad it took him till the end of the campaign to do so.

RALPH NADER: WORST SPIN OF ALL

I do think that Al Gore cost me the election, especially in Florida.

—*Ralph Nader*

No one can excuse Al Gore for running such an inept campaign. But, despite all his mistakes, Gore would still have handily won the election if it weren't for spoiler Ralph Nader.

There was no way Nader could win. He knew that. His only hope was to steal enough votes from Gore so that Bush could win. And he accomplished his goal by spinning that there was no difference between the two major parties or their candidates.

"The difference between George W. Bush and Al Gore is the velocity with which their knees hit the floor when corporations knock on their door," Nader preached. Otherwise, he insisted, there was no difference.

Put that down as the most dishonest spin of the entire 2000 campaign.

Enough said about Ralph Nader.

JOHN MCCAIN: THE EXCEPTION THAT PROVES THE RULE

If George W. Bush is a reformer, I'm an astronaut.

—*John McCain*

In 2000, the exception to politics being all about spin, the one candidate who defied the laws of spin was John McCain. Of course, I can't say too much, or I'll be accused, like the Bush camp accused all other reporters and commentators, of being in love with McCain and giving him nothing but positive publicity.

The Bush campaign never understood McCain's appeal. How could they? He talked straight, and they didn't know how to.

They didn't get it then, and they still don't get it now. The reason reporters write good pieces about McCain is because he's so strikingly different. Like a breath of fresh air. He's as close to the real thing as you can find in politics. He doesn't bullshit you. He doesn't spin. He just talks straight—and lets the chips fall where they may.

Not for nothing was his campaign bus called "The Straight Talk Express" (a name given it by spinmeister Mike Murphy). I only took one ride, but it was quite an experience. The Sunday before the New Hampshire primary, we went from his hotel to the quaint village (what New Hampshire village isn't?) of Peterborough, for the last of 114 town meetings he held in the Granite State. A small selected group of us (journalists were rotated in and out of the Senator's presence by McCain staffers) boarded the bus. We all sat up front, clustered on sofas and chairs around one big armchair, reserved for the big guy. One camera crew rolled for all the networks. In a few minutes, the Senator hopped on board with his wife, Cindy. She proceeded to join the staff in the back of the bus. Looking chipper, cup of coffee in hand, McCain sat on his throne, wished everyone "Good morning" and, as the bus pulled out of the parking lot, took his first question.

He never stopped for the next forty-five minutes. Occasionally, he might wince, sometimes in jest. But he never ducked a question. Never refused to answer. Never danced. Never spun. Day in and day out, he left himself wide open like that—as no other politician could or would dare. After all the bullshit they got from every other campaign—where candidates make self-serving statements, or hold meaningless photo opportunities, and then rush off without answering any questions—no wonder McCain got such favorable press. He earned it. He deserved it.

A year earlier, I had a similar experience with McCain. While filling in for radio talk show host Ronn Owens on KGO Radio, San Francisco—which I was able to do by satellite from ABC's Washington headquarters—I invited McCain to join me in the studio. He happened to come in the morning after the Senate had debated the patients' bill of rights. There were already rumors he might run for president. I was ready for him. I honestly thought I had him in the crosshairs.

I looked him right in the eye and said: "Yesterday, the Senate debated and voted on the patients' bill of rights. Included was an amendment that said simply, that if a woman has a mastectomy, she and her doctor—and not some insurance company accountant—should make the decision whether or not she spends the night in the hospital. Senator, you voted against that amendment. How can you go around the country running for president and defend that vote?"

"I can't," McCain said without hesitation. "I've been thinking about that vote all night. Every once in a while, you cast a bad vote. That was a bad vote." I, of course, had nowhere to go next. He had totally disarmed me. Imagine asking Al Gore that same question. Or George W. Bush. And the bullshit response you would get.

But if McCain appealed to the hard-bitten reporters, he also appealed to voters. The very same way. Just by being himself. I walked around that town meeting in Peterborough, watching the audience rapt with attention while McCain was speaking. I'd also carefully observed the crowd at another town meeting, two days earlier.

Now, I've been to hundreds of political gatherings in my life. But I was struck by how different these were, because the people there were so different. They weren't political regulars. They hadn't been bused in by the state party. They were ordinary citizens—young, old, men, women, military veterans and peaceniks—who had come out to see someone they'd heard about and admired. Their connection with McCain was tangible because, unlike any other politician they'd ever heard or seen, here was one who just stood up there and told them the truth: what was good, what was bad, and how he intended to fix it.

The thing that I found so amazing about McCain was that he was able to inspire people to believe in politics and politicians again. They may have walked into his town meeting a cynic; they walked out a believer and a doer. American politics needed that shot in the arm.

OK, I wasn't born yesterday. I recognize that McCain could be just pulling everyone's leg. The fact that he doesn't spin may just be his own version of spin. (How's that for cynicism?) But, it's still mighty damned refreshing.

In the end, though, straight talk would only get McCain so far—as far as giving a speech for Bush at the Philadelphia convention, which was not exactly his career goal. It was spin, not truth, that won the day. Spin dominated the campaign—and the grueling five weeks after the campaign.

THE FLORIDA RECOUNT: SPINNING OUT OF CONTROL

These people care more about the spin than the law.
—Bruce Rogow, Counsel
Palm Beach County Canvassing Board
(After phone calls from Gore attorneys
Warren Christopher and Alan Dershowitz)

There will never again be a world of spin like the Florida recount. Thank God. It started at the Florida state capital on election night. It ended at the U.S. Supreme Court on December 12. In between were five weeks of pure spin by the nation's master spinners: five weeks in which not one person involved ever told the complete truth.

For a documentary on spin, Hollywood could not have assembled a better cast than the real-life, actual players in the Florida recount. The candidates themselves, of course. But, also, for Al Gore: Warren Christopher, David Boies and Bill Daley. For the Florida Legislature, House Speaker Thomas Feeney. And, most of all, for George Bush: James Baker, Katherine Harris, Karen Hughes—and five members of the U.S. Supreme Court. It would be hard to decide who gets first prize.

Warren Christopher kicked things off, announcing that the Gore campaign was seeking a manual recount in three counties only, because—hear him spin!—that's where most of the complaints came from. Baloney. The Gore campaign wanted recounts in those three counties only because that's where most of the Democrats were, and that's where Gore was sure to win.

In desperation, some Gore supporters even stooped so low as to play the Holocaust card. Since Palm Beach county contains a large Jewish population, including many Holocaust survivors, Congressman Robert Wexler and others painted the ballot snafus as the worst suffering Jews had experienced since . . . well, you know . . . It was too unbelievable: even for spin, even for Florida.

And so was the Republicans' contention that all those votes in Palm Beach for Pat Buchanan had nothing to do with the fact that the butterfly ballot was so confusing. It was really because, insisted GOP spinners, those elderly Jews actually *intended* to vote for Pat. This was too much spin, even for Buchanan to swallow. "Well, look, I don't want any votes that I did not receive, and I don't want to win any votes by mistake," he said on November 9, two days after the election. "It seems to me that these 3,000 votes folks are talking about, most of them are probably not my votes. And that may be enough to really give the margin to Mr. Gore."

SPIN HALL OF FAME NOMINATION

⤜✦⤛

By Al Franken

NOMINEE: Karl Rove, top Bush political adviser

OCCASION: November 9, 2000, attempting to explain large number of votes for Pat Buchanan in Palm Beach County.

SPIN: "There are a disproportionate share of Reform Party members in Palm Beach County. For example, while there are 16,695 Palm Beach County residents who have registered in the Reform Party, in the nearby county of Broward, there are only 476 individuals registered to this party." (Actually, Rove was off by 16,354. There were only 341 residents of Palm Beach County registered in the Reform Party.)

TRANSLATION: "I'm a shameless, lying hack."

I'm not sure if an outright lie actually counts as spin, but I'm pretty sure you can find instances where Rove has managed to spin without lying.

Al Franken is a comedian and author.

In fact, when the dust settled, the *Palm Beach Post* revealed how damaging the butterfly ballot had been to Gore's chances. A total 5,330 ballots were thrown out because they were punched twice, for both Gore and Buchanan. But only 1,131 were tossed out because they were for Bush and Buchanan.

And then slick Jimmy Baker, rested up from Papa Bush's cabinet, rode into town, insisting from the beginning—hear him spin!—that all the Bush campaign wanted was a "fair and accurate count." More baloney! All they wanted was to shut down the vote while Bush was still ahead—which, later on, thanks to the U.S. Supreme Court, they were able to do.

As counties started, stopped, and restarted their recounts, depending on the daily whim of unpredictable Florida judges, the Bushies settled on their ultimate spin—first offered by Baker in Tallahassee, then echoed by Karen Hughes and Bush himself in Austin—that the votes in Florida had already been "counted once, counted twice, counted three times and some of them, even counted four times." Which, of course, was a big lie: They may have been run through the voting machines more than once, but the machines never registered them. Which means they were left uncounted: over 10,000 of them, still never counted. But the spin sure sounded good. It even fooled the U.S. Supreme Court.

The logical subset of this spin was that manual recounts were suspect; only machine recounts could be trusted. Or, as Baker solemnly pronounced, "The more often ballots are recounted, especially by hand, the more likely it is that human errors, like lost ballots and other risks, will be introduced. This frustrates the very reason why we have moved from hand counting to machine counting."

The official Bush position became, as a supporter's T-shirt summed it up: NO HAND JOBS. Writing for *Slate* magazine, Mickey Kaus suggested the new party slogan: "They trust the people. We trust machines."

This was a strange position to take, especially for a governor who, three years earlier, had signed a bill making hand recounts the preferred way to settle close elections in Texas. It was also difficult to understand for all those who had ever experienced a breakdown of their car, computer or ATM machine (who hasn't?), but were now expected to believe that machines were foolproof. Still, Republicans stuck to their professed faith in machines, until, in May 2001, Governor Jeb Bush proudly signed into law a set of reforms designed to fix, once and for all, Florida's antiquated, erratic, unequal, undependable election process.

You guessed it. What do Jeb Bush's reforms recommend

when elections are too close to call? An automatic manual recount! Which proves that what both Bushes, Baker and
Katherine Harris were saying about the illegitimacy of manual recounts was total bullshit. But which, of course, came
six months too late to give Al Gore any comfort.

But, we're getting ahead of ourselves. Back to the recount. It was only months after the election that the full
hypocrisy of the Bush/Baker operation became known. According to an analysis of all overseas ballots performed by
the *New York Times,* at the very same time the Bush campaign was insisting that no questionable ballots be counted
in the four Democratic counties contested by Gore—and accusing Democrats of denying men and women in uniform the
right to vote—they were simultaneously bending the rules
and demanding that all questionable overseas ballots be certified in all Republican counties. Under pressure from Bush
campaign operatives, county clerks counted as legitimate:
ballots with no witness signature or postmark, as required by
law; ballots mailed after the election; ballots received after
the deadline of November 17; even ballots where people had
voted twice.

There is no way of knowing for whom those ballots were
cast, although in heavy Republican counties, one can make
an accurate guess. But applying the letter of the law and
denying those questionable ballots, says the *Times,* would
have reduced Bush's margin in Florida to 245 votes and may
even have thrown the election to Al Gore. Whatever the outcome, it certainly made a mockery of the Supreme Court's
final ruling on equal protection under the law. At the time,
led by James Baker, Republicans weren't interested in treating all ballots equally.

Baker wasn't the only Bush operative. In the Florida
legislature, he got a lot of help from the transparently
overeager House Speaker Tom Feeney. In order to protect
the people of Florida from having no representation in the
electoral college, he piously spun, the legislature had no
choice but to elect its own slate of electors, pledged to
George Bush. Nonsense. Florida already had one official

body of electors, certified by Governor Jeb Bush, and already pledged to his brother Dubya. There was no need for a second.

It was too easy to see through Feeney's spin. Republican legislators were not acting to protect the people of Florida. They were acting, in panic, and under orders from their Republican governor, to prevent Florida's twenty-five electoral votes from being cast for Al Gore—if, indeed, as expected, the recount showed Gore the winner in Florida. By sending a second set of electors to Washington, the legislature hoped to force the election into the Republican-controlled House of Representatives, where Speaker Dennis Hastert could be counted on to deliver enough votes to decide the issue once and for all.

Baker had one more ally: Spinning frenetically in the middle of it all was Florida Secretary of State Katherine Harris, the Linda Tripp of the Florida recount. Poor soul, she attempted several different spins to justify her Ice Queen behavior: "I must protect the integrity of the ballots." "I'm just doing my job." "I have no choice under the law." "I'd like to be flexible, but I can't." Nothing worked. It was clear, she was just a marionette, doing whatever Governor Bush told her to do. The only question was: Which Governor Bush was pulling the strings, George or Jeb?

Throughout the entire ordeal, Harris insisted she was fiercely nonpartisan. But her mask came off later, when she confessed her nightly ritual to the *Washington Post*'s Dan Balz: "Propped before a flickering set in the wee hours, she rooted for conservative commentator Tucker Carlson on CNN's 'The Spin Room.' " Obviously, she was not rooting for Bill Press, which I took as a badge of honor. Tucker and I invited Harris to be our guest on the *Spin Room* several times, but she declined to appear on the show as long as I was co-host. Wonder why?

Harris was further exposed as a partisan zealot when records of her office computer hard drives were released in August 2001. Even though the hapless Harris had insisted she had erected a "firewall" during the election between her office and the Republican party, her office computer contained one document titled "George W. Bush Talk Points" and another speech written for her in which she declares: "I am a bit biased. I co-chair the campaign effort of George W. Bush. I hope it will be 'W.' "

She was not alone. Harris's office was a nest of Republican operatives, including her former campaign manager, Marc Reichelderfer, whose online i.d. was "gopspinner." Some firewall. Only Al Gore got burned.

For James Baker, Thomas Feeney, Jeb Bush and Katherine Harris, there is but one consolation: a report by the *Chicago Tribune* in July 2001 that defective election equipment in Chicago's Cook County was responsible for invalidating 39,000 votes cast in the presidential election. That makes Illinois, not Florida, the most problem-plagued state in the 2000 election.

Recount, anyone?

In the end, the election from spin was decided, not in the state of Florida, but in the citadel of legal spin, the United States Supreme Court. Read their final brief and you will discover how fine legal spin can be spun:

- We respect states' rights, insists the Court—therefore we are overriding the State of Florida.
- We affirm the right of every citizen to have his or her vote counted—therefore we are shutting down this election with tens of thousands of votes still uncounted.
- We sincerely encourage the Supreme Court of Florida to promulgate a new standard for counting ballots and call on all counties to complete their recounts by the deadline of 5 P.M. on Wednesday—therefore we are waiting until 10 o'clock on Tuesday night to issue our opinion.

And, finally, the Court's most outrageous spin, articulated by Justice Antonin Scalia: that the Court must act to prevent the "irreparable harm" that might result to George Bush, then ahead by 500 votes, if the count were to continue—and he were to lose. Which, of course, ignored the "irreparable harm" that *did* result to Al Gore, who won the popular vote but, thanks to the Supremes, lost the presidency.

Harvard Law Professor Alan Dershowitz is no fan of the Rehnquist Court. In the recount, he even represented several thousand Palm Beach residents who complained that, confused by the county's butterfly ballot, they intended to vote for Gore and ended up voting for Buchanan. Still, Dershowitz's comments on the Court ruling are surprisingly strong. This ruling, he argues in his book *Supreme Injustice,* was worse even than previous Court decisions on slavery or segregation, because in those cases, at least, Justices were voting their judicial philosophies. Here the majority of the Court voted their personal political preferences. As a result, says Dershowitz, Bush v. Gore "may be ranked as the single most corrupt decision in Supreme Court history."

Actually, he was being kind. Former Los Angeles District Attorney Vincent Bugliosi was even more biting. When Clarence Thomas and William Rehnquist insisted in later speeches that politics played no part in their decision, Bugliosi snorted to *The Nation* magazine: "Well, at least we know they can lie as well as they can steal."

In the end, it was left up to Jay Leno to sum up the entire election: "You know, it shows how old I am. I can remember the good old days when the president picked the Supreme Court Justices instead of the other way around."

Result? George W. Bush: the first president not elected to office, but *spun* into office.

Not surprisingly, a presidency born in spin has already exhibited a great proficiency in spin.

SEVEN

PRESIDENT BUSH: NEW SPINNER IN THE WHITE HOUSE

The legislature's job is to write the law.
It's the executive branch's job to interpret law.

—George W. Bush

Here's something you never thought you'd hear me say. In fact, I can't believe I'm saying it myself: I was wrong about George W. Bush.

There, I said it. I'll say it again. I was wrong about George W. Bush. After eight spinful years of Bill Clinton in the White House, I figured we were in for four years (please, no more than four!) of dullsville. He is known, after all, as the "Bogus Potus." But I have been pleasantly surprised.

Of course, it's early yet. As I write, we're not even one year into the Bush presidency. But, the man is already showing real promise for delicious spin. The Bush White House, in fact, may turn out to be as rich in spin as the Clinton White House. Just more low-key.

Take Saddam Hussein. After only three weeks in the White House, Dubya was already sending British and American fighter planes to bomb military sites near Baghdad. When news broke, Bush was on his first official state visit (more spin) to Mexico (yes, Mexico!), where he dismissed the bombing as no big deal. Aw, shucks, he told reporters, it was just "a routine mission." To hear him tell it, we were bombing Iraq two or three times a day.

Good spin. The truth is, Bush was sending Hussein a message. In fact, two messages. One, I may look like a pipsqueak, but I'm really macho. ("Don't mess with Texas.") Two, my daddy didn't finish the job ten years ago, but I will. ("Because Dick Cheney told me to.")

The administration also started off with one of the true hallmarks of the age of spin: the notion of bipartisanship. Everybody in politics knows that bipartisanship, or compromise, comes at the end of the process, not at the beginning. Sure, you agree to shake hands on an issue—but only after you've already beaten your opponent to a bloody pulp, or he's pummeled you black and blue—and not before.

Bush got it backward. Deliberately. He preached that he wanted to change the tone in Washington from the beginning. He insisted he would reach across the aisle to Democrats and seek their advice. But, once he got to the White House, he forgot all about bipartisanship. And, except for invitations to a couple of meetings or movies, he forgot all about Democrats. He even ignored moderate Republicans—ask former Republican, now Independent Senator James Jeffords—and acted as if he had a mandate to govern from the far right. He refused to meet Democrats halfway on his tax cut, campaign finance reform or the patients' bill of rights.

It soon became apparent that Bush's call for bipartisanship was pure public relations. What he was really saying was: Forget Al Gore. Forget the campaign. Forget compromise. *I'm* in the White House now. I'm in charge. Democrats should roll over and swallow my programs, just the way they are. For him, "bipartisanship" stands for "buy what my party says."

Here's one example of how the White House always has the advantage in the spin game. If Democrats do bend over for Bush, it's bipartisanship, for which he gets all the credit. If they don't, if they dare criticize one of his proposals, it's partisan politics as usual, for which they get all the blame.

Don't believe it? Listen to his puppets on the Sunday morning talk shows. And, remember, you heard it here first.

An important disclaimer: When we talk about George W. Bush as a good spinner, we don't mean him personally. We mean the people around him. Unlike Clinton, no matter how long he's in the White House, Bush himself will never be a great spinner because, frankly, he gets too tongue-tied. Let's be honest. In order to master spin, you must first master the English language, which Bush hasn't yet. In fact, sometimes, listening to him, you get the impression he's speaking a whole new language.

Slate magazine's Jacob Weisberg has collected some of Bush's verbal gaffes in a delightfully funny little book called *Bushisms*. I've kept a list of my own favorites:

- On John McCain during the primaries: "He can't take the high horse and claim the low road."
- On small business: "I understand small business growth. I was one."
- On sharing the wealth: "We ought to make the pie higher."
- On his budget: "It's clearly a budget. It's got a lot of numbers in it."
- On Africa: "Africa is a nation that suffers from incredible disease."
- On education: "If you don't know what you're supposed to know, we'll make sure you do early, before it's too late."
- On the Golden Rule: "We must all hear the universal call to love your neighbor just like you like to be like yourself."
- On the Cold War: "Then, it was us vs. them, and it was clear who the them was. Today, we're not so sure who the they are, but we know they're there."

See what I'm saying? He may be trying to spin, but you can't appreciate his spin because it's hard enough just to understand what he's saying. He makes Yogi Berra sound like Mario Cuomo.

I don't want to be too harsh on Dubya, however. I know his verbal clumsiness is not his fault. He inherited it from his father, the first President Bush. Editors of *The New Republic* magazine collected his most memorable public sayings, also under the title *Bushisms*. Like son, like father. In fact, Father Bush could have been speaking for both father and son when he once told reporters, "I am just not one who—who flamboyantly believes in throwing a lot of words around." Indeed, not.

Members of George W. Bush's administration, however, have already proven themselves very adept at spinning. They are bold, they are shameless, they are brazen. There is no limit to how far they will go. Starting with what may prove to be the greatest spin of Bush's entire presidency: that he's really in charge. Nonsense. When a deranged man with a gun starting blasting away across the White House fence early in February 2001, the president was never in danger. Even though it was almost noon, Bush wasn't in the office. He was in the basement of the White House, working out. As always, Dick Cheney was at his desk.

Check the records. That's not the exception, that's the rule. Bush's handlers schedule only one issue to work on every week, and usually only one public event a day. He sets aside at least two hours a day to exercise and another hour to jog. He's in bed by 10 P.M., on a late night. He spends every weekend either relaxing at Camp David or fishing at his ranch in Texas.

And yet he's still exhausted. On February 19, 2001, The *Washington Times* ran this headline: "Bush Goes Home to Rest for Busy Week." After drinking a few Diet Cokes with Vincente Fox in Mexico, reported the right-wing rag, Bush rushed home to his Texas ranch. It was a welcome relief for him to get home, said the *Times,* because "the pressures of the presidency have kept him away since taking the oath of office on January 20." Poor guy! Less than a month on the job, and he was already dying for rehab. All in all, out of his first 72 days in office, Bush spent 24 days away from the White House. Double the number of days Bill Clinton spent on travel during that same period of his presidency.

By the end of summer, he was really tuckered out. He left Washington on August 4 for a twenty-seven-day vacation at the ranch: just three days short of the modern record for longest presidential vacation set by Richard Nixon. The *Washington Post* calculated that by Labor Day, "Bush will have spent 42 percent of his presidency at vacation spots or en route." Which is probably better than having him stick around the White House.

The White House spin is that Bush has so much free time because he is such a talented manager. He runs the White House like a good CEO, delegating authority, assigning others the day-to-day tasks so he can focus his attention on the big picture. Dick Cheney even started that spin before the election was decided, telling *CBS News* on December 17, 2000: "Well, if he is chairman of the board, he's also the chief executive officer, without question. . . . He's a great boss."

Do they really expect us to believe that? Everybody knows that Dick Cheney's really running the country. In fact, the only time Dubya's been trusted with the helm was when Dick Cheney was under sedation for heart surgery.

Scary thought, isn't it? If anything happens to Cheney, George W. Bush is only a heartbeat away from the presidency.

When high gas prices hit in the spring of 2001, a CNN viewer e-mailed me word of a sign he had seen at the pumps of a Las Vegas self-serve station: "Don't blame my cashiers for the price of gas. Blame Dick Cheney and his understudy."

The second wholesale spin of the Bush era is that his White House is somehow above politics. Their holier-than-thou spin goes something like this: The Clinton White House may have had its War Room, and Bill Clinton may have taken a poll before making every decision, but not us. No, we're different. We're above polls. We just do what's right, without considering the political consequences. Again, that spin began even during the campaign. "A responsible leader is someone who makes decisions based upon principle, not based upon polls or focus groups," candidate Bush said in Kalamazoo, Michigan, shortly before the election.

The message carried over into the White House. For example, during the California energy crisis in the spring of 2001—when California Governor Gray Davis was begging for federal help and the Bush administration was telling him to solve his own problems—my good friend Mary Matalin, formerly co-host of *Crossfire* and now Dick Cheney's communications director, insisted that White House staffers were too steeped in energy policy to consider energy politics. "No one here has been political," she insisted to the *Washington Times*.

So much for the spin. The truth is that this administration has its finger to the political wind as much, if not more, than any in history. They may not call it the "War Room," but Bush aides have established the equivalent in daily political meetings, daily political messages, and weekly strategy sessions presided over by top political adviser Karl Rove. They have their own political pollster, Matthew Dowd, who surveys all issues in depth before Bush takes a public stand. "He [President Bush] does want polling done to test ideas before he has decided on them," Rove told the *Washington Post*. Dowd is paid by the Republican National Committee, just as Clinton's pollster, Mark Penn, was paid by the Democratic National Committee. Rove also regularly weighs in on important policy decisions, arguing the politically expedient imperative. It was Rove, for example, who convinced Bush to oppose the Navy's continued bombing of Vieques, over the objections of the Pentagon, in order to appeal to Latino voters. And Rove who persuaded Bush to limit federal funding for embryonic stem cell research, in order to appeal to Catholics. Karl Rove is George Bush's Dick Morris.

Now, there is nothing wrong with a political operation inside the White House. Indeed, we should all fear a White House without one. Who wants a president making decisions without first finding out what we the people think or want? Politics and policy are two necessary sides of the same coin.

What's silly is pretending you're above politics. To what end? Nobody believes it, anyway. It's not worth the spit to spin.

A couple other forms of spin preferred by the Bush White House deserve mention. Very early on, they learned that one of the best ways of spinning their way out of a problem is simply to give it another name. Change the name and the problem disappears. Unlike Clinton, Bush did not seek "fast track authority" from Congress; he sought the very same thing, but called it "trade promotion authority." He did not support "vouchers" for private and religious schools; but he did support "school choice" or "opportunity scholarships." He opposed federal "price controls" on electricity, but he supported "price restraints." And Republicans didn't gain any support for eliminating the estate tax until they started calling it the "death tax."

The right word or phrase can be a powerful type of spin, as Democrats learned, too. After losing the support of a lot of blue-collar voters over gun control, they suddenly started talking about "gun safety," instead.

It's also a trick exported around the world. When peace talks with the Palestinian Authority broke down, the Israeli government began a campaign of hunting down and killing militant Palestinian figures, usually with missiles fired from helicopter gunships. Do they call it "murder" or "assassination," which it clearly is? No way. They gently refer to it as a "policy of active defense."

One more tactic of the Bushies: labeling every legitimate question about any one of his policies as "the politics of personal destruction." This also started during the campaign. I used to laugh when Mary Matalin blurted it out, almost daily, on *Crossfire*. True, there is such a thing as "the politics of personal destruction." Republicans should know. They used it against Bill Clinton for eight straight years: attacking his personal life, not his public policy. (And, of course, Clinton gave them lots of ammunition.) But, so far, Bush has escaped personal criticism. Nobody's attacked his sex life, his appetite for fast foods, his temper, or his alleged drug or alcohol problems. Reporters even gave him a pass on his daughters' run-ins with the law over underage drinking (as they should have). Bush doesn't know from the politics of personal destruction. But the White House paints him as a victim of it, anyhow.

In practice, it becomes downright comical. Criticize Bush's tax cut, and you're practicing the politics of personal destruction. Question his support for faith-based charities: P.O.P.D. Suggest he's all wet on missile defense: P.O.P.D. again, big-time! You can't differ with him on anything without being accused of trying to destroy his reputation. Bullshit. There's a word for publicly disagreeing with a president's policy.

It's not "the politics of personal destruction." It's "democracy."

Sometimes, you get the feeling that the Bush White House doesn't believe in it.

Given both their predilection to spin and their skill in spinning, it's not surprising how the Bush administration has dealt with public policy issues. They have done little, but spun a lot. They have tried to resolve each and every issue by applying the maximum possible spin.

SPINNING FOREIGN POLICY

Foreign policy was candidate George W. Bush's weakness. Other than one mysterious teenage trip to Scotland (which, for some reason, nobody ever wants to talk about), and one trip to China to visit his dad, Ambassador Bush, Dubya had never been anywhere as an adult but Mexico. Not exactly a big adventure for a Texan. His lack of foreign policy experience, or even curiosity about foreign affairs, was troubling. Bush tried to make up for his own failings by appointing a lot of experienced foreign policy hands from his father's administration. But, once in the White House, the spin was soon out that Bush had become a foreign policy expert overnight.

If you don't believe it, look how well he gets along with foreign leaders. As *Newsweek* magazine first discovered, no matter who they are or what differences they bring to the table, Bush can be counted on to have a "good, frank discussion" with them.

- In the White House, one of his first sit-downs with a foreign leader was with Colombian President Pastana, after which Bush told reporters: *"We've had a very good discussion."*
- A week later, it was an Oval Office session with the president of South Korea, about which Bush had to say: *"We had a very good discussion."*
- The Prime Minister of Israel: *"We've just had a very frank and good discussion."*
- The president of Brazil: *"We've had a good, frank discussion about a lot of subjects."*

- The president of Egypt: *"My opinion hasn't changed after our good, frank discussion today."*

Word of advice to White House staff: *When you're teaching the boss to spin, at least give him a different 3×5 card* every once in a while. Otherwise, he sounds like a broken record.

Does Bush ever have a bad meeting? Not if you believe the White House spin. Even after his meeting with California Governor Gray Davis—who pressed Bush for price controls on the sale of wholesale electricity to California and, after he refused, walked out of the meeting and condemned the president on national television—Chief of Staff Andrew Card spun the session in the most positive terms: "It was a very friendly and constructive conversation." Obviously speaking from the same talking points, Karl Rove later described the encounter to reporters as "a very friendly and constructive series of meetings. . . . They continued on in a very friendly and very constructive and positive meeting. . . ." It was clear that, no matter what happened, the White House had determined ahead of time to spin the Bush-Davis summit as "friendly and constructive."

More foreign policy. It was not enough that Bush entertain foreign leaders at the White House—for good and frank discussions—the only way to really prove himself was to meet with them on their own turf. So Bush got himself a passport and went off to Europe twice in 2001. Neither trip was very successful, but the first was a disaster. Western European leaders listened politely, then proceeded to pronounce Bush wrong, and hopelessly naïve, on missile defense, global warming and other issues.

His first trip's biggest embarrassment came at the very end. Reminiscent of the presidential campaign, where Bush aides deliberately lowered expectations by spinning how poorly they expected their man to perform in the debates, White House staff sprayed gloom and doom about the president's last scheduled stop: his first meeting with the president of Russia. Vladimir Putin would probably eat Bush alive, they spun. And the media fell for it. For a whole week, there were reports of the upcoming big rumble, impending Armageddon, the biggest challenge yet, the acid test, for the happy glad-hander of Texas. Could his charm melt a Siberian glacier?

But, of course, it had all been carefully staged for the cameras. This was a case of global spinning. Kremlin and White House spinmeisters both agreed ahead of time that, since this was their first meeting, it was in the interests of both presidents that the meeting be brief, businesslike and, above all, "constructive and friendly." Afterward, as planned, they emerged from their meeting, not angry and growling, but grinning and gripping like asshole buddies. Bush had tamed the Russian bear. The spin worked!

Well, at least the spin worked until Bush, minus his cue cards and in the giddiness of the moment, went over the top. He had only spent 100 minutes with Putin, but that was all Bush needed to know him inside and out. The world may remember Putin as the former KGB leader, who built a successful career out of lying and teaching others to lie, as well as the Russian president who murdered the opposition in Chechnya and shut down Russia's independent print and broadcast media. But we were mistaken. Bush saw him differently. "He's an honest, straightforward man who loves his country. He loves his family. We share a lot of values. I looked the man in the eye. I found him to be very straightforward and trustworthy. We had a very good dialogue. I was able to get a sense of his soul." Even that was not enough. "I trust him," Bush added, and immediately invited him for ribs at his Texas ranch.

We were all left to wonder: who was spinning whom?

This sudden gushing over the man who most reminds us of the days of the Evil Empire was too much even for Bush's Republican defenders. Senator Jesse Helms suggested Bush should get a little more experience under his belt before canonizing foreign leaders. As if to prove Helms correct, one month after meeting with Bush, Putin met with Chinese Prime Minister Jiang Zemin. The two Cold War rivals embraced warmly for the cameras and signed a joint agreement—dubbed by the Russian media "an act of friendship against America"—to support China's sovereignty over Taiwan and oppose U.S. efforts to build a missile defense system.

Pretty damned effective, that Bush. Only he could get Russia and China back together again, lined up against the United States.

Bush's first excursion to Europe was such a disaster, he left himself wide open for criticism the second time around. In fact, Bush had barely left U.S. soil on his next trip, one month later, before Democrats questioned both the message he was bearing—anti-global warming and pro-missile defense—and his ability to deliver it. "I think we are isolating ourselves, and in so isolating ourselves, I think we're minimizing ourselves," Senate Majority Leader Tom Daschle told reporters as Bush was still winging his way to Europe on Air Force One. "I don't think we are taken as seriously today as we were a few years ago."

Daschle walked into the Bush White House trap. They knew harsh comments would be made back home, and they were ready for them with the pre-concocted spin that presidents were immune from criticism whenever they traveled overseas. "It's just wrong," thundered White House counselor, and master spinner, Karen Hughes. "It's really quite an unseemly departure from the long-standing United States custom of the bipartisan tradition of the way our foreign policy is conducted. It is a long-standing bipartisan tradition that both Democrats and Republicans stand together on United States foreign policy."

Such spin! Such nonsense!

Politics stops at the water's edge? Since when? If that tradition still existed, which I doubt, it was certainly trashed by Republicans once Bill Clinton became president. "I'm suggesting that the president of the United States cannot be believed. And I think it's reflective in his foreign policy," House Majority Whip Tom DeLay said on *Meet the Press* while Clinton was in the Middle East. "The Russian government should not be under any illusion whatsoever that any commitments made by this lame-duck administration, will be binding on the next administration," warned then-Senate Foreign Relations Chair Jesse Helms when Clinton was meeting with Russian President Vladimir Putin. Apparently, Republicans believe this shoe only fits one foot.

SPINNING THE PATIENTS' BILL OF RIGHTS

One of the biggest issues Bush faced in his first year was the quality of health care provided by HMOs. There were so many complaints about how managed care organizations were short-changing or mistreating their patients—some cases even resulting in death—that health care advocates in Congress crafted what was called "the patients' bill of rights." In the end—everybody agreeing that patients should have access to emergency care and the right to see a specialist—what it all boiled down to was whether patients should have the right to sue their HMO if the HMO screwed up and they, or a family member, were seriously injured as a result. Sides formed early on, but not along traditional party lines. Republican John McCain joined forces with Democrats Ted Kennedy and John Edwards in supporting a patient's right to sue. Democrat John Breaux and Republican Bill Frist offered their own bill, severely limiting the right to sue.

President Bush sided with Frist and Breaux. The problem for the White House was: how to spin the fact that the president was against letting patients sue HMOs for malpractice, when existing law allows them to sue private hospitals, clinics, or doctors? McCain and Kennedy were on the side of the angels on this one. Why was Bush opposed?

The answer was easy: a double spin, actually. First, Bush painted himself as a champion of a patient's bill of rights, not an opponent. "I urge Congress to bring a reasonable bill to my desk," he told reporters. But, he quickly added, he was talking only a bill "that recognizes patients are important, not lawyers." In other words, Bush was all for the rights of patients, as long as they were denied their ace in the hole,

their most powerful weapon: the right to sue. Allowing patients to sue would result in a flood of frivolous lawsuits,
Bush warned.

Now the parallel spin. Of course, Bush was all for a patient's bill of rights. He'd proved that, back in Austin. "I do
support a national patients' bill of rights," he told Al Gore
in the last presidential debate. "As a matter of fact, I
brought Republicans and Democrats together to do just that
in the state of Texas, to get a patients' bill of rights
through."

That, too, was pure baloney. Actually, Bush did everything he could to block passage of protection for patients in
Texas. The first year, he opposed the patients' bill of rights in
the Texas legislature, then vetoed it. Two years later, he again
opposed the legislation and then, perhaps with an eye to a future presidential campaign, allowed the bill to become law
without his signature. Texas, in other words, has a patients'
bill of rights despite Bush, not because of him. Not only that,
the Texas law, like the McCain-Edwards-Kennedy bill, includes the right to sue HMOs—which has not resulted in the
flood of meaningless lawsuits Bush warned about.

The point is, the White House spin worked. Bush was
able to have it both ways. Publicly, he was for the (phony)
patients' bill of rights. Privately, he was against the (real) patients' bill of rights. Nobody but those few Americans familiar with the details of both bills knew the difference.

SPINNING THE EXECUTION OF MENTALLY RETARDED

There is one area in which even his critics must admit,
George W. Bush leads the nation. As governor of Texas, he
presided over the execution of more people than any other
governor in American history: 152 death sentences carried
out in only five years. No one else comes close. It's a record
Bush is proud of.

After becoming president, Bush continued to support the
death penalty, with one exception. "We should never execute

anybody who is mentally retarded," he told a group of European journalists on his first overseas trip. This came as a surprise to American journalists back home, especially Texas reporters who remembered the case of Mario Marquez, judged to have the mental capacity of a seven-year old, executed in 1995. And, a couple of years later, of mentally-retarded Terry Washington and Oliver Cruz. Reporters also recalled Bush's opposition to legislation in 1999 outlawing execution of the mentally retarded. Had Bush experienced a White House conversion?

Quickly, the White House spin machine went to work. No, the president's statement was "not a change of policy," they insisted. He was merely using a different definition of "mentally retarded" than most people do. In other words, by society's definition, he had okayed the execution of several mentally retarded persons; by his own definition, he had not. How Clintonesque.

SPINNING GLOBAL WARMING

The scientific evidence that the world is experiencing global warming as a result of human activity, with disastrous economic, environmental and public health consequences to follow, is overwhelming. And the need for the world's industrial nations to start curbing emissions of greenhouse gases, as recommended in the Kyoto treaty—signed, but never ratified, by the United States—is obvious to most Americans. It's even obvious to Treasury Secretary Paul O'Neill, Commerce Secretary Don Evans and Environmental Protection Administrator Christie Whitman, all of whom have urged President Bush to stand up and take the lead in combating global warming.

Indeed, the need to act is obvious to every American, except the two who were elected president and vice president, thanks to gobs of money from the oil, gas, coal and power companies.

But the American people aren't dumb. They know global

warming is a problem. They want to preserve the environment. So how do you oppose doing anything about global warming without coming across like a dirty old polluter who doesn't give a damn about clean air? Summon the White House spin doctor!

On global warming, the prescribed cure was diabolical. Since science is what convinced most Americans, and most of his Cabinet members, of the reality of global warming, Bush's spin is: we need more science. The conclusions of 250 scientists who comprised a United Nations study panel and called for worldwide anti-global warming efforts are not enough, said Bush. We need still *more* science.

So he appointed his own panel of scientists.

Unfortunately, for Bush, two months later, they *also* concluded that global warming was real and recommended immediate action.

So what does the spin doctor recommend now? Stick to the script. Ignore your own scientists, and call for even *more* science. Bush will probably continue calling for more scientific research until he finds one scientist, somewhere on the planet—no doubt on the payroll of an oil or coal company—who will deny global warming. Then he will be brought to Washington and named the president's National Science Advisor.

Now, please don't jump to any conclusions. Don't accuse George W. Bush of always being in favor of more science. It depends on the issue. On his first trip to Europe, a reporter in Madrid asked President Bush the pesky question: "You say the scientific evidence isn't strong enough to go forward with Kyoto. So then how do you justify your missile defense plan when there is even less scientific evidence that it will work?"

Obviously, some people just don't understand. When it comes to science, you have to be flexible. The Bush rule is: *More science on global warming, where none is needed; and no more science on missile defense, where much more is needed.* That's the spin. And, as spin, it makes perfect sense.

SPINNING ENERGY

Bush came to the White House with two goals: cut taxes and drill in the Arctic. Both depended on finding the perfect spin. For drilling, he resorted to a combination of hope and fear: fear that the lights would go out if we didn't drill; hope that we could do so without destroying the natural habitat.

There was no energy crisis in 2001, so Bush invented one. "America in the year 2001 faces the most serious energy shortage since the oil embargoes of the 1970's," declared the first page of the administration's energy plan, written by Dick Cheney's task force. Nonsense! Sure, gas prices temporarily shot up to around $2 a gallon—that happens every spring—but then they came back down again. There were no long lines at the pumps, Americans were still driving their SUVs, the lights were still on, except in California, where they went off maybe an hour a week, and even that problem disappeared after a month or so.

What crisis?

Ask Jimmy Carter. He experienced a *real* energy crisis. In fact, he got kicked out of the White House because he couldn't deal with it. In a scathing *New York Times* op-ed piece, Carter exposed Bush's spin: "No energy crisis exists now that equates in any way with those we faced in 1973 and 1979." In fact, Carter showed, the gross national product of the United States has increased by 90 percent since 1980, but energy consumption has gone up only 26 percent. Americans are producing more, and consuming less. And it is only going to get better. With so many new power plants under construction, the libertarian Cato Institute's Jerry Taylor predicted an "electricity glut" in the near future.

The second part of Bush's energy spin was equally unconvincing. The former Texas oilman promised it was possible to drill for oil in the Arctic National Wildlife Refuge and leave "nothing but a footprint behind." Naturally, nobody believed him. We've seen too many oil fields, refineries, tank farms and oil spills. They ain't pretty. They're incompatible with a wilderness area.

This is one case, a rare case, where the spin did not work. Perhaps because it was too contrived. No matter how hard the White House spun, most Americans saw through the fog and realized that Bush and Cheney were just trying to serve their old buddies in the oil and gas business, the environment be damned. Their energy plan—which included Cheney's pipe dream of building one new power plant, every week, for the next 20 years—went nowhere.

Poor Dick Cheney. Since he did all the work, he was the one hurt most when his plan bombed. But, in a way, he asked for it. First, he ridiculed conservation as a "virtue" which might make you feel good, but does nothing to save energy. For that idiotic statement, he was almost laughed out of town. Then, he turned around and blasted people for using too much energy: "If you want to leave all the lights on in your house, you can. . . . But you will pay for it." That statement came back to haunt him, a few weeks later, when he asked the Navy to pick up the estimated $186,000 electric bill for the vice president's house in 2001.

Who's been leaving the lights on, Dick?

SPINNING THE ENVIRONMENT

One other area where the Bush White House spin fell flat: painting Bush as an environmentalist. No wonder.

To their credit, White House spin doctors tried their best to paint Dubya green. They dressed him in boots and jeans. They sent him to the Everglades of Florida and the giant sequoias of California. They gave him the right talking points, declaring his intention to make "the air cleaner, the water cleaner and the land more usable." It just didn't sell. As columnist Arianna Huffington wrote, it was too obvious the Bush administration's environmental agenda was "purely and simply about spinning." Standing under the California redwoods, Bush had the same lost look on his face Jesse Helms would if he'd stumbled into a meeting of the Senate Democratic Caucus: "What the hell am I doing here?"

The truth was, there was too much damage to overcome. Bush's image as the friend of polluters had been irretrievably set in his first weeks in office, when he gleefully climbed onto a bulldozer and destroyed as much of the environment as he could reach. In just a few weeks:

- He reversed his campaign promise to regulate CO_2.
- He repeated his plans to drill for oil in the Arctic National Wildlife Refuge.
- He suspended regulations to reduce the amount of arsenic in drinking water.
- He tried to reverse a Clinton administration ban prohibiting logging in 50 million acres of national forests.
- He called for new oil drilling off the coasts of Florida and Louisiana; and eased regulations on mining and drilling in national monuments.
- His administration also, briefly, announced plans to suspend testing salmonella for school lunches, then quickly backed off.

As late-night great Jay Leno explained: "I guess the Republican theory is you don't have to test for salmonella because the arsenic in the drinking water will kill the germs."

There was no way to dig George Bush out of that hole. Spin can only do so much. He will forever be known as pro-drilling, pro-mining, pro-logging, pro-pollution—and anti-environment.

SPINNING CHENEY'S HEART

Another issue. Dealing with his own health problems, Vice President Dick Cheney proved he could spin brilliantly—with the expert help of Mary Matalin. Not just his words, but his actions, were carefully orchestrated to give the appearance of "business as usual," despite having to check in every couple of months or so for a heart tune-up. Got a serious heart problem? Can't spin it any better than this.

- Thursday, June 28, 2001—Cheney himself tells reporters he will undergo a procedure to see if a new device is needed for his heart.
- Saturday, June 30—Cheney checks in, in morning. Has "pacemaker plus" installed. Checks out in afternoon.
- Sunday, July 1—Cheney rests at home.
- Monday, July 2—Cheney reports for work at 7:45 A.M. "With gusto." Puts in full day of meetings and media interviews. Declares himself fit as a fiddle.

To hear the White House spin it, Cheney's only problem is that he now has to hold his cell phone up to the opposite ear, in order not to interfere with operation of his pacemaker. This inconvenience, he can live with. But, you get the picture.

For successful cardiac surgery today, you need two doctors: a heart doctor and a spin doctor.

SPINNING TAX CUTS: SIX LAYERS OF SPIN

Of course, President Bush's major goal was an across-the-board tax cut—which, to his credit, he signed into law less than six months after taking office. (Not bad for anyone with twice his experience in Washington.) But it wouldn't have happened without major spin. More, indeed, than on any other issue. Six layers of spin, by my count.

SPIN LAYER 1. THE NEED FOR A TAX CUT

As a general rule, most economists would argue that tax cuts are needed during a recession to re-stimulate the economy. But, this time around, all bets were off. When George W. Bush first proposed a massive across-the-board tax cut, during the 2000 Republican primary, the country was still enjoying, under President Bill Clinton, its longest period of economic prosperity in history. So why did we need a tax cut? *To keep the economy strong,* said Candidate Bush.

Bush took office and the economy started to tank, and he changed his tune. Why did we need a tax cut then? *To get the economy moving again,* said President Bush—just the opposite of his campaign message. But that was just the beginning. He also told a group of businessmen we needed a tax cut *to encourage investment by small businesses.* And he told reporters in the spring of 2001 that the solution to high gasoline prices at the pumps was—you guessed it!—an across-the-board tax cut. Apparently, a tax cut would put more money into consumers' pockets so they could give more money to the oil companies.

Whatever the problem, a tax cut was the solution. You got the feeling that if there were a sudden outbreak of scarlet fever, Bush would have proposed an across-the-board tax cut as the surefire cure.

SPIN LAYER 2. THE COST OF A TAX CUT

Could we afford such a massive tax cut? That depends on how much it costs. Here the goal of White House spin was clear: keep it big enough to be impressive, but low enough to seem doable.

Bush's original proposal was for $1.8 trillion in tax cuts over 10 years. He compromised for a $1.35 trillion package. But that was just phony math, based on dishonest accounting. According to the nonpartisan Congressional Budget Office, without a meaningless, 10-year "sunset" provision inserted in the bill, the actual cost of the tax cut will exceed $4 trillion. Even *Newsweek* magazine reported: "The Big Lie is that it costs only $1.35 trillion."

In the end, of course, how large of a tax cut we could afford depended on the size of the surplus. That was the next level of spin.

SPIN LAYER 3. WHO SHRANK THE SURPLUS?

In Hollywood, they would call it "The Case of the Incredible Shrinking Surplus." Here's what happened:

- In January, when George Bush took over the Oval Office, the size of the 2001 surplus was estimated at $275 billion, based on continued economic growth of 4 percent a year. There was so much extra money sloshing around Washington, it made sense to give some of it back to taxpayers.
- Then a funny thing happened on the way to the bank. The economy sputtered, the market crashed, tax revenues dwindled—and the surplus disappeared.
- By July, when Bush budget director Mitch Daniels gave an update to Congress, the surplus was down to $160 billion, and still shrinking. Daniels tried to spin this as good news: "This year's surplus will still be the second-largest in the nation's history," he told reporters. "That is to say, world history, the history of man."

Great spin. Great math. Lose $115 billion and declare victory!

With far less money to spend than expected, the wise thing to do was to rethink and readjust the tax cut to reflect a smaller budget. The only problem was, it was much too late. The tax cut was already the law of the land. The money had already been spent.

Once again, Congress and the president had spent money they didn't have.

Was it just a coincidence that we were never told about the shrinking surplus until after the tax cut had already been signed into law? Believe that and you'll believe any spin there is. Actually, in this case, it was worse than spin, as Paul Krugman correctly noted in the *New York Times:* "In short, the claim that the tax cut was easily affordable, given other priorities, was what is technically known as a 'lie'."

SPIN LAYER 4. WHO BENEFITS?

There is nothing wrong with tax cuts. They are good public policy, as long as we can afford them. And as long as they go to the people who need them. Unfortunately, neither was true about the mammoth Bush tax cut. As seen above, there was less money to spend than he made us believe. And his tax cut went almost exclusively to those who need it the least.

The White House tried hard to spin the tax cut as egalitarian: something for everybody, all Americans treated equally. Nonsense. Check how much money goes where. The Bush tax cut didn't create a more level playing field; it further separated the haves from the have-nots. It was redistribution of wealth from the rich to the very rich.

Did all Americans benefit? Not at all.

- Twenty-one percent of Americans received no benefit from the Bush tax cut, because they pay too little, or no, income tax.
- The wealthiest 1 percent of Americans, those who pay the most taxes, reaped 38 percent of the goodies, or an average annual rebate of $46,000.
- Those in the middle, the hard-working middle class, receive an average of only $227 a year, over 10 years. Hardly enough to write home about.

Thanks to the *Nation* magazine, we know that most of Bush's Cabinet members, 12 out of 16 of whom are millionaires, made out like champs.

- Dick Cheney's income tax cut was close to $1.7 million.
- Treasury Secretary Paul O'Neill's cut was a mighty $3.5 million.

You can't say Bush doesn't take care of his buddies.

The *New York Times* broke it down even further. Under the Bush plan, showed the *Times,* the 400 wealthiest Americans—Bill Gates, Donald Trump and friends—will receive over $1 million a year in tax cuts. In just two and a half years, that's a gift of $1 billion we taxpayers will make to just 400 people. How generous we are.

This is one case where honesty would have been a better policy. Any time you have an across-the-board tax cut, there's no way to escape the fact that those who pay the most will get the most back. Better to defend that fact than pretend it's otherwise. Sometimes the truth is better than spin.

SPIN LAYER 5. HOW'S IT WORK?

At least, the Bush tax cut was easy to understand. There were four elements: tax rates were cut for everybody; the estate tax was eliminated; so was the marriage tax; and everybody received a tax cut. Right? Wrong! The reality was much more complex, and much more sneaky. So sneaky that *Newsweek* summed up the bill's provisions under the headline "Stupid Tax Tricks."

Take the estate tax, for example. It is gradually phased out, but not eliminated until the year 2010. But in 2011 it's back in full force. Which leaves you only one year in which to die tax-free. Set your Palm Pilot.

What happens to the so-called marriage penalty is equally silly. Nothing happens until the year 2005. It shrinks little by little until it disappears in 2009. One year later, it, too, is fully restored. As are the lower tax rates. In fact, ten years from now, unless Congress acts again, we will be right back where we started from before Bush took office. His tax cut is less a major shift in public policy than a temporary shell-game. Now you see it, now you don't.

SPIN LAYER 6. THE CHECK'S IN THE MAIL

In July 2001, the U. S. Treasury started mailing the first installment of the Bush tax cut: a check for $300 to every taxpayer; $600 to every married couple. And the Bush spin machine went into overdrive.

It started a month before checks were printed. On official stationery, the IRS sent letters to all taxpayers, informing them to expect a tax cut, compliments of President Bush. This made Bush the only president other than Richard Nixon to use the IRS for political purposes. Unfortunately, one complication developed when, because of a computer glitch, hundreds of thousands of taxpayers were promised twice as much money as they would actually receive. Oops!

Once checks started arriving, spinners had an orgasm. Republic National Chairman Jim Gilmore sent one million e-mails to party activists telling them to write letters to the editor, praising George Bush for the rebate. State party chairs were issued lists of what $600 could buy in their state. In Washington state, for example, a lucky couple could head home with two and a half months of groceries, forty packs of diapers, twelve nights out at the movies for a family of four, a year of cell phone service, 150 video rentals or forty Seattle Mariners baseball tickets. The RNC also mailed out ten thousand bumper stickers with the message: THANK ME FOR YOUR TAX REFUND—I VOTED FOR BUSH.

You have to admire the spin—but it was all phony.

Spinners failed to point out that, for the great majority of taxpayers, this was the last they would ever see of the great Bush tax cut. Over ten years, they would never receive another dime—while the wealthiest Americans would continue receiving chunky checks every year.

And, of course, nobody acknowledged that the $300 check was not George Bush's idea at all. It was not in his original campaign plan. It was not in the bill he sent to Congress. It was the brainchild of the Progressive Caucus of the House of Representatives, chaired by Democrat Dennis Kucinich of Ohio and Independent/Socialist Bernie Sanders of Vermont, two of the most liberal members of Congress. Bush was forced to accept it in order to round up enough Democratic votes. Republicans were taking credit for something proposed by a Socialist. Their bumper stickers should have read: THANK BERNIE SANDERS FOR YOUR TAX REFUND!

Then the final embarrassment: Not even half the checks

had been mailed when the *New York Times* reported that the Treasury Department had to borrow $50 billion to cover the tax refunds, because the projected surplus had disappeared.

George Bush is trying so hard to be like Ronald Reagan that he's even embraced deficit spending.

SPIN LAYER 7. WHAT HAPPENS NEXT?

Before taxpayers received their first $300 refund in the mail, sometime in the summer of 2001, a new challenge arose. Now that the surplus had disappeared, how was Bush going to pay for his tax cut without dipping into surplus Social Security or Medicare funds, as he had vowed not to during the campaign?

Calling White House spinners! Before you could say *"Best Little Whorehouse in Texas,"* they were on the job. First line of defense: *Blame Bill Clinton*. Bush's chief economic adviser Larry Lindsey stepped up to the plate: "The tax cut is not the true cause of the revenue shortfall. The shortfall is the result of an economic slowdown that began in September last year [when Clinton was still president]."

Second line of defense: pave the way for a raid on Social Security by downplaying the significance of Social Security funds. The crafty Paul Krugman of the *New York Times* predicted this development on July 7, 2001: "When it becomes apparent that the tax cut will cut into the Social Security trust fund too—quite possibly as soon as next year—we'll be told that this doesn't matter, that the trust fund is a mere accounting fiction." Lo and behold, as if on cue, the President's Commission on Social Security reported less than two weeks later that bonds in the Social Security trust fund are "not accumulated reserves of wealth but only promises future taxpayers will be asked to redeem." In other words, it doesn't matter whether we steal from the fund or not.

Then came official word from the Congressional Budget Office and Bush budget chief Mitch Daniels that, because of a shrinking surplus, the White House was already picking the lock of the Social Security lock box: "borrowing" $9–15 billion in 2001 for other government spending—and more in coming years. Another Bush campaign promise broken. Seniors of America, hold on to your wallets! Of course, that was before everything changed on September 11. Congress immediately gave the president $40 billion in new spending authority, with no debate about where it came from. Nobody worries about the Social Security surplus anymore.

ONE HUNDRED DAYS

As we have seen, the Bush White House is adept at spinning issue by issue. But it is especially adept at spinning the big picture, as it proved early on. With the approach of his first 100 days in office, Bush's spokespeople at first tried to downplay the significance of that traditional measure of a president's performance. It was purely an artificial ritual, they argued, kept alive only by the media. Trying to jump start the national economy during the depression, President Franklin Roosevelt had chalked up phenomenal success in his first 100 days in office, achieving passage of key elements of the New Deal. But no president had ever accomplished as much since and it was unfair to continue to measure presidents by his standard.

They were absolutely correct. The 100-days test is a stupid one to apply to any president. But the media just won't let go. This is, after all, early in every administration, a chance for reporters, editorial writers and pundits to tell the world, once again, how smart they are and how dumb the president is. Once the White House spin operation recognized this, they shifted gears: from ignoring the passage of Bush's 100 days to celebrating it as the greatest human triumph since Hannibal crossed the Alps. They puffed up the clumsy false-starts of the nascent Bush administration to make it appear as if they had actually accomplished something. And, to make sure all Republican operatives in the White House, on Capitol Hill, in the Republican National

Committee and around the country delivered the same message, they put out (unofficial) official White House talking points. All party hacks had to do was stick to the script.

The end product was a masterpiece of spin, here reproduced in its entirety. If you don't believe the Bush White House spins, read this. If you want to know why all Republicans sound alike, read this. If you want to see the perfect example of spin in action, read this—courtesy of the White House Communications Office.

PRESIDENT BUSH'S FIRST 100 DAYS

- President Bush is a strong leader who is doing what he said he would do.

- The President's plain-spoken and straightforward leadership is helping replace a culture of gridlock and cynicism with a constructive spirit of bipartisan respect and results.

- The President is leading with a steady and measured hand while tackling many of America's most pressing problems—from education to energy, from the economy to foreign affairs, from confronting poverty to racial profiling, from airline strikes to Medicare reform.

- The President is focused on his compassionate conservative agenda of education reform, cutting taxes, empowering faith and community-based groups, laying the foundation for Medicare and Social Security reform, and rebuilding our nation's military.

- The President's disciplined leadership and focus on results has led to notable early accomplishments:

  - The President has made bipartisan education reform the cornerstone of his Administration. The President wants to ensure that no child is left behind by holding schools more accountable and insisting on results. The President and Congress are near an agreement on a comprehensive, bipartisan education reform bill.

- The President has shifted the tax cut debate from a rancorous, partisan debate over IF there will be tax relief, to a bipartisan discussion of HOW MUCH tax relief Americans will have.

- The President's budget framework, which cuts taxes, funds important priorities and pays down historic levels of debt was approved by the House and Senate with bipartisan support. The budget was passed earlier than usual with the support of 15 Senate Democrats—proof that the President's emphasis on teamwork is yielding bipartisan accomplishments.

- The President put bipartisanship into action by meeting personally with more members of the opposing party in the opening days of his Administration than any other modern President.

- The President's plan to rally America's community and faith-based armies of compassion to help our most needy is moving forward in both chambers of Congress with bipartisan support.

- The President has personally taken his fair and responsible agenda directly to the people by visiting 26 states, appearing with leaders in both parties. The President's Cabinet has also traveled to 39 states to discuss the President's agenda and budget.

- On foreign policy, the President has been decisive, measured and realistic. He operates with a clear understanding of American interests and a commitment to work with our friends and allies to advance our common security in the world. During his first 100 days, the President traveled to Mexico and worked to strengthen alliances in our hemisphere at the Summit of the Americas in Canada, guided diplomacy that brought home our crew after an accident in China, and personally met with more than 20 world leaders to build relationships and discuss common interests and concerns.

- The President said in his Inaugural Address, "Civility is not a tactic or a sentiment. It is the determined choice of trust over cynicism." The President is keeping his word to bring a new way of thinking to Washington.

Notice the repetition of so many familiar themes: bipartisan, leadership, trust, compassionate conservative, plain-spoken, steady hand, new way of thinking, results. You'd never know they were talking about George W. Bush. But now you know why all Republicans sound the same on television: they're singing from the same hymnal—published daily by the White House.

Of course, the Clinton White House provided the same service to Democrats.

There is, of course, the remote chance that George W. Bush will start speaking straight to the American people. Remote, but unlikely. After all, why should he tell the truth when he get even more mileage out of spin?

Indeed, his first year indicates that Bush may very well take the art of spin to whole new heights. He's sure off to a damned good start.

The Bush spin has just begun.

EIGHT

SPINNING THE LEGAL SYSTEM

Jury: Twelve people who determine which client has the better lawyer.

—Robert Frost

Like journalism and politics, the legal profession is filled with men and women who spin for a living. This should come as no surprise. After all, most politicians are lawyers who started out practicing law—Bill Clinton even taught law!—and return to lawyering or lobbying once they retire or are thrown out of office. The only difference is, unlike full-time politicians, full-time lawyers don't believe their own spin.

It goes without saying. If the legal system is the arena of spin, it is certainly not the haven of truth. In the courtroom, an attorney's job is not to tell the truth. It's not to lie, either. It's to win. It's to persuade the judge or jury of a person's guilt or innocence. In order to do so, truth becomes an abstract. Truth is shaded, nuanced, compromised. Truth gives way to spin: painting the facts in the best possible light to help a client or win a case.

The foundation of all legal spin is the legend emblazoned over the portals of the United States Supreme Court: "Equal Justice Under the Law." Everybody knows that's not really

the case. It's more like: "Equal Justice Under the Law—
Sometimes"—as long as you have the money to pay for it, or
the right connections. But, still, we keep the equal-protec-
tion-under-the-law spin alive. Because it's just too depressing
to admit the truth.

PRE-TRIAL SPIN

In criminal cases, there's spin from start to finish: before the
trial, during the trial, and after the trial. The spin starts the
moment some poor sucker is charged with a crime. Forget
the theory of "innocent until proven guilty." Prosecutors, hoping to sway public opinion, immediately step forward and spin
the facts to demonstrate they have an airtight case against the
bastard. Who needs a trial? The guy's as good as dead.

District attorneys and their staffs see the worst in everybody. In fact, they're paid to. They believe everyone is guilty
until proven innocent. They take the facts and twist them to
nail every suspect. Their spin is: We're just following the evidence. The reality is: They're just trying to prove their pre-
mature conclusions.

Whatever happened to the "presumption of innocence"?
That's just spin used by prosecutors today to cover up their
own presumption of guilt. Same with the "burden of proof."
Don't believe the spin. In today's courtroom—especially in
cases with a lot of media attention—the burden is on the suspect to prove his innocence, not on the state to prove his guilt.

Poor Bill Clinton. He got saddled with just such a prose-
cutor, W. Hickman Ewing, Jr., one of the first assistants Independent Counsel Ken Starr hired when he took over the
Whitewater investigation in August 1994 from Robert
Fiske. As another Starr associate told the *New Yorker*'s Jef-
frey Toobin: "Most prosecutors at least say that they come
to things with open minds, but Hick says that he presumes
that a crime has been committed and his job is to proceed as
if there is criminal conduct and then be convinced otherwise." Which explains why Starr spent so much time on a

worthless Arkansas real estate deal—and how disappointed he must have been, after four years digging, to find Clinton guilty of nothing more serious than a blow job. Which, of course, he and Ewing were still able to parlay into an impeachable offense.

Of course, prosecutors make up just one side of the story. Defense attorneys spin just as fast, right from the get-go: spelling out all the reasons why there's no way their client could possibly be guilty as charged. But, again, that's their job: to take the client's problem and put it in the best possible light. A defense attorney might even know his man is guilty. It is still his obligation to do everything possible to defend him, short of putting him on the witness stand to lie. His goal ahead of trial is to convince the public of the poor sap's innocence. And not just the public. More importantly: any potential members of the jury who happen to be watching TV news that night. But they don't always do so successfully.

For example, when 24-year old Washington intern Chandra Levy was reported missing in May 2001, rumors immediately began—and were widely reported as news—that she was having an affair with California Congressman Gary Condit. Intending to quash the rumors, Condit's attorney Joseph W. Cotchett did just the opposite, insisting to CNN's Wolf Blitzer: "The congressman has come forward and said they were good friends—as he is with many interns." Hmm . . . Interns usually complain that, even after working in an office for six months, members of Congress don't even know their names. Apparently that is not the case with Congressman Condit. He has what you might call a good outreach program.

Actually, spin is in great demand for lawyers representing Washington politicians. Many D.C. residents remember Mayor Marion Barry's first encounter with the law, when he was caught on videotape smoking crack cocaine with a prostitute in a downtown hotel. Long after he went to prison, his supporters were still wearing T-shirts with the argument mounted by his defense attorneys: I SAW THE VIDEO. THE BITCH SET HIM UP!

Once out of prison, and out of public office, Barry continued to spin. He was later hauled into court on charges of exposing himself to a female custodian in a public restroom. Barry's excuse was: he had prostate problems, he really had to go, and if he hadn't pulled out his penis and waved it in front of the woman, he would have wet his pants. Spin that to the judge!

To be fair, it's not just politicians. Utah resident and fundamentalist Mormon Tom Green was arrested and charged with polygamy and, since his wives were only teenagers when he married them, also charged with statutory rape. We invited him to appear on *Crossfire;* and, to our surprise, he showed up with three of his five wives. When I suggested that he was using his religion as a pretext for having sex with teenage girls, Green roared with outrage. "It's got nothing to do with sex," he thundered. "We're too busy raising our kids to think about sex." I failed to point out—although I think it was obvious to all our viewers—that sex must have played some kind of role in producing his 29 kids. At least 29 times, he and his wives must have stopped whatever else they were occupied with long enough, not only to think about sex, but to do it.

On the civil side, pre-trial is also the time some lawyers will spin ridiculous cases, hoping someone will take them seriously. Remember: every time someone files what we call a frivolous lawsuit, there's a frivolous lawyer willing to file the papers. No doubt, you have your favorite list. Here are a few of mine:

- A college student in Idaho decided to moon someone from his fourth-story dorm room window. He lost his balance, fell out of his window, and injured himself in the fall (he's lucky he didn't kill himself). He sued the university for not warning him of the dangers of living on the fourth floor—or mooning from the fourth floor.
- A San Diego man filed a $5.4 million lawsuit against the city for the "emotional trauma" he suffered at an Elton John/Billy Joel concert held at the municipal stadium. No, he wasn't talking about the music. His problem was that, with so large a crowd, a group of women had infiltrated the men's restroom at intermission. He claimed he was

"extremely upset" at the sight of a woman using a man's urinal and his right of privacy was violated when he was forced to relieve himself in front of women waiting in line.

- A Houston minister and his wife sued a guide-dog school after a blind man learning to use a seeing-eye dog trod on the woman's toes in a shopping mall. The woman said she made no effort to get out of the blind man's way because she was curious to see if the dog would walk around her.

- A woman driving a car collided with a man driving a snowmobile. He died at the scene. She sued his widow for psychological injuries she suffered from having to watch him die.

- A New Jersey man sued McDonald's for injuries sustained in an auto accident. He claimed the crash was caused when the other driver spilled a chocolate milkshake, purchased at McDonald's, in his lap while reaching for a handful of French fries. He accused McDonald's of selling food to customers from their drive-through windows, knowing full well they would consume it while driving—but failing to affix a label on every container warning: "Don't eat and drive."

Believe it or not, some of these cases actually make it to the courtroom. And that's where the fun starts.

COURTROOM SPIN

Actually, there's so much spin in the courtroom, it would more aptly be called the "Spin Room." Think about it. What happens in a courtroom? Two lawyers stand up in front of the courtroom and make their best arguments on behalf of their client. The judge or jury then decides which is the better spinner. That's what the law is all about.

CNN's Greta van Susteren told me of one experience in the courtroom. As she was making what she thought was a powerful argument on behalf of her client, the judge interrupted and declared: "You're trying to make a silk purse out of a sow's ear." In other words, he was accusing her of spinning.

So, what did he expect? That's what lawyers are trained to do. Novelist and trial lawyer Tim Junkin reflected on his own courtroom experience in the June 2001 issue of *Washingtonian* magazine: "Litigators spend their careers this way, reconstructing facts, manipulating what information a jury will hear, ducking, weaving and spinning for the client, for causes the lawyers may not necessarily believe in. It's what the system demands."

Everyone with a law degree will tell you that one of the first rules of evidence taught in law school is to resort to spin as the ultimate defense. "If you're weak on the law," aspiring young Clarence Darrows are told, "pound on the facts. If you're weak on the facts, pound on the law. If you're weak on both, pound on the table!"

And the lawyers you really have to watch out for are the ones who profess to be too dumb to spin. "I'm just a poor country lawyer," apologized Senator Sam Irvin, who chaired the Senate's Watergate investigation, before proceeding to destroy Richard Nixon and all his men. Beware of self-negation among lawyers. It's too incongruous to be real.

THE INSANITY DEFENSE

In the legitimate interest of representing his client, there seems no limit to the amount of illegitimate spin a defense lawyer is willing to engage in. "Temporary insanity" is one of the more outrageous such claims. By definition any person who attacks another with a deadly weapon, except in self-defense, could be called temporarily insane. But that formal legal defense was enough to win Lorena Bobbitt freedom, even after she admitted cutting off her husband's penis with a butcher knife. You must admit, it does sound a bit insane.

The absurdity of the insanity defense is not lost on Hollywood. An early James Stewart movie called *Anatomy of a Murder* provides a classic example. Stewart plays a lawyer hired to defend a man already in jail and charged with murder. He doesn't deny the crime. He tells Stewart it was justified under the unwritten law of revenge because the man had raped his wife, so he got a gun, walked into a bar and shot him. Stewart tells him that neither the unwritten law nor anger is a proper legal defense. The only way out, Stewart warns, is to plead temporary insanity. He leaves his client with the request to think about it overnight and see if he can remember "just how crazy you were."

THE BLAME GAME

But movies don't just recount legal defenses. They have actually inspired their own, which I call: "Just Mad About the Movies." Only an idiot would believe seeing a movie would make someone go out and commit a crime. But that's how John Hinckley ended up in a mental hospital, not federal prison, for shooting President Reagan in March 1981. He was not in control of his own body, argued his defense lawyers, successfully. He was controlled by a pathological obsession with the movie *Taxi Driver* and, specifically, with its star, Jodie Foster.

More recently, an attorney tried the same defense for a man accused of shooting, stabbing and drowning his wife—allegedly inspired by having seen the movie *Crocodile Dundee,* a movie so bad it could understandably foster murderous impulses against the director. In this case, the man's far-fetched claim fell apart when it was discovered the wife was murdered a month before the movie came out. Blame it on the coming attractions?

Here's another: "My Parents Raised Me This Way." When kids get into trouble, just blame it on the parents. Even when kids kill their parents, still blame it on their parents. It worked for the Menendez brothers (at least for their first trial), who shot both parents dead in cold blood. After that, there's no weird behavior you can't blame on Mom and Dad.

If you can blame your parents, why not blame society and modern technology? Next thing you know, some defense lawyer is going to start spinning that his client is under control of the Internet. Surprise, surprise! It's already happened. In January 2001, a Florida lawyer argued that his client, an eighteen-year-old student, was not guilty of e-mailing threats to another student because he suffered from "Internet Intoxication." In other words, he lived in a virtual world and could not be held responsible for the consequences of his actions in the real world. A true sign of our wacky times.

And then, of course, there was the worst defense spin of all: the "Twinkie Defense." When Supervisor Dan White climbed through a basement window in San Francisco City Hall in November 1978, sneaked upstairs and shot and killed Mayor George Moscone and Supervisor Harvey Milk, his attorney argued he was not himself because he'd been eating too much high-sugar junk foods. Ridiculous spin? Yes. Successful spin? Yes.

THE JUDGE'S SPIN

Believe it or not, that distinguished old judge, sitting up there like an Old Testament prophet in his black robes, is not free of spin, either. Of course, judges insist that they bring a free and open mind to each new case. But, lawyers know, that's just spin. Give them a few years on the bench and judges are as jaded as everybody else in the process. Plus, they can't help but bring to the job their own political and personal opinions. After all, they're only human.

Still, despite their obvious human limitations, if not biases, our army of judges have long been accepted as the national repository of spin. Ever since 1803, when Chief Justice John Marshall wrote in *Marbury v. Madison:* "It is emphatically the province and duty of the judicial department to say what the law is." Nowhere in the Constitution does it say the courts have the power that Marshall asserted. But no one has ever successfully challenged it. Judges are supreme. Judicial spin rules.

And not just local judges. As with politics, so with the law: the higher the office, the greater the spin. Which, of course, makes Supreme Court Justices the best, or worst, spinners of all. Is there any doubt of how badly the Supreme Court can spin, after a majority of the Rehnquist court actually ruled that democracy was best served in the November 2000 presidential election by not counting all the votes?

The court's *Bush v. Gore* ruling was further proof of the smartest observation ever made about the Supreme Court, by Justice Robert Jackson: "We are not final because we are infallible, but infallible only because we are final." Why should we be shocked when the Court stops an election in mid-count and declares a winner? This is the same Court that once ruled that slaves had no rights; that separate but equal facilities for whites and blacks were constitutional; and that denying a political candidate the opportunity to buy an election was a violation of freedom of speech. Go figure. Go weep.

Back to the courtroom. When courtroom spin gets out of hand, there is really no one to blame but the judge. In the O. J. Simpson case, Judge Lance Ito clearly let Johnny Cochran go way overboard. "If the glove don't fit, you must acquit." Thanks to a series of friendly rulings by Ito, Cochran and his team were able to spin a double-murder case into an indictment of the Los Angeles Police Department. O.J. wasn't on trial, the LAPD was. And they, not O.J., were found guilty. Which, of course, enabled O.J. to get out of jail and devote the rest of his life to finding the real killers—on the golf course! Who knows, they could be stalking the back nine!

In fact, since the trial, O.J. has reinvented himself as— what else?—a victim. In an interview with the *New Yorker*'s Pat Jordan, he refers to the double murder and subsequent trials only as "my ordeal." *His* ordeal? What about Nicole Brown's or Ronald Goldman's ordeal? And he attempts to put a whole new spin on his relationship with Nicole: "The press created this guy who was hurting because his wife left him. That's bullshit! It was Nicole who wanted to come back to me after the divorce. She stalked me!" And, by extension, we can only presume it was Nicole who cut her own throat, after first slashing Goldman's.

In the same interview, O.J. falls back on one of the politician's favorite spins: blaming all of his troubles on the media. The reason everybody believes he's guilty of double murder is because reporters didn't do their job. "During my trial, the truth was known, but no one would write it," he absurdly insists. "It's a much better story if I'm guilty. They didn't look at anybody but me. I was set up." Do you hear echoes of Marion Barry here?

SPINNING THE JURY

Even juries get caught up in the cloud of spin that hovers over the legal system. We still refer to them as a "panel of peers"—even though few of our peers have ever served a day on jury duty, or ever will. It is small comfort to put your fate in the hands of a group of peers when all the so-called "peers" are retired persons or government workers: the only people not devious enough to get out of jury duty.

Recognizing that his spin is only as good as a jury will swallow, every lawyer worth his salt makes a great effort, ahead of trial, trying to tailor-make a jury and tailor-make his message for it. Many actually recruit people to sit on mock juries, then watch behind one-way mirrors as colleagues argue the case various ways, to see which spin works, and which doesn't. What they're looking for, says Arizona's Hale Starr—an expert who makes a good living advising attorneys on how to pick a jury—is what she calls the "3 A.M. test." Starr explains: "If you go to a juror and wake them up at three in the morning after the first day of trial and ask 'What is the attorney trying to say?', they'll use two or three words." That's the magic spin.

Once they're settled on the spin that works, lawyers are ready for the selection process known as *voir dire*, where they ask questions of prospective jurors, looking for the most fertile ears. It's like producing a play, although here you get to pick the audience. At least those sitting in rows one and two. And that's important, because they're the only ones that count.

The attorney's final step in winning over the jury is prepping the witnesses. Here again, truth is relative. Talking to witnesses ahead of time, the trial attorney first finds out what they know, then advises them how to spin the facts on the witness stand in order to reinforce the overall spin he's presenting and help convince the jury. The better the spinner, the better the witness. The biggest mistake any trial lawyer could make would be to put a witness on the stand without first giving him a crash course in Spin 101.

POST-TRIAL SPIN

But the spin doesn't stop when the courtroom empties and the jury goes home. At that point starts the post-trial spin—about the verdict. Equally predictable. Prosecutors insist that, even though the verdict was not so severe as they asked for (they're only going to keep him in prison for three consecutive life sentences), they're satisfied that justice was served. Defense attorneys counter that, even though he was slammed harder than he deserved, at least he's still alive. Plus, it goes without saying, they plan to appeal.

You may recall the big government case against Microsoft (later dropped by the Bush administration). Under President Clinton, the Justice Department accused Bill Gates's company of antitrust violations. After a federal judge found the computer giant guilty of monopoly practices and ordered that the firm be split in two, Microsoft appealed—and won. In the state of Washington, Bill Gates immediately declared victory. The appeals court ruling, he crowed, "removes the cloud of breakup from the company . . . and says clearly that we did not attempt to monopolize the browser market."

At the same time, in the city of Washington, government lawyers declared victory. "Today's decision represents a very significant victory for the antitrust division on the core claim in the Microsoft case that Microsoft engaged in anticompetitive conduct to preserve its monopoly position in computer operating systems," Charles James, the government's top antitrust enforcer, told reporters.

Now, wait a minute. This isn't soccer, where tie games are allowed. In any lawsuit, one side has to win, the other side has to lose. The verdict can't be a victory for both sides. Unless you spin it that way. And attorneys always will.

From the sidelines, Microsoft's competitors watched the game with obvious glee—and got in the last word. "When the nation's second-highest court rules seven-to-none that you are a monopolist that has violated the antitrust laws," an unnamed senior AOL Time-Warner executive told the *New Yorker*'s Ken Auletta, "it's not a good day, no matter how hard you spin it."

Another example. After San Francisco attorney Stacey Stillman was voted off the CBS reality show *Survivor,* she sued the production company, claiming the show was rigged against her. She says other contestants were told to vote against her so that all the older contestants wouldn't get booted off the show first. When SEG, the production company, immediately counter-sued her for breach of contract and defamation, a judge ruled that Stillman could not be sued for breach of contract, but could be sued for defamation. Again, both sides declared victory.

"I'm elated. I'm just thrilled that the judge has ruled I can't be sued for speaking truthfully about illegal activities," Stillman gushed. Countered SEG's attorney Andy White: "We're very pleased with the result and looking forward to getting in front of a jury as soon as possible."

What do we learn from this? Lesson #1: *No matter what the judge or jury rule, declare victory. Somebody may believe you.* Lesson #2: *Don't go on dumb TV shows like* Survivor. *They're all rigged.*

Legal spin is not limited to criminal cases. It's just as prevalent in civil cases. Especially divorce cases. In states where there is not yet no-fault divorce, lawyers still toss around meaningless words like "mental cruelty" and "incompatibility": spin for "I just can't stand the asshole anymore." Then comes the war over assets. The wife argues she's left with three kids, a big house to maintain and no means of supporting herself. Therefore, she's entitled to clean him out—and stake a claim on all future earnings. The husband complains that after paying for her graduate degree, vacation house and golf lessons and setting up a trust fund for each kid, he's barely got enough left to live on—let alone support his new girlfriend. Till spin do us part.

There's only one problem. Courtrooms are too small for everybody to witness and enjoy the great spin that happens inside. What about all those unlucky people who can't get seats? Problem solved! We'll take the most sensational trials and put them on national television.

COURT TV

An entire television network that does nothing else but broadcast courtroom proceedings live, from beginning to end? At one time, that seemed as crazy as Ted Turner's notion of a 24-hour news channel. After all, nobody cares what happens in probably 99 percent of all court cases. And a great part of those we do care about consists of boring recitals of facts, uninspiring statements or pointless interrogation of witnesses.

That notion seemed crazy to everybody but Steve Brill, back in 1991, who recognized courtroom spin as such a great form of entertainment it deserved the larger stage of national television! He knew people would watch it. And do.

The Court TV cable channel is a huge success because the drama of spin and counter-spin unfolds before our very eyes and ears with both the electricity of the stage and the excitement of real life. These aren't actors. These are real people, dissing other real people. Real lawyers spinning before a real judge. Sitting at home, we get to decide which one's the better spinner before even the judge does. We learn the verdict, we see the outcome in the courtroom, we hear the spin of winners and losers before we see it on the evening news. We were there!

No wonder Court TV is so popular. But, don't worry, if you don't have enough time or patience to watch an entire trial, you can also find the next best thing: little, bite-size trials, pre-packaged for your entertainment pleasure. *Judge Judy, The People's Court* and any one of a dozen other courtroom TV shows are also so successful because they're a spin-off of the real thing. Art imitating life.

And, of course, in the made-for-TV courtroom, the premise is the same. Only the lawyers are missing. But that's

OK. Plaintiff and defendant can spin for themselves. They each make their case, then the TV judge decides which is the better spinner. Warning. If Judge Judy tells you, as she did one complainant, "You're full of baloney, all right"—that means your spin is over the top. But still not as bad as the woman she told: "You're a liar. Oh, you're a liar. I'm going to tell you why you're a liar."

In the show *Divorce Court*, brave couples come up against an equally verbal tornado in the Hon. Mablean Ephraim. As in real-life divorce trials, the drama is usually confined to a man and wife spinning their best story in order to walk away with the most cash. Although the made-for-TV divorce battles are, fittingly, more bizarre than most. Natalyn was pregnant with their first child when she discovered her husband, Fred, was playing around. She left the state, moved back in with her parents, sued him for divorce—and asked Judge Ephraim to make the bum pay for her $320 bus ticket. Of course, if he gets off paying only $320, he's luckier than most.

Here's another one. Nikki, also pregnant, had only been married for three months when she found out hubby Richard was bedding down with two other women. She tossed him out and showed up on *Divorce Court* seeking an end to the marriage and $2505 dollars to pay for their wedding expenses, plus the nonrefundable deposit on the honeymoon they never took. And never will.

In the latest twist of television justice, combatants abandon the courtroom entirely—for the bowling alley. It's Comedy Central's *Let's Bowl!,* where plaintiff and defendant agree to forget all about judge and jury and let the winner be decided by a game of bowling. This is not recommended for criminal trials. But, for minor matters, think of all the lawyers' fees you save—and it sure beats bowling alone.

But it's not just people spinning for themselves. Judge Joseph Wapner, the first judge of *People's Court* and the godfather of court TV, has graduated to *Animal Court*, where people spin on behalf of their animals. It's like when animal trainer Jack Hanna appears on *Larry King*. There are more beasts on camera than people. Was the cat sicker when it was adopted or when it was returned to the original owner? Did the rare bird die of a sickness it acquired before it was purchased or once it was in its new home? Is the horse as healthy as the buyer claimed it to be? Take a look for yourself. On *Animal Court,* the horse is right there, in the courtroom.

It's just like the real court except more colorful and, like professional football, it's all rearranged into neatly-packaged, TV-size chunks of time in order to allow room for commercials. We interrupt this spin in order to bring you this spin. But that's the subject of the next chapter.

Before we get there, however, one final point about legal spin. It's not limited to the courtroom.

SPINNING LAW ENFORCEMENT

Fortunately for most people, their encounters with the law fall short of the courtroom. It could be as routine an experience as getting a speeding ticket. But that doesn't mean it's short of spin. Cops spin as much as lawyers or judges. And, sometimes, we get to spin back.

Think about it next time you're stopped for speeding and the cop walks up to your car. You are about to experience spin vs. spin, neither of them successful. He will try to spin you that he's kind, reasonable, and just doing his job. None of which you will buy. You will try to convince him that you are shocked, had no idea what the speed limit was and are even grateful he pulled you over to enlighten you. None of which he will buy, either. Or should.

The exchange offers endless possibilities:

Police Officer's Spin: Good morning. Are you on your way to a fire? Ha! Ha! Ha! Just a joke. I see you're from out of state and I hate to interrupt your travel, but I think you might have overestimated the speed limit back there. I'm sure you didn't mean to, but you were actually going 65 in a 35-mile-per-hour zone. I really don't want to write you a ticket, but the rules say I have no choice. If you would just sign right here . . . It doesn't mean you plead guilty, it just means you acknowledge receiving the citation. . . . You can always return to Maine in 60 days and contest the ticket. Thank you for your cooperation. Have a nice day. (It's that last comment that always kills me! The asshole just ruined any chance you could have a nice day.)

Police Officer's Translation: I just nailed your ass and I'm glad, because you're helping me make my daily quota. Of course, you can always appeal. Fat chance. You'll be long gone by then. So long, sucker!

Innocent Driver's Spin: I make a point never to speed. I might have been going 37, but no more. Obviously, the speedometer's not working. Besides, I wasn't paying attention. I was just following that car in front of me. Why didn't you stop him? I'm sorry. Did I tell you? I was distracted because my cat just died and I'm on my way to pick up my disabled brother. But that's not all. My car was stolen two days ago. I called the stupid hot line. They kept me on hold for four hours. So now I have to drive this piece of shit I borrowed from my other brother. And now, because of you, I'm going to be late for my fucking job. So please don't give me a ticket.

Innocent Driver's Translation: You know I'm guilty. I know I'm guilty. So how do I get out of it?

All of which applies, unless you happen to be African-American or Latino. Then, all bets are off. Whatever the policeman's spin, you're not guilty. You were stopped for only one reason: the color of your skin. You're black, you're brown, you're guilty. End of story.

Bottom line: any time you're confused about the role of the police officer, remember the words of wisdom of Chicago's colorful first Mayor Richard Daley: "The policeman isn't there to create disorder. The policeman is there to preserve disorder." He sounds like George W. Bush.

NINE

SPINNING TO SELL A PRODUCT

There's a sucker born every minute.
—P. T. Barnum

Advertising is legalized lying.
—H. G. Wells

Advertising is the 'wonder' in Wonder Bread.
—Jeff I. Richards

In selling products, there is wholesale spin and retail spin. Wholesale spin is mass advertising. Retail spin is the selling of individual products. We are suckers for both.

WHOLESALE SPIN

Do you want to see the spin of spins? Just look at any billboard, magazine ad, bus sign or TV commercial. That's all commercial advertising is: pure spin. That's what huge advertising agencies sell as a service: pure spin. And that's all good (or bad) salesmanship is: pure spin. Either we don't notice it, or we don't care. We recognize it for what it is: hype to sell a product.

Of course, the list is endless, because the opportunities to spin are so endless. It could be beer: "This Bud's for You!" Or soft drinks: "Things Go Better with Coke." Or toothpaste: "You Wonder Where the Yellow Went . . ." Or new cars: "Have You Driven a Ford Lately?"

What's amazing is how successful advertising campaigns are. We know it's spin, yet we still believe their exaggerated claims about products, because we want to believe them. "The common man, no matter how sharp and tough," master huckster P. T. Barnum also wisely observed, "actually enjoys having the wool pulled over his eyes, and makes it easier for the puller."

Commercial advertisers are so clever they've even convinced us to buy bottled water—water!—at $1.50 a pop, when most tap water is just as healthy. Ever notice that "Evian" is nothing but "naïve," spelled backward?

I should know better. I work in the world of spin. But I don't. A couple of years ago, sitting on the set of *Crossfire,* I noticed a commercial for an over-the-counter diet supplement with ginseng. On the screen were beautiful, happy, healthy men and women: frolicking, playing sports, laughing, full of energy. Perhaps because I was feeling badly battered by Pat Buchanan at the time, I thought: this is just what the doctor didn't have to order for me. The fountain of youth! Next day, I picked up a supply of pills at the corner pharmacy and started taking two or three a day. I continued taking them for almost a year, until one day I was visiting my cousin, a pharmacist on Maryland's Eastern Shore, and asked her how effective this magic pill was. "You might as well be taking nothing," she deadpanned. "What?" I asked. "You might as well be taking nothing," she repeated. So I stopped taking the pills. But, boy, was I a sucker for that spin.

No wonder Mark Hanna and others figured out that the best way to get politicians elected was to sell them like soap. They realized how gullible, or spinnable, the American people are. And they figured out they could trick us into voting for candidates just like we shop for a bar of soap: selecting one we know nothing about, but we've heard good things about on television. How right they were. What fools we are.

Occasionally, spin can go too far. Remember when the dairy industry was spanked for claiming: "Milk Does the Body Good." Turns out, milk does not do every body good because some people are lactose intolerant. So they had to change their ads to celebrities with milk mustaches. Except for Monica Lewinsky. That wasn't milk.

The maker of V-8 juice launched a similar campaign. Full-page newspaper ads trumpeting the claim: "This just in: Tomatoes are good for you." That ad, too, will last until some university researcher determines that tomatoes are not, in fact, good for people with some rare disease. Then that spin will be undone as well.

You expect spin from Hollywood. It's a city, indeed an entire industry, that thrives on spin: spinning actors and actresses, spinning scripts, spinning deals, spinning movies. If Paris is the "City of Lights," Los Angeles is the "City of Spin." But, even there, some spinners can go over the top.

Sony Pictures got into trouble when it decided it could not count on movie critics to put the right spin on their new releases—so they invented their own. This is especially funny since most movie critics are the biggest whores in the world, usually willing to bend over and gush the most enthusiastic praise for a new movie in exchange for nothing more than a stale bagel and cup of coffee. Still, not wanting to take a chance with real people, Sony invented fictitious movie reviewer David Manning, who "reviewed" four movies—two thumbs up for each, of course!—for the *Ridgefield Press,* a small Connecticut weekly. The whole scam worked beautifully until another reporter at the Ridgefield paper looked up Manning in the newsroom and discovered he didn't exist. Oops!

That wasn't Sony's only gaffe. At the same time, it was revealed they gave some staffers an extra job: paying them to pose as audience members on opening night, then leave the theater and praise the movie to waiting reporters. For both offenses, Sony got widely slammed in the media—and deservedly so. In the advertising world, it's easy to spin success-fully. The public will believe anything. There's really no need to lie.

Of course, these are exceptions to the rule. Most of the time, manufacturers or salespeople can get away with mak-ing almost any claim for their product. In fact, it often seems that the more outrageous the claim, the greater the spin, the more likely we are to believe it.

The general rule remains: see or hear advertising slogans, think spin. No matter what the line of product. One of the most successful slogans ever was: "Nothing Comes Between Me and My Calvins." Even if most of us were too old-fash-ioned, or too bashful, to wear no underwear under our blue-jeans, the boldness of that claim sent Calvin Klein to the top of the charts. It echoed an earlier, spectacularly successful and daring campaign by the makers of Maidenform bras. Imagine this: "I dreamed I stopped traffic in my Maidenform bra." Millions of women did enjoy the dream, even though they would never think of taking off a blouse and stopping traffic in their bra. Too bad.

Or, how about this one, from the giant Safeway grocery chain: "Since we're neighbors, let's be friends." The spin, of course, is: we may be a huge supermarket, but we'll be just as friendly as your old-fashioned neighborhood, Mom-and-Pop grocery store. Bullshit! We know that's not true. In a Safeway or other giant market, nobody knows your name, you can't find anything, you're forced to wait in long lines to check out and it's impossible to just run in for one item and run out. But we still fall for the spin. We still shop at Safeway.

When I was growing up, my father owned and operated his own Esso gas station, which later changed to Exxon. And I remember how sales soared when Exxon adopted its classic sales pitch: "Put a tiger in your tank." Yes, people actually believed that their old rattletrap of a car—complete with worn tires, dirty spark plugs, clogged filter and hole in the muffler—would pick up and roar like a tiger once they'd poured some of that magic into the gas tank. Silly slogan, silly spin—but great sales.

HIT PARADE OF SPIN

Creation of a successful advertising slogan is the pinnacle of spin. The genius lies in identifying the very essence of a product, its singular appeal—and then expressing that unique quality in a catchy phrase that people will notice, understand, like, repeat and never forget. We might not be able to recite Gerard Manley Hopkins by heart, but every one of us could rattle off the most famous lines of Madison Avenue, even if we never bought the product. Here's a familiar list.

Alka-Seltzer	"Plop, plop. Fizz, fizz . . . I Can't Believe I Ate the Whole Thing."
Allstate Insurance	"You're in Good Hands with Allstate."
American Express	"Don't leave home without it."
AT&T	"Reach Out and Touch Someone."
Avis Rentals	"We're Number Two. We Try Harder."
Barnum & Bailey Circus	"The Greatest Show on Earth."
BVD Underwear	"Next to myself, I Like BVD best."
Campbell's Soup	"Mmmm Good."
Chevrole	"See the USA in a Chevrolet."
Crest	"Look, Ma, no cavities!"
General Electric	"We Bring Good Things to Life."
Kellogg's Rice Krispies	"Snap! Crackle! And pop!"

Kentucky Fried Chicken	"Finger-lickin' Good."
Lay's Potato Chips	"Betcha can't eat just one."
M&M's	"M&M's melt in your mouth, not in your hand."
Maxwell House	"Good to the last drop."
New York Times	"All The News That's Fit to Print."
Texaco	"Trust Your Car to the Man Who Wears the Star."
Timex	"It takes a licking, and keeps on ticking."
United Airlines	"Fly the Friendly Skies."
United Negro College Fund	"A Mind is a Terrible Thing to Waste."
United States Army	"Be All That You Can Be."
Wheaties	"Breakfast of Champions."

Despite all these great slogans, nobody has done a better job of memorable product branding than America's most well-known, most popular and most successful product: Coca-Cola. Coke is the world's best-selling soft-drink. Diet Coke is #3. Coca-Cola owns roughly half of the worldwide market for all soft drinks. In fact, it is so famous worldwide that "Coke" is the planet's second-most recognized expression. Second only to "OK." And it's hard to imagine Santa Claus without a cold bottle of Coke in his hand.

Coca-Cola would be nowhere, of course, without a superior product and its still secret formula. But even so, Coke would still be only a big name in little Atlanta if, from the very beginning, it had not developed lasting brand recognition through powerful slogans—and, of course, bombarded us with those slogans until they are ingrained in our daily language.

Knowing that, in marketing, to stand still is to die an early death, the makers of Coca-Cola change or modify their slogans every year. But, looking back, it is amazing to see what a long shelf life some of their better advertising campaigns have had, and still have. Here's a glimpse at Coca-Cola through the years.

1886	"Drink Coca-Cola"
1910	"It Satisfies."
1920	"Delicious and Refreshing."
1929	"The Pause That Refreshes."
1943	"It's the Real Thing."
1963	"Things Go Better with Coke."
1982	"Coke Is It!"
1993	"Always Coca-Cola."
2001	"Life Tastes Good."

But spin works, not just to sell products as relatively benign as Coca-Cola. With enough creativity, and in the absence of any moral standards, it's even possible to spin cancer as good for you. Cigarette manufacturers didn't hesitate to do so. I never smoked a day in my life, yet one of the earliest and catchiest advertising tunes I remember is: "You get a lot to like in a Marlboro. Filter, flavor, fliptop box." Yeah, sure. All of that and, by the way, lung cancer thrown in for free. Unfortunately, not enough people thought about the possibility of lung cancer. They were lured in by the cigarette's siren song of pleasure and the glamorous photos in the ads.

Others fell for such killer slogans as: "I'd Walk a Mile for a Camel." Or "Winston Tastes Good Like a Cigarette Should." Or "LSMFT: Lucky Strike Means Fine Tobacco."

When all else fails, you can always "Come to Marlboro Country."

But, of course, it was difficult to think about the danger of inhaling when cigarette manufacturers, well aware of the health risks of smoking, spent millions of dollars advertising the health benefits. The makers of Camels not only asked you to walk a mile for one of their cigarettes, they said it would be good for you: "For Digestion's Sake—Smoke Camels." L & M bragged that their cigarettes were "Just What the Doctor Ordered." And the makers of Old Golds dismissed the entire health issue: "We're Tobacco Men . . . Not Medicine Men. Old Gold Cures Just One Thing. The World's Best Tobacco."

If you think cigarette manufacturers have turned over a new leaf, forget it. In the summer of 2001, Philip Morris released a report, prepared by Arthur D. Little International, aimed at rebutting claims that public health costs from smoking illnesses were a financial drain on the Czech Republic. Not so, concluded the report. Just the opposite. When smokers die prematurely, they concluded, the government actually saves money on health care, pensions and housing. Conclusion: the more people who smoke, the more people who die of lung cancer, the more money Czech taxpayers save. Philip Morris apologized and withdrew the report. Why did they release it in the first place?

Speaking of spins on smoking, one of the most memorable commercials appeared way back in the 1950s, for Muriel cigars. A sultry female voice left no doubt about what smoking a Muriel could lead to when she sang: "I'm today's new Muriel, only a dime. Why don't you pick me up and smoke me sometime?" And this was 45 years before Monica Lewinsky and Bill Clinton made use of a cigar as a sex toy famous!

SPINNING FOR WOMEN

Women are the target of most advertising campaigns, and not just to buy home products they don't need. More insidious than that. The object of most marketing drives aimed at women is to con them into thinking they can become the perfect woman they see in the ads—thin, rich, smart, sexy, worldly, sought after and fought after—if only they use the same shampoo, tampon or underarm deodorant. Camay Soap reminds them: "You Are in a Beauty Contest Every Day of Your Life." Virginia Slims cigarettes congratulates them: "You've Come a Long Way, Baby." Clairol Hair Products teases them: "If I've Only One Life, Let Me Live It As a Blonde!" Even Listerine warns them about the first step to take if they ever want to walk all the way down the aisle: "Often a Bridesmaid, But Never a Bride. For Halitosis, Use Listerine."

It's enough to give a young, or grown, woman a complex. She can never be as beautiful or seductive as the women on the TV screen or in the magazine ads, no matter how many Virginia Slims she smokes. The goal is at once irresistible and unattainable. Before she started counseling Al Gore on how he should conform himself to the image of the perfect Alpha male, Naomi Wolf wrote a book on the impact of advertising on women. In *The Beauty Myth,* she compares the image of beauty portrayed in ads to the "Iron Maiden" of the Middle Ages: a spike-filled box, painted like a woman, inside of which victims were strapped and tortured. "Like the Iron Maiden," notes Wolf, "the beauty ideal enforces conformity to a single, rigid shape. And both cause suffering, even death, in their victims."

Of course, what makes the ideal even more impossible to achieve is the fact that none of the models are real. Oh, they're real people, all right. Stunningly beautiful women, in fact. But nowhere near as perfect as they appear in their photos because the photos have been retouched: every blemish, wrinkle, freckle, birthmark or stray hair airbrushed away. In researching their insightful study on this subject, "Sexism and Sexuality in Advertising," Kent State's Michael F. Jacobsen and Laurie Anne Mazur interviewed veteran New York retoucher Louis Grubb. He told them: "Almost every photograph you see for a national advertiser these days has been worked on by a retoucher to some degree. . . . Fundamentally, our job is to correct the basic deficiencies in the original photograph or, in effect, to improve upon the appearance of reality." Jacobsen and Mazur put the icing on the cake: "In some cases, a picture is actually an amalgam of body parts of several different models: a mouth from this one, arms from that one, and legs from a third."

Even with retouching, most models burn out by the time they're thirty. Carmen Dell'Orefice is the one, great exception. As this book was written, she was still sought out for ads, having just celebrated her seventieth birthday! She is not only the most long-lived model working today, she may also be the most honest, more than willing to puncture the mythology of the perfect woman she portrays in the magazine ads. "People shouldn't look at me and think life is one big piece of glamour," she told the *New York Times*'s Alex Witchel. "That's the marketing, the spin."

Nonetheless, the sad fact is that the advertising spin of drop-dead glamour for the asking is so successful it not only convinces millions of women to buy beauty products—$8 billion a year in the United States on cosmetics alone—it drives many of them into taking unnecessary risks with their bodies: $33 billion spent annually on weight loss products in 2000; $15 billion on cosmetic surgery.

Until fairly recently, women alone were under siege. Men were thought to be oblivious to such silliness, until some smart advertiser figured out that men were every bit as vain as women. Hence today's cascade of advertising campaigns and magazines like *GQ*, *Men's Health* and *Esquire*, devoted to projecting the ideal male image: rich, successful, tan, creased, buff, sexy, and surrounded by beautiful women. And, did we mention, with a full head of hair? Rogaine makes no secret of what it's all about: "Don't You Think She Wants You to Have Hair?" It's all an extension of those early Charles Atlas ads: "You Too Can Have a Body Like Mine."

ICONS OF SPIN

Some advertising campaigns have been so successful that the mythical figure portrayed in the ads has been adopted as an honorary American citizen. Everybody knows who they are and what they stand for. Just mention their name and the spin kicks in from memory. They augment and personalize the verbal spin of ads and slogans. They become, in fact, the embodiment of spin. For a walk down advertising memory lane, check out the the Museum of Advertising Icons's Web site at toymuseum.com. Procter & Gamble's "Mr. Clean" may have been the first. The more recognizable ones today all have to do with food.

- **Ronald McDonald.** The best known of all. So famous he was invited to march in Macy's Thanksgiving Day Parade. Recognized by a scary 96% of American children. If only their parents had read Eric Schlosser's *Fast Food Nation,* Ronald and his fast-food dispenser might not be so popular. But that's another story.
- **The Colonel.** There is no connection between fried chicken and a dignified old Southern gentleman in white suit, black string tie, white goatee and black cane. At least, there was none before we were bombarded with millions of dollars in very clever advertising. Today we all know that Colonel Sanders, modeled after KFC founder Harland Sanders, stands for finger lickin' good breasts and thighs. All we have to do is see his picture and our stomach starts growling.
- **Bob's Big Boy.** According to the legend, which is itself probably just spin, Bob Wian was trying to figure out how to publicize his family restaurant—Bob's Pantry in Glendale, California—when a fat little boy in red suspenders walked in with his parents. Voilà! The perfect symbol. Bring your kids to Bob's Big Boy and they'll all walk out looking as fat and happy as. . . . Bob's Big Boy.
- **The California Raisins.** I know what you're thinking: Only

in California! But, still, you gotta love it. The dancin', soul-singin' California raisins became a national sensation: making a dried-up old fruit a lot more exciting and boosting sales of raisins and Post's Raisin Bran Cereal.

And don't forget the Jolly Green Giant, Tony the Tiger and Spuds McKenzie. The list goes on and on.

SPINNING STOCKS AND BONDS

When we think of advertising spin, we automatically think of selling bars of soap, soft drinks, cigarettes, cosmetics, shampoos and other personal products. Ways to make us spend our money. But spin is also employed as an enticement to invest our money.

In fact, with so many Americans owning stock today and taking a more active interest in managing their own money, the vortex of commercial spin must be the kingdom of financial institutions: firms like Charles Schwab, Merrill Lynch, and Bear-Stearns—all competing for the same dollar by promising to turn that dollar into multiple dollars through sound investment strategy. They will never guarantee an instant profit—that would be illegal—but they come as close as they can. Even the mighty *Wall Street Journal* offers itself as the instant cure to your stock portfolio blues. "The Benefits of the Journal Begin Immediately" boast subscription ads. In other words, just read the *Journal* and watch your stocks soar. If only it were that simple.

Of course, we no longer have to depend on the *Journal* as the principal source of information about the market. It merely reports on yesterday's gains and losses. That's too late to act or react. Far better to track the market's moves as they happen: on CNBC, CNNfn, Bloomberg Financial Services or the Internet. Or stopping by your local brokerage office. With all that instant information, it should be easy for individual investors to make smart decisions. Right? Wrong! No matter how much chatter they hear, they still can't be sure how to respond because Wall Street professionals speak in a language all their own which is purposely designed to confuse the public.

In his *Journal* column, "Getting Going," Jonathan Clements often writes about the special lingo of Wall Street, which he has dubbed "Street-Speak." He could just as well have called it "Street-Spin," for that's just what it is. The problem for average investors, Clements points out, is that "professional and amateur investors don't always say what they really mean." In other words, they spin. To help people like you and me navigate the DOW rapids, Clements and a few expert friends have put together a glossary of Wall Street spin, complete with translation. Here are a few examples, every one of which you have heard from some investment house bullshitter on television:

Spin: "We're cautiously optimistic."
Translation: "We can't figure out what's going on."

Spin: "The bull market remains intact."
Translation: "Stock prices have been sliding for a month, but we are pretending to be long-term investors."

Spin: "You've got to be selective here."
Translation: "The market is down 15% and falling fast, but we have deluded ourselves into thinking we can still make money."

Spin: "It's a market of stocks, not a stock market."
Translation: "Sure, most of our holdings have been creamed, but we do have this one winning stock, which we boast about endlessly."

Spin: "We believe there's a support level at 9000 on the Dow."
Translation: "We're praying stocks don't fall farther than that."

Spin: "We always knew it was a bubble."

Translation: "Why, oh why didn't we sell our stocks a year ago?"

Spin: "We're getting close to a bottom."
Translation: "Panic!"

Only rarely do you meet the honest broker like William Dudley, director of domestic economic research at Goldman Sachs. When government figures showed unemployment rising in July 2001 to 4.5 percent, creating even more uncertainty in an already uncertain market, Dudley told *Newsweek:* "You cannot spin this report to make it sound positive; there is nothing positive about it." Hear, hear!

Another problem individual investors have in seeing through the Wall Street spin is that analysts hide their own financial connections to companies they comment on or recommend to investors. There's a good reason why, according to *First Call,* only 1 percent of 28,000 stock recommendations in 2000 were calls to "sell." The reason is that analysts themselves had invested heavily in dot.com stocks and didn't want anyone to abandon their favorite holdings. So, they gave artificially optimistic reports, enthusiastic even, hoping against hope as long as they could—and thereby deliberately deceiving unwitting investors who counted on them for the straight skinny. That problem may be solved by a recommendation of the National Association of Securities Dealers that analysts be required to disclose their ownership in companies before giving advice to buy or sell. Merrill Lynch has gone even further: barring its 600 stock analysts from buying shares of companies they cover.

THE PIONEERS OF SPIN

As Mark Hanna was the father of political spin, so there are those who are revered as the pioneers of advertising spin. Two deserve particular credit.

You probably never heard of Rosser Reeves. I never had, until I read Garry Wills's book *Reagan's America.* But he is a man who had a great influence on Ronald Reagan—and continues to have a huge impact on your life and mine through the advertising messages we are bombarded with from all sides, many times every day.

Reeves came up with the basic, but powerful, concept of the "Unique Selling Proposition" or USP: *What is the single strongest claim that can be made for this product in terms of its desirability?*

In searching for that unique identity, Reeves cautions in his book *Reality in Advertising,* it is important to remember that the USP must be true, though it need not be the whole truth or a truth specific to the product of which it is asserted. Or, as we would say today, it must be somewhat true, but not necessarily entirely true. It must be good spin.

Once the USP is found, the advertiser must never tire of repeating it, or lose faith in its efficacy, simply because he has become bored with it. "A great campaign will never wear itself out," preaches Reeves. Now you know why Reeves became famous for repeatedly delivering the same speech. Now you know where Reagan learned the same trick. Now you know why we hear the same commercials and the same slogans, over and over again. Blame it on Rosser Reeves.

Here's the key. The USP will gain "penetration," Reeves demonstrated, as long as it is simple to understand and is repeated early and often. This is true, even if it makes a claim that competing products could also legitimately claim. In their case, it will be too late; your product will have already preempted the field. In his book, Reeves talks about Listerine as an example.

"Who can steal "STOP HALITOSIS" from Listerine? Dozens of other mouthwashes stop halitosis. Many tried to move in on this great classic USP until it became almost a source of embarrassment to them, seeking ways to phrase their imitation, so that they did not advertise the leader. This USP, in the public's mind, belongs to Listerine."

Unique selling proposition: Doesn't that sound like a political campaign? Is it any wonder that Rosser Reeves went from Listerine to politics, creating the first television commercials for Dwight D. Eisenhower in 1952.

But if Rosser Reeves was the prince of puffery, Edward Bernays was the king. He's even memorialized as *The Father of Spin* in Larry Tye's biography, published in 1998. Generally recognized as the man who invented today's world of public relations, Bernays excelled in creating and promoting the images of both products and people, especially his own. And he did so with flair.

To knock down the taboo against women smoking, he organized ten fashionable ladies to march up Fifth Avenue on Easter Sunday, as part of New York's Easter Parade, while conspicuously puffing their "Torches of Freedom"—and so was born the women's liberation movement. Over cigarettes! To conquer kids' dislike for soap, he convinced Proctor & Gamble to sponsor a National Soap Sculpture Contest. One million bars of soap a year were carved into swans, ducks, flowers, faces and other sudsy features. To promote the Russian ballet, he persuaded the lead female dancer to pose for photographs at the Bronx Zoo with a live boa coiled around her. To generate enthusiasm about electricity in the home, he mounted a worldwide celebration of the fiftieth anniversary of the invention of the light bulb called "Light's Golden Jubilee"—secretly paid for by General Electric. And, in perhaps his greatest challenge, to spice up the image of dour Calvin Coolidge in the 1924 presidential campaign, he brought Al Jolson and forty other Broadway artists to perform at the White House.

In 1930, Bernays was hired by Simon & Schuster and other major publishers with the goal of getting people to buy more books. He rejected the notion of promoting individual books. He decided to promote reading, instead. There followed a classic Bernays campaign. He recruited prominent celebrities to endorse the value of reading for civilization. Then he enlisted the help of professional organizations of architects, contractors and decorators: persuading them to design and build bookshelves in all new homes. To Bernays, the goal was simple:

"Where there are bookshelves, there will be books." It worked. Book sales shot up. It still works. Who can look at empty shelves today without filling them up with books?

Bernays also pioneered the art of promoting war—by associating it with a worthy cause and giving it a noble name. He came to the aid of President Woodrow Wilson, mobilizing support for World War I by packaging the war under the slogan "Make the World Safe for Democracy." It's a public relations tactic used in every war by every president since: right down to the first George Bush's "Desert Storm"; Bill Clinton's "Desert Fox"—which, because it just so happened to occur in the middle of the Lewinsky scandal—was also dubbed "Operation Wag the Dog"; and the second George Bush's at-first awkwardly named "Operation Infinite Justice," for the response to the terrorist attacks of September 2001.

There is little difference between public relations and propaganda, Bernays argued. "Intelligent men must realize that propaganda is the modern instrument by which they can fight for productive ends and help to bring order out of chaos." Ironically, Josef Goebbels later adopted Bernays's propaganda theories and applied them to the rise of Hitler's Nazi Germany.

However, it was not just for his clever public relations campaigns, or his government propaganda, that Bernays is most celebrated as a pioneer spinmeister. His genius lay in recognizing that the publicist's mission—get this!—was not to change the product to fit the customer, but to change the customer to fit the product. This was not something Bernays learned in school. It was in his blood. He was the nephew of Sigmund Freud. And, like "Uncle Sigi," Bernays knew that the secret to influencing people's behavior was to get inside their minds and dreams. Once he did so, he was able to mount public relations campaigns that today would be considered diabolical.

For example, when Lucky Strike realized it was losing women smokers because its then red and green package clashed with most women's clothes, Bernays didn't advise Luckies to change their colors (they did, much later, switch to red and white)—he set out to make green the color of choice. He sponsored a "green" charity ball. He persuaded fashion designers to include green accessories in their new lines. He planted newspaper stories calling green chic. And, lo and behold, suddenly green was in. And so were Lucky Strikes. Cigarettes and clothing color-coordinated. How cute.

The "green" campaign illustrates one of Bernays's most important insights: that sometimes the best way to sell one thing is actually to sell another. That's how he had such success selling bananas. Yes, bananas! Hard to believe today, perhaps, but it wasn't long ago that bananas weren't so popular. They looked weird, they didn't taste all that special, and it was impossible to grow them in the United States. That's when Bernays went to work selling the lowly banana. First, he promoted it as the peerless remedy for indigestion. Then, he spun eating a banana as a patriotic duty—because United Fruit freighters carrying bananas from Guatemala were also standby ships in case the country ever went to war. He didn't sell bananas, he sold patriotism. Got the message? Love your country, eat a banana, keep the ships afloat! When Guatemalan president Jacobo Arbenz Guzman began cracking down on United Fruit in the early 1950s, Bernays escalated the banana wars. He helped brand Guzman as a communist, turning American public opinion against him and paving the way for the CIA-sponsored coup that drove him from office. If there were ever any doubt, the powerful spinmeister demonstrated to the world the ultimate power of spin.

WE SPIN TOO MUCH

What's curious is that, despite all the constant onslaught of commercial advertising—on radio and television, in newspapers and magazines, on billboards, bus stops, subway station walls and banners pulled behind small planes—nobody seems to care about what is really exploitation of the masses and a gross invasion of privacy, not to mention an insult to our intelligence. Indeed, the American people not only accept

the mighty spin of advertisers without complaint, they seem
to consider it a public service. The only serious complaints
about advertising techniques have come, not from outside
the industry, but from inside.

In 1964, a disgruntled group of professionals calling
themselves "Adbusters" first surfaced. They published a
manifesto, "First Things First," asking colleagues to
protest the pressure on them as writers, designers and photographers to join the mass advertising fraternity's efforts
to sell cat food, deodorants and fizzy water, despite its obvious lucrative opportunities. There were more important
causes on which they should be devoting their time and en-
ergies, said organizers. In all, twenty-two brave souls
signed up.

But some people never give up. Adbusters resurfaced in
2000. In their second manifesto, the message is the same: beware those who recommend advertising as the most lucrative, effective and desirable use of their talents. Following the
herd, they argue, will result in a life spent in well-paid, but
meaningless, work. "Encouraged in this direction, designers
then apply their skill and imagination to sell dog biscuits, de-
signer coffee, diamonds, detergents, hair gel, cigarettes,
credit cards, sneakers, butt toners, light beer and heavy-duty
recreational vehicles. . . . The profession's time and energy is
used up manufacturing demand for things that are inessential
at best."

Devoting one's lifetime to inventing spin to sell products,
say Adbusters, is not only bad for the individual professional, it's bad for society because it reinforces the emphasis
on acquisition as a sign of success. He who dies with the
most toys, wins. And it reduces language to a collection of
slogans. In the words of the manifesto: "Designers who devote their efforts primarily to advertising, marketing and
brand development are supporting, and implicitly endorsing,
a mental environment so saturated with commercial messages that it is changing the very way citizen-consumers
speak, think, feel, respond and interact. To some extent we

are all helping draft a reductive and immeasurably harmful code of public discourse."

Once again, Adbusters are calling on writers, photographers and designers to boycott product advertising and employ their talents for more noble causes. That in itself is a noble cause. But it is also a hopeless one. They will never persuade professionals to abandon advertising spin, because we consumers are too gullible. We will fall for their spin every time. And, as long as we do, they will keep on spinning. In the immortal words of Lay's Doritos: "Crunch All You Want, We'll Make More."

RETAIL SPIN

If wholesale commercial spin is bad, retail is even worse. Harness all the energy of mass advertising into one laser beam and focus it on one product and one individual—and that's the intensity of spin you and I feel from every merchant, car salesman, or telephone pitchman we encounter. "Buy it, you need it. But even if you don't need it, you'll like it."

I love to shop. Outside of sex, nothing makes me feel better, in fact, than spending money. After all, I earned it. I deserve it. And there's nobody better to spend money on than myself. But, personally, I much prefer anonymous shopping. I'm ready to walk out of a store the moment anybody says: "Can I help you find something?" I even resent it when they say "Good morning!" I don't want to be seen, spoken to, pitched or pinched until I've found what I want—all by myself, thank you—and walked up to the cash register to pay for it. Then, of course, I want to be helped out the door as fast as possible.

And I'm not alone. That, I believe, explains the appeal of those cavernous, ugly, god-awful, impersonal warehouse stores like Costco. It's not just that you can find everything from groceries to hardware to books to prescription drugs all under one roof. The best part is, you're left to roam around, even get lost, all on your own. Hell, you couldn't find a salesperson if you had a snack attack. But that's what people want. They don't want to be spun while shopping.

The only thing better than the superstores is online shopping. Sure, it's convenient. No need to leave the house. No need to get dressed. You can even shop naked. But the best part is: you find the Web site, you select the item, you make the choice, you order, you pay—and you never talk to another human being, never suffer through one more sales pitch. Oh, happy shopping!

There's a good reason most people prefer silent shopping. It's not just that we don't want to be bothered while participating in such a self-fulfilling activity as spending money. It's also that we know we're weak. We know that, if spun, we'll give in. So we go out of our way to avoid temptation.

Of course, salespersons know that, too, after centuries of playing us for suckers. So they woo us like the expert spinmeisters they are, using all the tricks of the trade.

MY FAVORITE SPIN

After sex and shopping, I like eating out the most. Just something I enjoy about being with friends in a good restaurant, surrounded by happy people, no cell phones and no cigarettes. And, almost every time I'm out in a restaurant, I see someone fall for the waiter's classic spin. The conversation goes something like this.

Customer: "Do you think I should have the ravioli [$15] or the swordfish [$28]?

Waiter: "Well, it's up to you. But the ravioli we offer every day, while the swordfish was flown in special this morning from Norway and there are only three servings left. It's delicious."

Customer: "I'll have the swordfish."
  Waiter: "Excellent choice! It's my favorite dish on the
            entire menu."

I'm always tempted to shout: "Bullshit!" Better yet, I want to follow the waiter around to other tables throughout the evening to see how many other (more expensive) dishes he identifies as his "favorite dish." Of course, he'll use the same tactic to convince us to buy a more expensive bottle of wine.

On a much larger scale, personal endorsement is a trademark of talk-radio hosts. Have you ever noticed how often, in pitching products, they'll toss in a little secret: this is the car I drive, the mattress I sleep on or the cruise my wife and I went on for our honeymoon? Don't believe it. It's all spin. I'll tell you another little secret: they're paid to say that, even though it's not true, because the sponsor knows you'll be impressed—and run out and buy the same product. You can wear the same brand of underwear Rush Limbaugh does. Big deal.

I love talk radio. I still work as talk-radio host from time to time, filling in for megastar Ronn Owens on KGO Radio in San Francisco. But I'll never forget my first encounter with the personal pitch, many years ago, on a Los Angeles station. It was the middle of the night. I was sitting in for a vacationing host on the graveyard shift, taking calls and reading commercials. In the middle of one, I found myself routinely reading: "This is the same mattress my wife and I sleep on. . . ." when I stopped. I couldn't continue. I mumbled something like: "No, we don't. I'm just filling in tonight. This must have been written for somebody else." Ever since, I have carefully read ad copy *before* reading it to make sure I'm not offering some phony personal endorsement. Frankly, even if they do own the product, I don't believe talk-show hosts should be giving personal endorsements. In so doing, I think they damage their credibility. They should stick to being a good talk-show host, not a slick huckster.

THE PICK-UP-YOUR-PRIZE SPIN

This is one of the oldest tricks in the books, but it must still be working because shysters are still using it. You've probably experienced it yourself. Here's the spin: Congratulations! You're the lucky winner of $100 in top quality merchandise at Mrs. Mayberry's. To redeem your prize, all you have to do is buy at least $2000 worth of products in the next 12 months, then we'll give you a coupon worth $100 off your next purchase. Get it? Spend $2000, save $100. Great prize.

It happened to me, not long ago. I called AOL's service line to get advice on a computer problem. The problem was easily and readily fixed, whereupon the technician said: "As a reward for calling our service line today, we're going to give you $25 free. Hold on for details." Before I could say "You've got mail!," a pitchman was on the line explaining that all I had to do to get my "free" $25 bucks was to sign up for AOL's online shopping mart, first three months free, after which I would, of course, have to pay a monthly premium for the privilege of shopping there—but I could cancel at any time.

No deal. If you're going to give me a present as a valued customer, give it to me flat out, no strings attached. Don't make me buy it. Don't spin it as a gift.

THE LOOK-AT-ALL-THE-MONEY-YOU-SAVE! SPIN

A related spin, favored by new car dealers, is to advertise big bucks—$1000, $1500, $2000, you name it—off the purchase price of a new car. Buy a new Chevy today and we will take $2000 right off the top!

How can you resist? Easily, one would hope. Isn't it obvious? All they do is jack up the list price, then pretend to lop off $2000. You don't save a dime. In fact—here's the value of the spin—lured by the promise of saving two grand, you'll probably end up spending more on that new car than you planned to.

It's like the old joke about the woman who comes home wearing a new fur coat and tells her husband she just saved $5000. The coat cost $15,000, understand, but she got it on sale for $10,000. Warning: Don't try it. I have, as justification for spending obscene amounts of money on rare books—on sale, of course. "Look at all the money I saved," I told Carol. She wasn't impressed.

THE OL' BAIT AND SWITCH

That's not the only spin salespeople use. There's also the "This low price is available only until midnight, so it's now or never" line—which gives you no opportunity to go out and comparison shop. Or the related: "This is the very last one. There will never be another [boat, house, car, plane, toaster, computer or electric shaver] like it on the market." Meaning, if you believe the spin, you will either buy it now or die a loser.

But the most transparent gimmick may be the old bait and switch. You see an ad for a great new wraparound sound system at an unbelievably low price. You shlep over to the music store, only to be informed that (a) the last model available at that price just walked out the door, as you were walking in; and, besides, (b) even though it was a great bargain, there were lots of features lacking in that system. You'd be much better off buying this other, more expensive system—which, of course, they just happen to have plenty of in stock.

The same snake tactic works for any product. Real estate, too, for example. I have never bought a house yet without buying a more expensive one than I originally intended. Funny how a good salesperson can spin any product to make you spend more money and still feel good about it.

THE GOING-OUT-OF-BUSINESS SPIN

Nothing subtle here. Big banner across the front of the store: "GOING OUT OF BUSINESS. ALL ITEMS MUST GO!" It's so phony. Just for the hell of it, keep track of the next "going out of business" sale you come across. Notice how many weeks, months or years later the same store is still there, with the same sign and the same spin.

Years ago, when I was living in San Francisco and working in Marin County, there was an Oriental rug store off Highway 101, at the southern entrance to Mill Valley, that was never in business. It was always going out of business. Luring customers in with promises of give-away prices since their doors would be closing any minute. Twenty-five years later, I'll bet it's still going out of business.

THE WONDERMAN OF SPIN

While Rosser Reeves and Edward Bernays were the pioneers of wholesale commercial spin, retail spin also has its founding father: Lester Wunderman. As Malcolm Gladwell relates in *The Spin Myth*, if Bernays was the father of "Big Think," then Wunderman was the father of "Little Think—the small but significant details that turn a shopper into a buyer."

Want to know one of my pet peeves? Those pain-in-the-ass subscription cards inserted in every magazine. I don't just dislike them, I *hate* them. They either fall out or stick out of every magazine I open, and I read nine or ten magazines a week. In fact—call me obsessive, I don't care—I can't even read a magazine without first flipping through, pulling or tearing out all the subscription cards, and throwing them away. Every time I do, I curse Lester Wunderman. He was the first to come up with the idea of stuffing subscription cards in magazines; and first to sell magazines on late-night television with an 800-number (so-called "per inquiry" commercials you see all over cable television, whereby how much advertisers have to pay the station depends on how many responses they get to their ad). Wunderman was also the first to use scratch-'n'-sniff ads; and first to persuade newspapers to insert special advertising sections in their Sunday editions—a curse we still suffer today.

Wunderman also raised the "pick up your prize" art of

salesmanship to new heights. Assigned to build up membership in the Columbia Record Club, he first convinced the company to offer subscriptions—where else?—in tear-out cards inserted in popular magazines. Next he sweetened the deal: buy four records and choose three free records from a selection of twelve. Membership soared to one million. Then he sweetened it even further: choose three free from a selection of thirty-two. The membership doubled. It's a tactic still used today by book and record clubs because people still respond when they think they're getting something for nothing.

THE BOTTOM LINE OF SPIN

The bottom line is that spin is what drives the world of advertising and sales. In many subtle and not-so-subtle ways we are persuaded to buy a certain brand of necessary products—and to fill our homes with piles of ever more expensive, unnecessary ones. The spin can be misleading or confusing. Sometimes it can even be helpful. But, once again, it's up to us to sort it all out and make an intelligent decision.

We are capable of doing that, but only—caveat emptor—if we don't take the spin at face value. As in politics, it's our task to look through the spin and try to find the truth lurking behind it. That's important when we vote, but even more important when we're spending our own money. We must turn on our spin detectors before spending a buck. Remember the immortal words of Yogi Berra: "A nickel ain't worth a dime anymore."

Even then, there's no relief. Buying and selling is just one of the many ways spin fills and colors every hour of our every day.

TEN

EVERYDAY PEOPLE, EVERYDAY SPIN

GIVE US THIS DAY OUR DAILY SPIN

6:30 A.M.   Alarm goes off, hit snooze button.
Spin: "Just nine more minutes, that's all I need."
Truth: I can't stand one more day at that goddamned job.

7:30 A.M.   Finally roll out of bed, quick shower, kiss your wife good-bye.
Spin: "Have a nice day, sweetheart. I'll hurry home to help get ready for the kids' big party."
Truth: What bad breath she has in the morning. I can't believe you invited over all those unruly kids.

7:32 A.M.   Backing out of driveway, spot neighbor watering his lawn.
Spin: "Hi, Ed. How ya doin'? Looks like a great day."

Truth: I hate that asshole. Why doesn't he get a job?

8:30 A.M. Arrive half-hour late for work.
Spin: "Sorry to be late, but traffic was really tied up on the freeway."
Truth: Good thing there were no accidents this morning, I wouldn't be here for another half-hour.

9:20 A.M. Run into boss, who wants progress report.
Spin: "I was just going to call you. It's almost finished."
Truth: Shit! I'd better get started.

9:30–Noon Burrow yourself in your cubicle.
Spin: "Just what I need. Two and a half hours of uninterrupted worktime."
Truth: After reading the *New York Times* online, answering my e-mail, playing Solitaire, checking out the market and trying to find a discount airline ticket for Thanksgiving, I can't believe it's already time for lunch.

12:15 P.M. Reminded of monthly brown-bag staff lunch.
Spin: "Sorry I can't make it. I have an important lunch date downtown."
Truth: Finally a chance to swing by the golf center and try out that new Rescue club.

5:30 P.M. Invited to join gang for drink after work.
Spin: "OK, but just one quick one, because I'm due home to help with my kids' party tonight."
Truth: Any excuse will do.

5:31 P.M.   Call home.
Spin: "Honey, wouldn't you know it? Tonight, of all nights, I have to work late. I'll be home as soon as I can."
Truth: Whew!

9:00 P.M.   Arrives home.
Spin: "Oh, no! Everybody's already gone home and the kitchen's already cleaned up?"
Truth: Perfect timing!

9:05 P.M.   Collapse into favorite armchair.
Spin: "I brought a lot of paperwork home I need to look over."
Truth: Zzzzzzzzzzzzz.

10:30 P.M.   Crawl into bed.
Spin: "Good night, sweetheart. I love you."
Truth?

Politics, law, advertising, sales, media—if you've stuck with us so far, you're no doubt breathing a sigh of relief. At least I'm not one of them, you think. I'm not in a spinning profession. I'm not one of the spinning class.

Wrong! The world is not divided into spinners and non-spinners. Spin isn't restricted to any one profession or calling. In some way—whether tennis pro, CEO, bank teller or bus driver—we all spin. The spin is always with us. From daybreak to sunset, spin gets us through the day. Whether we're spinning ourselves, our family, our co-workers or friends, we're spinning all day long. There are many times we spin to get ourselves out of a jam, to avoid embarrassment, or simply to shade the truth.

Here are a few of the more common ways and places we may find ourselves spinning.

FAMILY VALUES

> O, *what a tangled web we weave,*
> *when first we practice to deceive.*
> —*Sir Walter Scott*

Okay, let's start with the premise that husbands and wives, parents and kids—family members all—we all love each other. But that doesn't mean you always tell them the truth, the whole truth and nothing but the truth. Sometimes you don't want to, you shouldn't or you can't. At the same time, you don't want to lie. So, you spin.

Let's start with parents. One of the first examples of spin I remember—don't we all?—is my father, yardstick in hand, prefacing my spanking with the classic cop-out: "This is going to hurt me more than it hurts you." Yeah, sure, Dad. Spin away.

What good Mom or Dad always tells kids the unvarnished truth? There are some things kids don't need to know—yet. There are other things kids should do without having to be told all the complicated reasons why. So parents resort to harmless, age-old nostrums.

Here are a few I remember from my own childhood.

- It's important to eat your carrots because "carrots improve your eyesight." After all, my father used to ask us kids: Did you ever see a rabbit with glasses?
- When eating watermelon, it's important to spit out the seeds. Otherwise, "a watermelon might grow in your stomach." For the longest time, when I saw a pregnant woman, I thought she'd swallowed a watermelon seed. I certainly didn't want to look like her!
- And what enabled us to survive those long rides in the car except the solemn reassurance of my father that "we're almost there." One hour later, we were still "almost there." It's a wonder, come to think of it, that his nose didn't grow—like mine would, if I ever told a lie.

- And, of course, no little boy ever played with his penis again after being warned that "if you keep playing with it, it will fall off."

There were also incentives to be good little boys and girls. It wasn't a good idea to try to get away with anything because, even if we thought we got away with it, we couldn't fool Santa. He sees all, he's keeping a list, he knows who's been naughty—and he'll punish the bad ones on Christmas Eve. We shouldn't worry about getting credit for doing good things, either, because "no good deed goes unrewarded." Someday, we'll get our reward. (I'm still waiting.) And, of course, the main reason for eating our peas, finishing our homework and cutting the grass was that every boy and girl in America has an equal chance to grow up and become president of the United States. (But an even better chance if your last name is Bush or if you're a multimillionaire or famous actor.)

See what I mean? They're not exactly lies. But they're not the truth, either. They're somewhere in between. They're spin.

The one I remember best was about swimming. My extended family—including my own parents, brothers and sisters, grandparents, aunts, uncles and all the cousins—used to spend almost the entire summer at the beach in what was then Fenwick Island, Maryland (now part of Ocean City). As kids, we wanted to be in the ocean every hour of the day—which, in the days before professional lifeguards protected that stretch of beach, meant that one or two of the grown-ups had to stand by the water's edge and keep an eye on us. There was one rule that nobody dared violate: after eating, we were told, we had to wait one full hour before going back into the water, or else we would get cramps and sink to the bottom. I still remember that gang of us cousins, after wolfing down peanut butter and jelly sandwiches for lunch, huddled on the beach blanket, checking our watches every couple of minutes, true believers, waiting impatiently for that seemingly interminable hour to pass. It wasn't until years later that I realized it was all spin. There was no danger of drowning by not waiting an hour before returning to the water. Why an hour? Why not thirty-nine minutes? Are our bodies as carefully calibrated as oven timers? The whole story was nothing but a ruse to give our parents, aunts and uncles a lunchtime break. I don't blame them.

And, of course, how often were we told that we simply had to put up with that slap on the behind, that home confinement or that lack of allowance for two weeks because "it was for our own good"? Two things for sure: all kids fall for the spin. And, when they grow up, they'll use the same spin on their own kids.

But kids don't wait till they grow up to spin. Following our good example, they start to spin early. Parents beware! "I don't feel good" may be nothing but spin for "I don't feel like going to school today." Did she finish her homework? "Yes, it's finished" could be spin for "I've finished as much as I want to. I'll scribble the rest in the bus on the way to school tomorrow morning." Then there are all the ways to hide, or explain away, a lousy report card. And how about the creative stories kids come up with when they've broken something and are afraid to admit it?

At the same time, why should we be surprised how well kids spin at such an early age? They learned it from us. They knew what was going on when they heard their father say: "I really don't feel like going to that stupid cocktail party tonight. I think I'll just call and tell them we're both sick." They were listening when he told an obnoxious friend: "Oh, I'm sorry I didn't return your call. I never even got your message. This damned answering machine keeps skipping messages." And they were proud to be recruited as spinners-in-crime when their mother asked: "Oh, honey, there's someone at the door. Please tell them I'm in the shower and can't come to the door." The apple doesn't fall . . .

Talking about kids spinning parents reminds me of the classic film *A Christmas Story*. Remember? Mommy and

Daddy constantly tell their son he can't have a BB gun because he might shoot his eye out. Finally they give in and get him the gun from Santa. And, sure enough, Christmas morning, he almost shoots his eye out. He runs back into the house and tells his parents he got stuck with an icicle.

Clever, these little gremlins. And wait till they start dating. "Mom, don't be silly. He's just a friend" could mean anything from first base to third base. "Yes, we were in the bar, but we weren't drinking beer." How many times did George and Laura Bush hear that one from daughter Jenna? With kids, like politicians, you always have to read between the lines. And even then you can't be sure.

SPIN HALL OF FAME NOMINATION

By Tucker Carlson

NOMINEE: Joe Carollo, mayor of Miami

OCCASION: In February of 2001, Carollo was arrested for spousal abuse. During an argument in their kitchen, Carollo threw a terra cotta tea container at his wife's head, striking her and leaving a lump the size of a golf ball. The couple's ten-year-old daughter called 911. "My dad is hurting my mom," the girl cried. "Please come." Carollo went to jail. Once he got out, he held a press conference to offer the explanation above.

SPIN: "I love this city so much that I worked tirelessly, I worked day and night to save it from financial ruin, to root out corruption and to reignite international

investment in our great city. My commitment and dedication to the city has
come at unbelievable and personal
cost. The biggest cost being my marriage, and my family."

TRANSLATION: "Sometimes you love a city so much
you have to beat your wife."

Tucker Carlson is co-host of CNN's Crossfire *and former co-host of* The Spin Room.

The relationship between husband and wife is so close, you might think it would be spin-free. Not at all. Husbands still spin their wives; and wives, their husbands. Every day. And both fall for it.

"You know, sweetheart, you don't look a day older than when we got married." Such spin! But what wife doesn't want to hear it? Of course, one good turn deserves another, so she hurries to assure him: "Don't be silly, honey, nobody notices you have a bald spot." If he's really lucky, she might even add: "You still look very trim for your age. I can't even tell you've gained any weight." Unlike my wife, Carol, who bluntly told me, one morning: "Bill, you're getting too fat!" I immediately started the Atkins diet.

Then there are always the old standbys. He knows he can't lose with: "This meal is delicious!" or "I love that new dress." or "I'm so happy that your mother, your brother and his wife, both sisters and their husbands and all their kids are coming for Thanksgiving again this year." She evens the score with "Of course, I don't mind if you go out with the boys again tonight. Have a good time."

A healthy supply of spin is necessary for any successful marriage or relationship. If couples always told the naked truth, the divorce rate would double. But marriage is not the most sacred temple of spin. There's also religion.

SPIN HALL OF FAME NOMINATION

By Mary Matalin

NOMINEE: James Carville

OCCASION: Speech to Missouri Democratic Party on July 18, 2001

SPIN: "We are the party that brought America together. They are the party that rips it apart. . . . They didn't even want to count the votes in Florida."

TRANSLATION: George W. Bush is in the White House. Al Gore lost Tennessee and West Virginia. He blew this election. But we'll never admit it—we'll just keep living in denial and whining about Florida.

Mary Matalin is Assistant to the President, Counselor to Vice President Dick Cheney, and former cohost of Crossfire. *She has never even met James Carville.*

FAITH OF OUR FATHERS

Say what you will about the Ten Commandments, you must always come back to the pleasant fact that there are only ten of them.

—H. L. Mencken

Religion plays an important role in the lives of most Americans. And religion is also a great repository of spin. It is hard to generalize here, because there are so many different faiths. But they all share a basic set of beliefs: There must be something more than this. This human life is too painful to be all there is. What makes it all worthwhile is the divine dimension to life. We are created by God. The same eternal God who taught us right from wrong, and watches over us here below. And the same loving and forgiving God who, based on how well we do, will welcome us to an eternal life of bliss or condemn us to the eternal pain of roasting in hell.

For starters, the nonbeliever would say this is all spin. That may be the case, but it sure has worked for a long time. Having been raised a Catholic and received a degree in theology, I've struggled with these issues my whole life. I don't think it's all spin, even though an awful lot of it is. But I do know this: it's more difficult to separate spin from nonspin in religion than in any other field because, in questioning any religious creed, you are easily branded a heretic or atheist— and, besides, if you're wrong, lightning will strike you dead on the spot. Nevertheless, onward Christian soldiers!

There is so much spin in religion, in fact, that every brand of religion has its own official category of spinmeisters. Whether they are called priest, minister, ayatollah, nun or rabbi, they are ordained to spin. The Catholic Church even honors a High Priest, or Pope—which raises the interesting possibility, and reality, of Papal Spin.

One of their more frequent assignments is spinning death. This is never a problem when the person has lived a long time. It's easy to celebrate the end of a good life, extolling the person's few virtues, while ignoring his many vices. But what happens when a tragic accident or illness kills a child, a parent with young kids or a person in their most active and productive years? That's when the official spinmeister falls back on the basic spin. This is all part of God's plan. We can't understand it. We can only accept it, knowing it's for the best. Maybe He, or She, is just testing us. Only this we can know for sure: little Johnny is better off now because he's already with God in heaven.

Now, this may work for you. But I'm never convinced. I can't explain it, either, but that answer is much too simplistic for me. I can't believe a kid getting struck and killed by a drunk driver is part of God's plan. Nor is widespread genocide in Rwanda, a woman dying in childbirth, or thousands of innocent Americans killed by fanatics who take over commercial airliners. What kind of diabolical God would wish that on anybody? I had an experience like this in my own family. One of my uncles lost his first wife when she died giving birth, leaving him with three young children and a new baby. As he related it to me, her doctor had warned her about getting pregnant again but, a devout Catholic, she listened to her parish priest instead, rejecting the options of birth control or abortion. When, immediately after her death, the priest suggested that, "in the eyes of God, she's much better off now," my uncle threw him out of her hospital room and never went to church again.

Another tough assignment, short of death, is spinning suffering. Why does it happen to some people and not to others? Worse yet, why does so much suffering happen to the same unlucky people—and almost none to the same lucky ones? Damned if I know. It's the question that haunts Morton Kondracke of Fox News about his wife, Milly. In his powerful story of her struggle with Parkinson's disease, *Saving Milly,* Mort agonizes: Why her? Why not me? What did she do to deserve such a miserable fate? It's a difficult question, but one that deserves an answer—and one for which there is none.

In my experience, the person who's come closest to providing an answer is Rabbi Harold Kushner in his phenomenal best-seller *When Bad Things Happen to Good People.* Building on his personal grief and doubts over the loss of his own son to a rare disease, Kushner says we should not blame God's cruelty or our own sins for misfortune. We just have to accept the fact that we live in an imperfect world where things are not always connected and where sometimes, under God's plan, things happen for no reason at all. Even terrorism.

In other words, shit just happens. That is true, but I still find that small consolation. And, as Rabbi Kushner points out, trying to make some sense out of personal tragedy inevitably leads to the fundamental question of faith: if God allows such terrible things to happen to those who believe in Him, love Him and obey Him—what good is He? Where's the plus here? What's in it for me? Spin your way out of that one.

Archaeology proves that, as long as there has been

human civilization, there has been some form of organized religious worship. So, religion is a necessary and positive part of life. But religion, like other good things, has also been perverted to negative ends—religious spin justifying religious sin. One of the most common is pride: Look at us. We're so good, we're so holy, we're God's special people. In fact, God loves us so much that He would deny anybody but us Catholics (substitute Protestant, Jew or Muslim) membership in his exclusive country club. As governor of Texas, even George W. Bush believed that only Christians could get to Heaven—until his mother convinced him otherwise.

It's national pride that links religion and patriotism. Indeed, for most Americans, religion and patriotism are one and the same. We are a God-fearing country, created by our God-loving founding fathers, based on Judeo-Christian values. We can do no wrong. If, as a nation, we poison the atmosphere with greenhouse gases, support Salvadoran death squads or drop two atomic bombs on defenseless cities, it must be God's will. Because God is on our side. God bless America.

It's self-love that drags religion into politics. Here again, the spin is that God is a member of our team. Ask Tom DeLay, he'll assure you that God is a conservative. Nonsense. Take it from me—God is not a conservative. She is a liberal. Just read the New Testament.

Seriously, the only sound theological truth is that God is neither conservative or liberal, Republican or Democrat. God does not identify with any political party. Nor does He, or She, take a stand on political issues. There are sincere believers on both sides. It was wrong for John Cardinal O'Connor to suggest that Catholics should not vote for Geraldine Ferraro, a devout Catholic, just because she happened to be pro-choice. It was wrong for the Christian Coalition to tell its members that God was in favor of the flat tax and increased defense spending. I once asked former Coalition director Ralph Reed where in Scripture it says that Congress shall enact a flat tax, but never got an answer. Because there is none.

And God sure as shit does not endorse political candidates, although many candidates try to spin themselves as anointed by God to run. This was especially loathsome during the 2000 presidential campaign. Never have candidates been so shameless about trying to wrap themselves in Jesus. It started during the primaries with George W. Bush. In one of the early debates, moderator Tom Brokaw asked the panel of presidential hopefuls to name their favorite "political philosopher." Bush, obviously primed beforehand to mention Jesus somewhere in the hour and a half, blurted out: "Christ!" My first thought was that he was swearing out loud at how dumb the question was! But, no. He added after a considerable pause: "Because he changed my heart."

At least John McCain had the nerve to point out: "I thought we were talking about philosophers!" And Alan Keyes lectured Bush on the truth that Jesus was neither politician nor philosopher. But, later in the same debate, when Brokaw asked each of the panelists for a final comment, Keyes one-upped Bush in Jesus-speak, by asking his fellow candidates to join him in prayer.

Unfortunately, the Democratic candidates were equally offensive in evoking Jesus. Al Gore said he never made any decision without first asking himself: "W.W.J.D.—What would Jesus do?" Is that really what we want in a president? Would Jesus really exaggerate like that all the time? And every Joe Lieberman political rally turned into a prayer rally. In his first speech as vice-presidential candidate, Lieberman used the God word 13 times in just 90 seconds. Enough already! It sounded like he was running for chief rabbi.

Other calls upon religion have been much, much worse. In the early days of the AIDS epidemic, there were conservative "Christian" voices declaring that this was God's way of punishing homosexuals for flouting God's law. The same God who, according to Pat Robertson, might send an earthquake, tornado, hurricane or meteor shower to destroy Orlando after Disneyworld hosted a celebration called "Gay Days." "You're right in the way of some serious hurricanes and I don't think I'd be waving those flags in God's face if I were you," he warned Orlando from his TV pulpit. Just what kind of hateful, vengeful God does he worship?

How many wars have been fought, how many millions of people killed, in the name of God? Still today in the Middle East, extreme Jewish militants kill Arabs and extreme Muslim factions kill Jews, both deluded into believing they're obeying the will of one and the same God. Catholics and Protestants are still fighting in Northern Ireland. Hitler was a Christian.

While people of all faiths around the world united in prayer and sorrow after the horrific events of September 11, 2001, that tradgedy too was an occasion for some to show the worst side of organized religion. The suicide bombers were convinced by some demented Islamic clerics that they were flying straight to heaven. And, here in the United States, conservative Christian preachers Jerry Falwell and Pat Robertson immediately suggested that God was punishing us for our sins. With Robertson nodded his approval, Falwell told viewers of the *700 Club*: "What we saw on Tuesday, as terrible as it is, could be minuscule if, in fact, God continues to lift the curtain and allow the enemies of America to give us probably what we deserve."

Who deserves what? Who's responsible for what? Falwell wasted no time in naming names: "The ACLU's got to take a lot of blame for this . . . and I know I'll hear from them for this. But, throwing God out of the public square, out of the schools. The abortionists have got to bear some burden for this because God will not be mocked. And when we destroy 40 million little innocent babies, we make God mad. I really believe that the pagans, and the abortionists, and the feminists, and the gays and the lesbians who are actively trying to make that an alternative lifestyle, the ACLU, People for the American Way—all of them who have tried to secularize America—I point the finger in their face and say: you helped this happen."

Falwell and Robertson later apologized, sort of. Too late. They'd already domonstrated they're just as full of misdirected hate as their Ayatollah counterparts.

In the Catholic Church, religion has been used since the Council of Trent to justify treating women like second-class citizens, still not considered candidates for ordination to the priesthood. The spin is, this is God's will. The reality is, this is just how male authorities choose to interpret the Scripture.

But religion need not be all that serious. For comic relief, there are always the TV evangelists. Their entire ministry is spin, and it usually comes in two categories: virtue and money. First, they tell you how righteous they are; then, they demand your money.

The proof these hucksters are so virtuous is that God talks to them, personally, several times a day. Unfortunately, as we've discovered, God may be trying to talk to them, but they're not always listening because they're otherwise preoccupied. Jimmy Swaggart was obviously preoccupied when he was busy picking up prostitutes in Palm Springs. And Jim Bakker certainly had his direct-line-to-God-cell-phone turned off when he and John Wesley Fletcher were cavorting in Room 538 of the Sheraton Sand Key Resort in Clearwater, Florida, with an attractive twenty-something church secretary named Jessica Hahn. Praise the Lord!

How do we become as holy as they are? Send money! What will make God love and forgive us? Send money! What's my ticket to salvation? Send money! After all, that's why God created us. To send money! And, of course, they're still on television because enough poor suckers do.

The most shameless example of religious money-grubbing was Oral Roberts, back in 1987. This was even more shameless than 1980, when Roberts told his TV congregation he'd been visited by a 900-foot tall, barefoot Jesus. OK, we know Jesus might have been 900 feet tall—but barefoot? Really, Jesus. What happened to your sandals?

In 1987, Roberts went on television with a very scary message. God had told him he needed to raise $8 million in the next two months. If he didn't, Roberts relayed, God had promised to strike him dead. At the time, I was a television commentator on KABC-TV in Los Angeles. I recognized what a great opportunity this was to prove, once and for all, the existence of God. Here's what I urged our viewers on February 7, 1987:

"Now, wait a minute. Before you feel sorry for Oral Roberts, before you dash off a check, think about it.

This is the ultimate test of Christianity. This is the one time to know, for sure, whether God really exists or not.

Nothing is proven if ol' Oral gets his $8 million and stays with us, except that we were suckers for one more television preacher's pitch.

The real test will come if Oral Roberts doesn't make it. If he falls only $2.98 short, then we'll see God in all His glory go 'Zap! Zap! Too bad, you didn't make it, Oral. Hallelujah!'

What a glorious opportunity to prove, once and for all, the existence and power of God. It will be like the Old Testament in our time.

If you really believe in God, don't send Oral Roberts one bloody cent so that God can manifest Himself, as He promised.

In all Christian charity, it's not that we wish Oral ill; it's just that we wish God well."

Unfortunately, our signal didn't reach enough people. Oral Roberts ended up getting his money. So we still don't know for sure whether there is a God or not. Sometimes when our favorite team loses, we seriously doubt it.

THE SPIN GAME

Slump? I ain't in no slump. I just ain't hittin'.
                                              —*Yogi Berra*

Sports, too, is full of spin. Spin is as much a part of athletics as it is part of politics, law, business, family and religion. Not for nothing does the term "spin" derive from baseball pitches and billiard shots.

True, the winners and losers of a sporting event or game are ultimately decided by which team or individual plays the most skillfully or with the most passion. That being said, there is still plenty of room for spin to make a difference on the final scoreboard. Whether by throwing a fastball high and inside ("chin music") to keep a great hitter out of his comfort zone, sprinting by someone in the tenth mile of a marathon to throw off their pace, or quietly clearing one's throat just before a rival makes a key putt on the green, there are plenty of ways that athletes use spin to psych out an opponent at critical moments of a contest.

In fact, there are plenty of not-so-subtle ways to do so as well. These days, trash-talking has become so ingrained in basketball at every level that it's almost considered one of the finer points of the game. Fearsome trash-talkers like Reggie Miller, Gary Payton, Charles Barkley and the venerable Michael Jordan are consistently given high marks by sportswriters for their ability to psych out their opponents.

I must admit, it might be unsportsmanlike, but this type of spin can make watching or reading about a game so much more fun. Who can forget Barkley's aside to the strongly religious A.C. Green: "A.C., if God is so good, how come He didn't give you a jump shot?" Or Michael Jordan's scowl at his opponent after a particularly vicious dunk? He didn't have to say anything. Or one of Deion Sanders's endzone dances after a long return? Or the trademark finger-wagging of Philadelphia center Dikembe Mutombo after a block? All highly effective displays of athletic spin.

While these ballplayers may have perfected the art of trash-talking, in fact its roots are much older than that. As early as 1961, chess champion Bobby Fischer proudly proclaimed to all potential challengers: "There is no one alive I can't beat." Whoa! Good thing he never met Deep Blue.

Arguably the greatest trash-talker of all time was a great athlete, the Greatest himself, Muhammad Ali. Ali was famous for his pre-bout spinathons, in which he'd regale the assembled sports reporters with such zingers as: "I'm so fast that last night I turned off the light switch in my hotel room and was in bed before the room was dark." Or, sounding like an early Jesse Jackson: "If you think the world was surprised when Nixon resigned, wait till I kick Foreman's behind."

Ali even acknowledged the importance of spin to his game when he later said: "I figured that if I said it enough, I would convince the world that I really was the greatest." He was right. It worked.

To his credit, Ali backed up his spin in the ring. In fact, he even used it to his advantage. Take the classic "Rope a Dope" strategy of the "Rumble in the Jungle" of 1974, in which Ali stayed back on the ropes and let his opponent, George Foreman of lean grilling machine fame, tire himself out, swinging for a knockout. Then, in a late-round clinch, Ali leaned over and taunted Foreman, whispering in his ear: "That all you got, George?" Soon, Ali had won back his world heavyweight title, and Foreman started considering a career as pitchman, instead.

Ali's "Rope a Dope" isn't the only athletic spin to double as effective winning strategy. In fact, every sport has its own built-in feints and ruses, from faking the blitz in football, to throwing the slider in baseball, to tossing up a head-fake in basketball. In each case, an athlete is spinning his opponent into thinking he's doing something he's not.

Indeed, in some contests, spin is an integral part of the rules of the game. Hence the bluff in poker: good spinners are rewarded for their spin with large amounts of cash.

And spin isn't restricted solely to the players. Many an athlete and coach spend a good part of every game trying to spin those all-important and theoretically impartial judges in black and white, the referees.

In fact, it's considered an essential part of a coach's job in any sport to spin the refs. So, coaches spend all game jumping up and down on the sidelines: pleading, cajoling and screaming at the men in stripes.

It's customary these days for the players, the coach, the manager and everyone else in a sports organization to blame a particularly horrible loss on the referees, even by denying to do so. "I'm not allowed to comment on lousy officiating," bemoaned Jim Finks, general manager of the New Orleans Saints, after a close loss in 1986.

Spinning the referees is especially important in a playoff series, when two teams will meet several times in a row and are playing for high stakes. Coaches will whine about certain calls—just to make sure they don't happen again, later in the series. Example: after losing the first game of their best-of-five, first-round playoff series against the Los Angeles Lakers in April 2001, the Portland Trail Blazers' head coach Mike Dunleavy blamed it all on the refs. Speaking of the way the Lakers' Shaquille O'Neal likes to lean in with his elbow before he shoots, Dunleavy complained: "Nobody else is allowed to do that. For a stretch of a time, maybe Karl Malone got away with it, but the whole world bitched about that, too. He would lead into you with his elbow and clear people out, same thing. Basically, it's not a legal play."

Sounds a bit desperate, doesn't it? But, two years earlier, the shoe was on the other foot. In 1999, when Dunleavy's Blazers handed Phil Jackson his first loss as coach of the Lakers, it was Jackson who blasted the officials for not calling enough fouls. "I'm disappointed in the referees," he growled. "They were awful. They let Shaq be attacked and then he is the villain. They were flagrantly fouling him. They humped on his back and flagrantly fouled him, whipping the ball across his chest and beat him in the face." Poor Shaq! Jackson makes it sound like the 350-pound hulk got mugged on the court. All spin. All part of the game.

And, like courtroom judges, their counterparts in the legal arena, referees are highly susceptible to spin themselves. Ask any fan. Certain players will get the "superstar treatment" from refs by virtue of their real or assumed greatness, while rookies and journeymen won't be given anywhere near the same latitude. As comedian Colin Quinn noted on *Saturday Night Live* after Michael Jordan's second retirement in 1998: "MJ says he's retiring because he wants to do more traveling. Yeah, like he could do more travelin' than he did in the Garden against the Knicks."

Speaking of Michael the Great, another fundamental sports spin is the myth of the super athlete. From "Say, it ain't so, Shoeless Joe!" to "Where have you gone, Joe DiMaggio?" to "I wanna be like Mike," America has a long and rich history of hoisting its sports heros on top of a pedestal. Which, of course, prompts professional sports leagues to create these heroes, just so they can sell TV time, T-shirts and other memorabilia.

For example, thanks in part to his own innate talent, warm smile and good looks—plus the savvy marketing of the NBA under Commissioner David Stern—Michael Jordan went from being just a talented basketball player to a near superhuman figure: the All-American Hero. In fact, according to *Compton's Encyclopedia,* Jordan is now the most recognized athlete on the planet and, according to Fortune magazine, he's generated approximately $10 billion for the U.S. economy. Not counting what he's pocketed for himself. Now, that's some spin job.

While MJ is the most well-known, there are other athletes in recent years who have felt the Midas touch of the sports hero's spin. Baltimore Orioles' legendary first baseman Cal Ripken, for example, is revered as the "Iron Man" because he played a record 2,632 consecutive baseball games in a row. But if your postman compiled a similar perfect attendance record over the course of many years, rain and shine, would you also consider him an American hero? Or just a guy who's too dumb to take a vacation?

Sadly, Honest Cal sounded like a politician when he announced his retirement on June 18, 2001. Sure, he was proud of his baseball achievements, he said. And he knew no one could play forever. But there were other priorities in life, he insisted. "I'm ready to do other things. I'm ready to be home and be available to my kids and family." Next June, somebody should check with his wife and kids, to see how much they've seen of Cal since he retired. Maybe he meant it, but it sure sounded like so much political spin.

Example: Knicks guard Latrell Sprewell went from Public Enemy No. 1, after choking his Golden State Warriors coach P. J. Carlesimo, to Mr. Congeniality, after only one full season in New York City. His good behavior helped, but so did his playing in a big media market in desperate need of a new sports hero to replace the aging Patrick Ewing.

Similarly, the Philadelphia 76ers' star guard Allen Iverson's public image recently changed from corn-rowed street thug to hardworking, big heart—partly because of his out-standing play, but also because David Stern and the post-Jordan NBA decided after several years of worrying about his "urban look," to embrace Iverson as one of its new and exciting top stars. Spin in action.

Yes, sports leagues and sports drinks spend millions, spinning us into believing that certain players are superhuman. But that doesn't mean the players are above spinning themselves. Just the opposite. Especially after a bad game, bad season, or bad year. Then the spin really starts flying.

How many times have we fans heard variations on the same theme after a bad loss: "We didn't bring our A-game"? Or "We just didn't get the breaks tonight"? Both pure spin for "We lost, fair and square. We got our asses handed to us."

It's not just professional sports. Every New Year's day, we hear some coach trying to put the best possible spin on getting creamed in a nationally-televised college bowl game: "We may not have won the final game, but we were one of only two teams that made it all the way to the Orange Bowl. And, for that, I'm proud of our team. We have nothing to be ashamed of." Oh, yes, you do. You lost, dumbo! You might just as well have stayed home.

That phony "we won, even though we lost" reasoning has its roots in the sports spin all kids are taught when growing up—whether it's Little League, Saturday morning soccer or tennis camp: "It's not whether you win or lose, it's how you play the game." Not so! Sports is all about winning. We only remember the winners. Only winners get prizes. *New Yorker* cartoonist Pat Byrnes made the point forcefully by drawing a father telling his little son, about to walk out on the baseball field: "Just remember, son, it doesn't matter whether you win or lose—unless you want Daddy's love."

That's why, sometimes, sports spin only goes so far. "It was a rebuilding year," the coach might say. "We had a great year, even if we didn't make it to the playoffs." Nice try. But don't expect fans to think it was such a great year, if they couldn't even make it to the big dance.

But, in the end, you can't blame the spinners. When a

season ends poorly, there's a good chance some athletes will be traded and some coaches, fired. So, it makes sense for players and coaches both to spin the season the best they can. For them, it's called self-preservation.

Of course, that doesn't quite explain the occasional strange outburst. Like the one by Boston Celtics coach Rick Pitino in March 2000. He found something new to blame: the city! After an embarrassing loss to the Toronto Raptors, Pitino lashed out to the Boston press: "Larry Bird is not walking through the door, fans. Kevin McHale is not walking through that door. And Robert Parish is not walking through that door. The negativity that's in this town sucks! It sucks and it stinks and it sucks!"

That's some spin. It's not Coach Pitino's fault. It's not the team's fault. It's Boston's fault! Small wonder Pitino was out of a job the following year. Even though he was president of the team, he admitted it was time to fire himself.

Once again, for the model of sports spin, we turn to Hollywood. In the great baseball flick *Bull Durham,* veteran minor league player Crash Davis, played by Kevin Costner, takes rookie pitcher Nuke LaLoosh (Tim Robbins) under his wing. One day, sitting in the locker room after a game, Crash Davis gives Nuke LaLoosh a lesson in spin.

LaLoosh: "Teach me something new, man! I need to learn! Teach me something."
Davis: "You got something to write with? Good. It's time to work on your interviews. Whenever reporters ask you anything, just repeat the following: 'We gotta play 'em one day at a time.' "
LaLoosh: "Sounds pretty boring."
Davis: "Of course, it's boring, that's the point. Write it down. 'I'm just happy to be here, hope I can help the ball club.' I know, write it down. 'I just want to give it my best shot, and the good Lord willing, things will work out.' "

For spin of all kind, that's a real keeper. Play ball!

ELEVEN

SEX AND DATING: WHERE SPIN BEGINS . . . AND ENDS

I used to be Snow White, but I drifted.
—Mae West

By now, I know what you're thinking. There must be one area of human endeavor which is so intimate, so personal, so private, it is spin-free. And that could only be the most intimate of personal activities: sex. Wrong again! The intricate dance of words, gestures and actions—sometimes graceful, sometimes beautiful, sometimes downright silly—that comprise the pursuit, enjoyment and afterglow of sex are full of spin, from beginning to end. And then some.

Sex is so central to our lives, you'd think we would have it all figured out by now. But no. We still struggle with all its dimensions: when it's okay, when it's not okay; with whom it's okay, with whom it's not; what counts as sex, what doesn't; how important a part of a relationship it is, or should be. We talk about it a lot but, when it really counts, we hesitate to talk about it at all. We make jokes about it, but there's nothing we take more seriously. The fact is, despite thousands of years of human experience, sex is still one big mystery. We know more about how fruit flies do it than humans. And many people are determined to keep it that way.

Growing up, it's hard to get a good fix on sex, especially when the deck is stacked against you. On the one hand, your friends, who don't know any more about sex than you do, are consumed by it. On the other hand, your parents, who— by proof of your existence—presumably have had some sexual experience, pretend it doesn't exist. To compound the problem, add the mixed signals from other authority figures. Starting with religious leaders.

As a Catholic, I was totally confused. When I was still in grade school, our parish priest, Father Lawrence Ward, used to thunder from the pulpit every Sunday: "Before they get married, no young person should touch another young person, either by kiss or by sex." Knowing what "kiss" meant, but not "sex," I would run home and look it up in the dictionary. No luck. Without pictures, I was never sure what this sex thing was that I wasn't supposed to touch.

Bad as it was for schoolboys, it wasn't much simpler for married people. Here's the difference. They were allowed to have sex, I was taught in Catholic high school—by which time, thanks to several Boy Scout outings, I knew what sex was—but never just for pleasure, and never for any purpose other than to conceive a child. This was even more confusing. How could you be sure you hit the bull's eye? If you only wanted three kids, did you really only get three turns at bat? In your entire lifetime? And, since you couldn't masturbate without hair growing in the palm of your hands, what else could you do?

I learned the answer to that in the seminary, where I spent a few years: you played sports. Every single day, rain or shine. You ran, swam laps, worked out, shot hoops, did push-ups, played football, tennis, softball, volleyball. If all else failed, you walked around the block. Fast—100 times.

Anything to work up a sweat and release all of your energy so you wouldn't be tempted to jerk off. Except we all did anyhow. Which explains my reaction when our freshman biology professor at Niagara University solemnly informed his co-ed class: "Ninety-five percent of all men masturbate." Adding, after a pregnant pause: "The other five percent are liars." I laughed out loud. I was the only one.

So, when I was growing up, sex was even more cloaked in mystery than it is today. But just when I think people may be starting to take a healthier attitude toward sex and be more open about sex with kids, I'm reminded of how much like mushroom farmers we operate: treating kids like mushrooms by keeping them in the dark and feeding them manure. That's exactly what the so-called Medical Institute of Austin, Texas, is trying to do.

In June 2001, the Institute released a report with the startling conclusion that, for teenagers, having sex was more dangerous than smoking cigarettes. The reason, argues Institute founder Dr. Joe McIlhaney, is that, by engaging in sex, teens can get an instant case of genital herpes, vaginal warts, or some other sexually-transmitted disease. Girls could even get pregnant. But whatever complications they get from smoking won't show up until they're a lot older.

I didn't make this up. Here's Dr. McIlhaney's spin: "Sex is more dangerous than smoking. Sex hurts them when they're teenagers. Smoking will hurt them later." Here's Dr. Press's translation: "Sex is not OK, because you might get herpes next week. But smoking is OK because, even if you get lung cancer, it won't hit until you're middle-aged, when nobody cares anymore whether you live or die."

What bullshit! And what a dangerous lesson for anybody. No wonder kids tune out when grown-ups start pontificating about sex. Sure, abstinence is the only surefire way to prevent pregnancy or disease. We should teach kids that. But, let's not kid ourselves. In 1990, the *New England Journal of Medicine* reported that 40 percent of high school freshmen had had sex; for seniors, it was up to 72 percent. That number is probably even higher today. Realizing that most teenagers always have and always will have sex, we should also teach them how to act responsibly and how to practice safe sex. Scaring kids out of sex just won't work.

There is one part of the Medical Institute's report I agree with, however. They debunk the theory, held by many teens, that oral sex is not real sex—that vaginal sex is the only thing that counts. Says one sixteen-year-old girl in the study: "With oral sex, you don't get the emotional attachment that comes with intercourse. Oral sex isn't really sex; it's much more casual, and it comes with a lot fewer responsibilities." By their definition, and Bill Clinton's, when he professed: "I did not have sex with that woman, Miss Lewinsky"—he was telling the truth!

This, too, is nonsense. Oral sex, as wonderful as it is, for both giver and receiver, is still sex. It should not be done casually. And it does, too, come with responsibility. A girl won't get pregnant from giving a blow job, but she could just as easily get herpes or HIV. Again, safe sex is the answer. And girls who willingly give blow jobs (or Lewinskys, as they may be better known today) should stop kidding themselves. They're no longer virgins, even if their hymen is still intact.

That being said, oral sex should not be against the law, as it still is in many states, which include oral and anal sex under the banned category of "sodomy." *Esquire* magazine defines the oral variety of sodomy as a "Slurpee." The following states make Slurpees illegal: Alabama, Arizona, Florida, Idaho, Louisiana, Massachusetts, Michigan, Minnesota, Mississippi, Missouri, North Carolina, Oklahoma, South Carolina, Texas, Utah, and Virginia.

As *Esquire* magazine suggests, if I lived in one of those states, I would put a bumper sticker on my car: WHEN SLURPEES ARE ILLEGAL, ONLY OUTLAWS WILL GET SLURPEES. These stupid sodomy laws should all be wiped off the books. The great Dr. Kinsey said it best: "The only unnatural sex act is the one that's impossible to perform." Among consenting adults, everything else should be legal. Starting with flirtation.

COURTSHIP DISPLAY

It is not easy to find, or hold onto, a life partner. Doing so often requires considerable energy and creativity. But at least we have it easier than members of the bird or animal kingdoms. Science writer Natalie Angier described for readers of the *New York Times* the elaborate dance carried out by male and female great-crested grebes:

> As one bird dives and swims toward the other,
> its partner arches its back and fluffs itself up,
> cat-style, until the diver bursts through the water
> right next to it in the "ghost display," wings
> extended, body erect. The two part, plunge back
> under and re-emerge with weeds clutched like
> roses in their beaks. Pressing their breasts together,
> they rise up and begin trampling their feet on the water,
> heads turning back and forth.

Thank God we weren't born great-crested grebes. If we were required to give such a strenuous hello, we'd be too worn out to have sex. Our task is a lot easier. First of all, all we have to do is come up with a good opening line. That's where spin comes in.

Be honest. What are all those good pick-up lines, if not spin for: "Wanna fuck"? When a woman says: "Would you like to come up to my place for a nightcap?" she's not just planning to show him her rare book collection. Although what she will show him is pure poetry. When a guy reaches across the dinner table on their first date, strokes her hand and asks: "Do you feel a certain chemistry here?" he's not talking about his chemistry set. He's talking about his erector set. As the old saying goes: "Love is a matter of chemistry; sex is a matter of physics."

The worst pick-up line I remember from my dating days in San Francisco in the late 1960s: "What's your sign?" If they're so into astrology, why do they have to ask? And who the hell cares?

BAITING THE TRAP

Of course, before you try out your best, or worst, pick-up lines, you must first meet the lucky, or unlucky, person. After high school or college, that becomes more difficult. Suddenly everyone we know is either married or about to be. So begins the hunt. And, this being a country where we don't take kindly to parents prearranging our future spouses, we set out to snare the prey ourselves: in a mindless blur of bars, mixers, cocktail receptions, dinner parties, subway rides or walking the dog—during which we hope Mr. or Ms. Right will trip and fall right into our lap. Seldom happens. Then, especially after a certain age, and certain sad experience, comes the final indignity: the personal ads!

In the dating game, placing or responding to a personal ad may be the last resort. It is also the first place to look for spin. Each ad, in fact, is a little masterpiece. We never spin so well as when we are spinning ourselves. And, in so doing, modesty must never be allowed to get in the way.

From the *Washington Post* personals, I culled these samples of great personal spin. Like partners, they come in all shapes and sizes, and are organized in distinct categories. Sell, baby, sell.

WOMEN SEEKING MEN

Blonde, Gorgeous. I'm a sexy, big-sized Lady ISO secure, nice Guy, open-minded.

Have Fun? Me: SWF, 37, active, slim, independent, ISO buddy: walks, talks, hikes/biking, movies, drinks, coffee, dinner . . . ? You: SWM, secure, active, fun, easygoing, little baggage.

Sweet Summer Sensation. ISO special, successful SPM, smart with degree, down-to-earth, mentally and financially stable, honest, kindhearted, N/S, 30–45, any race. I'm SPF, 38, no kids, 5'7", BA, MA, full-figured, enjoys swimming, hiking, dancing, also music, art, nature, foreign films, exotic cuisine. I'm warm, fuzzy, outgoing, spiritual, not religious. Call now.

There is a good reason why no photographs accompany the personal ads. You might as well postpone the disappointment, because you know that no one comes close to the person described in the ads. If they did, they wouldn't have to advertise for dates in the newspaper. Women, of course, aren't the only offenders. Men are equally bold and even more verbose in describing how wonderful they are. Just ask them, they'll tell you, and tell you, and tell you again.

MEN SEEKING WOMEN

A Great Catch looking for the same. I am an attractive, bright, charming DWM (52). I enjoy fine and simple dining, travel, sports (getting better at golf), willing to try almost anything. You are smart, very attractive, slim. You have a great life and are looking for someone who, too, has a great life to join together and have a supergreat life. You have or like kids and sometimes just enjoy quiet times at home. If you are my next best friend, please answer now.

Five-Star Rated! Handsome, charming, great sense of humor, sophisticated, bright, eccentric, romantic, adventurous, successful CEO loves to boogie, travel, exercise, kiss, fine dining. Naughty, gentle, very nice 5'9" SWPM ISO exceptional Lady, knockout looks, great attitude, great shape, 36–48, same qualities/interests. Could be soulmates forever.

Renaissance Man. SWM, 49, creative (photographer, writer and dreamer), romantic ("candlelighter," slow dancer and beach stroller), analytical (organizer, planner and builder), athletic (runner, bicyclist and hiker), musical (choir singer, dancer and music listener), humorous (speaker, conversationalist and "facilitator"), traveler (foreign voyager and weekend "getawayer") w/blue eyes and two cats (Mickey and Angie). ISO SF, 35–45, like mind/spirit, soulmate.

Frankly, I think this last guy needs a mirror. He'll never find someone he loves as much as he loves himself. Except maybe another cat.

Reflecting reality, the *Post* does not limit itself to heterosexual ads. It includes homosexual personals, although they are nowhere near as graphic as you will find in gay publications. But, for a family newspaper, some of them are still pretty direct.

MEN SEEKING MEN

Retired Military bear seeks life with broad-backed, thick-chested GWM.

BIWM, TV, seeks other TV who enjoys fine lingerie, discreet and healthy, no games.

WOMEN SEEKING WOMEN

Beautiful Lesbian. BF, 36, ISO pretty, caring, passionate, full-figured F, 38–45, only.

Much Fun, much joy, more to come. SBiF ISO SBiF to give me that joyful feeling.

Here's one more reflection of the times. People are living longer and healthier lives. And, with more years than they once thought possible ahead of them—plus the rise of Viagara—they no longer feel they have to move in with their kids or check into the rest home. Widowed or divorced, they can search for a partner to share their Golden Years. Now the spin never dies.

SENIORS SEEKING SENIORS

**Attractive, 112# ** WiWF ISO SWM, 70s, for companionship and caring, good times.

SWF, 64, seeks N/S Gentleman who likes long walks, quiet talks and holding hands.

WiWM, 70s, 6′+, slim, good sense of humor, romantically inclined, like movies at home, trips by car, dining out. ISO WF, any age/height/weight, for long-term, close relationship.

Finally, just to prove that hope springs eternal, the *Post* opens its pages to the timid, the meek and the cowardly— who saw the man or woman of their dreams passing on the street or sitting on the subway, but didn't dare say hello or ask for a phone number. Damn! I blew that opening. But give me another chance, and I'll score. Provided, of course, I can just find that hunk or babe somewhere.

You must admire their determination. But, somehow, I can't imagine anyone answering a personal ad like this.

YOU CAUGHT MY EYE

Metro Red Line, Thursday. You called me a jerk. I didn't pass gas, it was the lady. Need second chance.

Now, multiply that spin of personal ads by ten and you still won't come close to the level of deception found in computer chat rooms. This is the ultimate masquerade party. People can take on any identity, because no one will ever know. Except for those few who are foolish enough ever to want to meet someone in person they'd only met online, there is no way they will ever know who you are, nor no way you will ever know them. The mystery remains a mystery. That sexy, young woman you're making virtual love to on the computer screen could be as ugly as sin, as old as Grandma Moses or underage. Or, she may not be a she at all.

Even if he/she sends you a photograph, you still can't be sure it's a genuine photo of the person you're talking to.

That, more than anything, must explain the phenomenal success of computer chat rooms. Yes, they provide instant access to the lonely or stay-at-homes. Jumping into a chat room is a lot easier than taking the time to develop and maintain a real-life friendship. You don't have to put up with all the nonsense. But, most attractive of all, I believe, is the fact that, because they're so anonymous and impersonal, the chat room enables us to be whomever we want to be at the time: one person, one minute; another, the next. We can keep reinventing ourselves. We can spin ourselves to the moon.

Whether in person, online or in print, in the dating world, spin is just verbal foreplay. Even the word "dating" itself is a creature of spin. It used to mean just what it says: dating, as in going out on dates. Today, when we say he and she are dating, we mean they're sleeping together.

As shown in the personal ads, the spinning we do to get a date holds true for both heterosexual and homosexual relationships. Here's another example. A friend of mine owns a male phone-sex service. As a businessman, he occasionally listens in on calls—not to eavesdrop for curious and lascivious purposes; heavens, no!—but only in order to monitor the quality of his phone line. (Think about who's listening in, next time you're tempted to spend $6.99 a minute.) Almost every phone conversation, he says, begins with both men spinning about the size of their equipment. And who said size doesn't matter?

Just goes to figure. Has any man ever walked into a drugstore and asked for "small" condoms? Don't be silly. They don't even make small condoms; only large and extra large. You know what they say about men with big feet. Dream on.

PUTTING ON A GOOD FACE

We don't think of it this way very often, but clothing and makeup are both part of the dating spin game. You don't go out for the evening, hoping to meet someone special, dressed like a dog. Whether to the beach, the dinner party or the symphony, you put on your most attractive outfit, one that shouts: "Hey, look at me. I'm here. I'm beautiful. I'm available. Talk to me."

The instant appeal of a certain style of clothing also works for men, but is especially effective for women in sending a powerful signal. After all, the plunging neckline, the strapless dress, the bustier, the slit skirt and short shorts were not just designed to allow more freedom of movement. They're made to highlight what you're not wearing more than what you are.

Makeup also sends a message. Some women are very attractive with no make-up. Many would rather be dead than be seen without it. Tastefully done (not applied with a trowel like Tammy Faye Bakker or Katherine Harris), makeup is part of the overall package—clothes, shoes, fragrance, body language—that help a woman spin who she is and, perhaps, what she is looking for.

There are those, however, who see too much symbolism in makeup. Researching this book, I read about a PBS documentary hosted by Desmond Morris, author of *Intimate Behavior* and *The Human Zoo,* in which the noted biologist argues that humans share many responses with all other animals and, more importantly, that much of the behavior that we regard as uniquely human has a biological basis in being. Like wearing makeup.

"Let us take the wearing of lipstick as an example," Morris explains. "It is easily argued that the wearing of lipstick is for cosmetic reasons; it is to make the woman more attractive. Such an assertion implies that there are really some ugly women out there who need to cover up their shortcomings. But in actuality, the wearing of lipstick has more to do with mimicking the sexual response that women experience during intercourse, thereby serving as a reminder to both sexes that propagation is essential to survival. During intercourse, the woman's [vaginal] lips redden as blood flows to them."

Is this really why women wear lipstick? I don't think so. I think this guy has been spending too much time with the gorillas.

PLAYING HARD TO GET

Of course, we have to remember that the search for a partner is a two-way street. The hunter and the prey are not always spinning themselves the same way. Sometimes, though rarely, it's the woman who's aggressive and the man who's passive. Most of the time, it's the other way around: the horny male making an ass of himself; the equally horny, yet unwilling-to-admit-it female, playing hard to get.

Why is it that women spin themselves as so hard to get? Don't they know how dangerous that is? Don't they realize that, sooner or later, we men just might give up and move on? Not a chance. They've got us figured out for the hopeless, predictable fools we are. It's never been a level playing field—women always outfox men—but, alas, it became even more one-sided with the 1995 publication of *The Rules* by Ellen Fein and Sherrie Schneider.

Their best-selling book's full title is: *The Rules: Time Tested Secrets for Capturing the Heart of Mr. Right*. They might as well have called it *Time Tested Secrets for Playing Hard to Get*. Their philosophy is: the more a woman holds back, the more a man will step up the pursuit. And nobody's proven them wrong. The way, they say, to spin yourself a boyfriend or husband is not only to play hard to get, it's to be downright rude. Of course, all that changes once he persists, persists and persists—and she finally agrees to be his girl-friend and wife. Right? Not on your life! Not according to the gospel of Ellen and Sherrie.

Check out their Rule #18: "Even if you're engaged or married, you still need the rules." Jesus, give a guy a break!

GETTING DOWN TO BUSINESS

Having broken the ice, the next step is to figure out how to get your dreamboat in bed. Here, too, spin comes in handy. Like spinning that sex is really not your main, or only goal. "Don't get me wrong. I don't want you to think I'm attracted to you just because of your body. You have a great mind. You are so smart and so funny, I could spend hours just talking to you." While the whole time you are panting, hoping she'll hurry up and take her clothes off. The last thing you want is for her to believe you're really interested in her mind.

Another standby is to spin yourself as relatively inexperienced and not the obscene, sleep-around pig you really are. "I've only done this with x number of men before." In one survey, 47 percent of men and 42 percent of women admitted they would understate the number of their previous sexual partners in order to convince someone to have sex. On this matter, comedian Chris Rock gives the best advice of all: "Don't ask, 'cause you don't wanna know."

Another step down what you hope will be a slippery slope is to promise privacy in a variety of ways: "I'm very discreet" or "This is just our secret" or "Nobody will ever know." Sure, nobody will ever know—except all the boys in the locker room, all the girls in the sorority and everyone around the office water cooler. Next time you think having sex will ever be kept a secret, remember Monica Lewinsky and Chandra Levy. It certainly never remains a secret long with twenty-four-year-olds.

The last resort, for men at least, is to spin themselves as responsible human beings, capable of exercising self-restraint. The hollow promises of "I'll pull out in time" or "I won't come in your mouth" should be banned from the English language.

DOING BUSINESS

If the long dance of flirting and courting is full of spin, so is the sex act itself. Nobody believes the line: "Wow, this is the best sex I've ever had"—but everybody loves to hear it. When he says "We fit so well together, we must be made for each other," she knows he's just spinning, but she purrs nonetheless. When he assures her: "I'll still respect you in the morning," she knows she's lucky if he even remembers her name. Or the color of her eyes. Tip from *Esquire:* If you can't remember the color of her eyes, don't guess. "Cut your losses, plead drunkenness, and admit that you forgot." *Esquire* also correctly warns: "Knowing her name or the color of her eyes becomes even more important on multiple-night stands, such as in, for example, a marriage."

There are those so sexually-repressed they can't even bring themselves to say the words "make love" or "have sex," let alone "fuck." For those poor souls, *Esquire* magazine published a book called *Things a Man Should Know About Sex,* in which they have a list of the "Top Ten Euphemisms for Sexual Intercourse," that includes "Interior Decorating," "Parallel Parking," and "Lead the Llama to the Lift Shaft."

Speaking of welcome spin (and lifting shafts!), what swells a man with pride more than those three little words, the most wonderful words in the English language: "It's so big!" Telling each other what you like, or how much each of you enjoy what the other is doing, can double your satisfaction. And in bed is the one place you can get away with talking dirty and using all those bad words for certain body parts, as long as your partner agrees—or, better yet, gets into it, too. For some people, learning to talk dirty is like learning a whole new language. But it's certainly worth the cost of the Berlitz records. It may well be that the better the spin, the better the sex.

Sometimes silence during sex can be the best spin of all. Constant chatter can be a turn-off, especially if the person is always talking outside of bed, too. I'll never forget when Tucker Carlson and I hosted Dr. Ruth as a guest on *The Spin Room* on Valentine's Day 2001. Before we could even say hello, Dr. Ruth jumped in: "Good evening. I am so happy to be on your show on Valentine's Day. And I have an important assignment for you. Right after the show, I want you two to go home and make love—not with each other, but with your wives or girlfriends [she really didn't have to add that; Tucker's not my type]—and tonight, for something special, I want you to try a position you've never tried before!"

Remember, this was on live television. Tucker just blushed and laughed. I also blushed, but managed to stammer out: "Dr. Ruth, after all this time, I think I know and have tried all the positions. Do you have a particular one in mind?"

"For you, Bill," she immediately advised, "I would suggest remaining silent." How did she know?

But, of course, the greatest spin during sex is the fake orgasm. In one survey I saw, 70% of women and 25% of men admitted to faking an orgasm. I think the others were liars. Especially the men. Harder for them to hide the fact they did not really have an orgasm, but men fake it, too.

If the orgasm's not coming on its own, why fake it? The answer: spin! The most common reason both men and women give for faking an orgasm is to make their partner happy. In other words, to spin that the sex was good. Not great, but good enough. Some do so in order to encourage their partner's orgasm. Some because they don't want their partner to feel inadequate. Others because they're just not into it and they want to get it over with. In which case, the fake orgasm is spin for "Enough already. Let's roll over and go to sleep."

Of course, that assumes the lucky couple even got that far, and were not derailed by the classic spin of sex: "I'm sorry, dear, but not tonight. I've got a headache." Which you can probably get away with most of the time, as long as you're not a porcupine. Believe it or not, biologists tell us that a porcupine couple copulates every day, 365 days a year, whether it's breeding season or not. You see, it could be worse.

BREAKING UP IS HARD TO DO

If spin plays a role in starting and enjoying a relationship, it also plays a role in ending one. Unless you want to be downright cruel and hurt someone, it's always better to spin your way out gently, rather than give the real reasons you want to hit the road. And, no matter how corny, you'd be surprised how long the rejected party will cling to that spin as a faded souvenir of good times and a faint glimmer of hope for getting back together.

It's like that great scene in *Dumb and Dumber.* He: "What are my chances?" She: "Not good." He: "You mean, not good like one out of a hundred?" She: "I'd say more like one out of a million." He: "So, you're telling me there's still a chance?"

In case you can't come up with a good spin line yourself, the Web is full of them. Among other sites, here are a few that "Inspired Living Humor" (www.inspiredinside.com/humor) suggests for her to offer him.

Spin: "There's a slight difference in our ages."
Translation: "I don't want to do my dad."

Spin: "I've got a boyfriend."
Translation: "I prefer my male cat and a half gallon of Ben and Jerry's."

Spin: "I want to remain friends."
Translation: "I want you to stick around, so I can tell you in excruciating detail about all the other men I meet and have sex with."

There are two other basic spin-off lines that former girlfriends have used on me. First: "I still love you, I just don't love you that way anymore." This is slightly better than saying flat out "I can't stand the sight or touch of your naked body," but not much. It's small consolation to know that, even though she's throwing you out of her life, she's still willing to be in the same room with you and two hundred other people.

Same with: "I will always keep a place in my heart for you." Yeah, that's nice, but there will always be a place in your heart for your brother, too. Don't you get it? I don't want to be just in your heart. In fact, if I can't be in your arms, and someplace else, I don't even want to be in your heart. So there.

And there you have it. From beginning to end, sex and spin are inseparable. You can have spin without sex, but you can never have sex without spin. But, as with spin in politics, the law, or advertising, that's no reason to walk away from sex (as if one ever could). It's just a good reason to master spin and add it to your repertoire of sexual techniques.

Mae West had the first word in this chapter. For those who can't get enough spin or sex, she also gets the last: "Too much of a good thing is wonderful."

TWELVE

CLOSING
COMMENTS

At the end of each *Crossfire* show, after our guests are out of the studio and the dust has settled, the co-hosts get the final word. We never get more than a minute, but it's time enough to sum up, make one more important point or get in one last jab. We call it "Closing Comments." And, sometimes, it's the best part of the show.

Here we go.

To sum up. Spin is a way of fudging the truth without trampling on it. Politicians are most often associated with spin, but they're not the only ones. Everybody spins: teachers, preachers, salesmen, CEOs, hair stylists, bankers, boyfriends, psychiatrists, athletes. Kids learn to spin at an early age. We even spin ourselves. There are no known cases of dogs or cats spinning.

Some people take spin too far. They use it to betray or deceive, or tell an outright untruth. That's bad spin. That's a lie.

But, most of the time, spin's an innocent form of speech. It gets us by when telling the whole truth is too awkward, too embarrassing or too painful—and maybe even unnecessary. It helps us survive. It gives us self-confidence. It can also help us achieve a greater goal, like preserving a friendship when telling the brutal truth would destroy it.

To make one more important point. It's pretty clear why we spin. There's no biological imperative. We are not chameleons, or caterpillars or scorpionfish who have to change our color in order to protect ourselves from natural enemies.

Spin is not a matter of life or death. There's no sociological imperative, either. In fact, it's just the opposite. From the time we start to talk, we are told always to tell Mommy the truth, the whole truth and nothing but the truth—even if she doesn't.

So why do we spin? Because we can. And because it generally makes things go a lot smoother. There's nothing wrong with that. So, relax. Learn to recognize, even appreciate, spin. Spin unto others, as you would have others spin unto you. And never swallow whole anything anybody tells you. No matter who it is, remember: 75 percent of what they're telling you is probably just spin.

To get in one last jab. Despite recent scandals, Democrats don't have a monopoly on extramarital affairs. And Democrats don't have a monopoly on spin, either. Politicians of both parties spin as much as they can get away with. Trent Lott spins as much as Tom Daschle. George Bush spins as much as Bill Clinton. And talk-show hosts and TV pundits spin as much as all of them combined.

So, the next time you hear someone in politics or in the media brag about being "spin-free" or "spin-proof" or operating in a "no-spin zone," don't you believe it. That is pure puffery and pure baloney. In fact, that is pure spin.

Now, one friendly request. In these pages, I focused on the spin I've encountered in politics, in the law, in religion, in the business world and in the most important of all human activities—sex! But I realize that I have only scratched the surface. There's a lot of spin going on even I don't know about. Reading these pages, you have no doubt thought of other examples of spin, even more outrageous, in your own lives. Spin from your chiropractor, boss or gardener. Who knows where or when?

I'd love to hear about them. Our *Spin Room* show was interactive. I'd like this book to be interactive, too. So please take the time to e-mail me your personal experiences and examples of spin to spinthis@aol.com.

Thanks for traveling this far. May the Spin always be with you.

ACKNOWLEDGMENTS

I would love to be able to say that I am the sole author of this book. That I came up with the idea, lived it, researched it, wrote it, refined it and brought it to life entirely on my own. But that would be the worst of spin.

The truth is that, like putting a television show on the air, getting a book from thought to print is never a solo event. It requires a lot of minds and hands, working together, pulling together and building together, from start to finish. And this book is no exception.

I owe a great debt, first of all, to my *Spin Room* collaborators: Gail Evans, who first proposed the show; my irrepressible co-host Tucker Carlson; Executive Producer Don Smith; and the incredible, enthusiastic team of Libby Schlatcher, Amy Farrar, Kate Albright-Hanna and Susan Toffler. Plus our entire studio and control room support staff and all those wonderful viewers. They helped bring spin alive. There was never a more fun TV show to work on.

A special thanks also to the daily support and insights of our great staff at *Crossfire,* my home for the last five years. To Rick Davis, brave enough to hire me. To Jennifer Bloch, our longtime and very talented executive producer. To a formidable array of co-hosts: Geraldine Ferraro, Robert Novak, Pat Buchanan, John Sununu, Mary Matalin and Tucker Carlson. And today's outstanding line-up of Chris Guarino, Kristi Schantz, Kate Farrell, Jennifer Yuille, Amy Farrar and Terri

Revis. *Crossfire* is the oldest and still best political debate show on television and I'm proud to be part of it.

Washington's a great town to live and work in. Friendship crosses philosophical and party lines. I'm grateful to friends Margaret Carlson, Mary Matalin, Bob Novak, Paul Begala, Tony Blankley, Kate O'Beirne, Ollie North, Cal Thomas, Hendrik Hertzberg, Al Franken and Tucker (again?) for pitching in with their favorite spin moments. It's fun to leave the Beltway occasionally, return to California and appear on Bill Maher's *Politically Incorrect*. It's always a gas. Bill Maher's always out of control. So are his guests. That makes it a great show. Thanks, Bill, for adding your personal take on spin.

For over twenty years, I've been a faithful subscriber to the *New Yorker,* and the first thing I look for in every issue is the latest George Booth cartoon. For some reason, I identify with his wacky world. He's become a close friend. It's an honor to have an original Booth in these pages. And my thanks also to Douglas Page of Tribune Media Services for making available the political cartoons of Mike Peters, Dan Wasserman and David Horsey.

When you start talking about spin, everybody chimes in with an example of their own. Many, many friends did. Thank you all. A special word of thanks to John Andrews for his insights on Shakespeare. And to fellow traveler David Corn for reviewing the draft and suggesting valuable modifications.

Three people deserve most of the credit for making this book happen. Ron Goldfarb is more than an agent, he is a good friend who quickly adopted this project as his own. Research assistant Kevin Murphy, as focused as I was scatterbrained, worked around the clock digging up great material. For my first book, I could not have found a better guide or teacher than my editor, Mitchell Ivers. He immediately understood what the book was all about and helped shape both its construction and content.

I could not have undertaken or completed the book without the strong support of Carol. She not only put up with my long nights and entire weekends at the computer, she even agreed to read and edit the manuscript. Greater love than this no woman hath.

Finally, there are three people who had a powerful influence on my life and, at least indirectly, contributed to this book. Peter Behr always told the truth, sometimes to my dismay, and tried to pass his truth-telling on to me. Alas. Sidney Galanty introduced me to television and encouraged me just to relax and have a good time. I still do. Seth Warner implanted in me a burning liberalism and a healthy skepticism about every human utterance. It's still there.